Lesson Masters

THE UNIVERSITY OF CHICAGO SCHOOL MATHEMATICS PROJECT

PRECALCULUS AND DISCRETE MATHEMATICS

INTEGRATED MATHEMATICS

Further practice on
SPUR objectives

Scott Foresman
Addison Wesley

Editorial Offices: Glenview, Illinois • Menlo Park, California
Sales Offices: Reading, Massachusetts • Atlanta, Georgia • Glenview, Illinois
Carrollton, Texas • Menlo Park, California

http://www.sf.aw.com

Contents

ISBN: 0-673-45919-5

1 2 3 4 5 6 - PO - 0 1 0 0 9 9 9 8

Name ______

Questions on SPUR Objectives
See pages 71–75 for objectives.

Skills Objective A

1. Is the following statement universal, existential, or neither? *Some integers are prime.* ______

Skills Objective B

2. Rewrite the following statement using universal and existential quantifiers.
Every number is greater than some number.

______

Skills Objective D

In 3–6, let $p(x)$ be the sentence $6x^2 - 7x + 2 \leq 0$. Determine whether the given statement is true or false.

3. $p(0.68)$ ______

4. $\exists$ *an integer x such that* $p(x)$. ______

5. $\exists$ *a rational number x such that* $p(x)$. ______

6. $\forall$ *real numbers x such that* $0.58 \leq x \leq 0.62$, $p(x)$. ______

Properties Objective E

In 7 and 8, determine whether the given sentence is a statement. If it is a statement, determine whether it is true or false.

7. $\frac{x}{x} = 1$ ______

8. $\forall x, \frac{x}{x} = 1$ ______

Properties Objective F

9. Given $\forall x, x \neq 1, 1 + x^1 + x^2 + x^3 + \ldots + x^n = \frac{1 - x^{n+1}}{1 - x}$, use the Law of Substitution to prove that $\forall k, k \neq 1$ and $k \neq 0$, $1 + k^{-1} + k^{-2} + k^{-3} + \ldots + k^{-n} = \frac{k - k^{-n}}{k - 1}$.

Name

▶ **LESSON MASTER 1-1** *page 2*

Properties Objective H

10. Consider the following statement. *The sum of any nonzero real number and its reciprocal is greater than the original number.*

a. Write this statement in the form ∀ *x in S, p(x)*.

b. Provide a counterexample to show that this statement is false.

Uses Objective I

In 11–15, refer to the table below, which gives the number of Gold (G), Silver (S), and Bronze (B) Medals won by six countries in each of four different sporting events in the 1998 winter Olympics held in Nagano, Japan.

	Alpine Skiing			Figure Skating			Cross-Country Skiing			Speed Skating		
Country	**G**	**S**	**B**	**G**	**S**	**B**	**G**	**S**	**B**	**G**	**S**	**B**
Germany	3	1	2	0	0	1	0	0	0	2	3	1
Norway	1	3	0	0	0	0	4	3	2	1	0	0
Russian Fed.	0	0	0	3	2	0	5	2	1	0	0	0
Austria	3	4	4	0	0	0	0	1	1	0	0	0
Canada	0	0	0	0	1	0	0	0	0	1	2	2
United States	1	0	0	1	1	0	0	0	0	0	1	1

Let *C* be the set of the six listed countries and *E* be the set of the four listed sporting events. Use the table to determine if each statement is true or false.

11. ∃ a country *c* in *C* such that ∀ sporting events *e* in *E*, *c* won a medal in *e*.

12. ∀ sporting events *e* in *E*, ∃ a country *c* in *C* such that *c* won a Bronze medal in *e*.

13. ∀ countries *c* in *C*, ∃ a sporting event *e* in *E* such that *c* won a Gold medal in *e*.

14. ∃ a sporting event *e* in *E* such that ∀ countries *c* in *C*, *c* won a medal in *e*.

15. ∃ a country *c* in *C* and a sporting event *e* in *E* such that *c* won Gold, Silver, and Bronze medals in *e*.

Name

LESSON MASTER 1-2

Questions on SPUR Objectives
See pages 71–75 for objectives.

Skills Objective C

In 1–4, write the negation of the statement.

1. *All true wisdom is found on T-shirts.*

2. $\exists$ *real numbers x such that* $x^2 + 1 = 0$.

3. *At least one integer is irrational.*

4. $\exists$ *a real number x such that* $\forall$ *real numbers y,* $x - y \neq y - x$.

Skills Objective D

5. Consider the statement let *p: Some parabolas have no lines of symmetry.*

a. Write $\sim p$ as a universal statement.

b. Which is true, *p* or $\sim p$?

Properties Objective E

6. Suppose *p* is a false statement. Is the statement $\sim(\sim p)$ true or false?

7. Suppose the statement $\forall$ *z in M,* $\sim r(z)$ is true. What is the truth value of $\exists$ *z in M such that* $\sim p(z)$?

8. Suppose the statement $\exists$ *x in S such that* $\sim p(x)$ is true. What is the truth value of $\forall$ *x in S,* $\sim p(x)$?

Uses Objective I

In 9–11, let *m*(*x*) be the sentence *x is male* and *f*(*x*) be the sentence *x is female*. Tell which is true, the statement or its negation.

9. $\forall$ *U.S. Presidents y, m(y).*

10. $\exists$ a *U.S. Vice President v, such that* $\sim f(v)$.

11. $\forall$ *U.S. Secretaries of State z,* $\sim f(z)$.

Name

Questions on SPUR Objectives
See pages 71–75 for objectives.

Skills Objective B

In 1–4, express the inequality by writing out each implied *and* or *or*.

1. $m \leq -5$

2. $0 \leq k < 1.2$

3. $|z| > 3$

4. $|t - 1| < \frac{1}{2}$

Skills Objective C

In 5–7, use De Morgan's Laws to write the negation of the statement.

5. *Jill is well and Mel is ill.*

6. ∀ *integers x, x is odd or x is not prime.*

7. ∃ *real numbers x and y such that x < y and y < x.*

Skills Objective D

In 8–13, suppose the statement *p* is true and the statement *q* is false. Determine the truth value of the given statement.

8. *p and q*

9. *~(p and ~q) or (~p or ~q)*

10. *~p or ~q*

11. *~p and ~q*

12. *(~p or q) or ~(p or ~q)*

13. *~(p and q)*

Properties Objective E

14. Use DeMorgan's Laws to show that the statements of Questions 12 and 13 are logically equivalent.

Name

▶ **LESSON MASTER 1-3** *page 2*

Properties Objective H

15. Show that the following statement is false. ∀ *real numbers x,* $x \geq 0$ *or* $\sin x \leq 0$.

Uses Objective I

In 16–18, refer to the table below, which lists the amenities available at five hotels with rooms reserved for an upcoming convention. H = Handicapped Access; FC = Fitness Center; IP = Indoor Pool; L = Lounge; R = Restaurant; D = Distance to Convention Center; S = Single Price

Hotel	H	FC	IP	L	R	D	S
1	*	*	*	*	*	15 blocks	$180
2	*				*	6 blocks	$100
3	*					4 miles	$146
4	*	*		*	*	12 blocks	$175
5		*		*	*	15 blocks	$109

Use the table to determine whether the given statement is true or false.

16. ∃ *a hotel h such that h has an indoor pool and* $S < \$180$.

17. ∀ *hotels h, h has a restaurant or* $D > 3$ *miles.*

18. ∀ *hotels h, h has a restaurant and lounge or h has handicapped access.*

Representations Objective L

19. Use a truth table to show that *p and (q or r)* ≡ *(p and q) or (p and r).*

Name

LESSON MASTER 1-4

Questions on SPUR Objectives
See pages 71–75 for objectives.

Representations Objective K

1. Consider the following network.

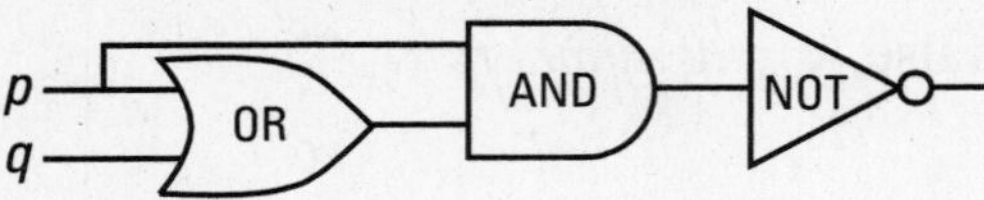

a. Write an input-output table for the network.

b. Draw a functionally equivalent network that has only one logic gate.

2. Consider the following network.

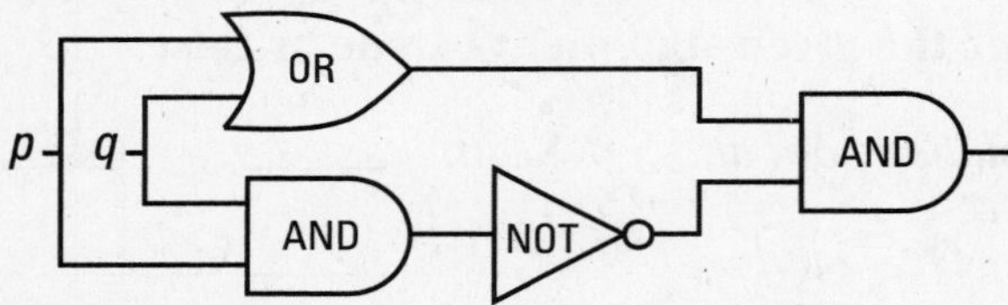

a. Write the logical expression that corresponds to the network. ______________________

b. Write an input-output table for the network.

Name

▶ LESSON MASTER 1-4 *page 2*

3. Are the two networks shown below, each with four inputs *p*, *q*, *r*, and *s*, functionally equivalent? Justify your answer.

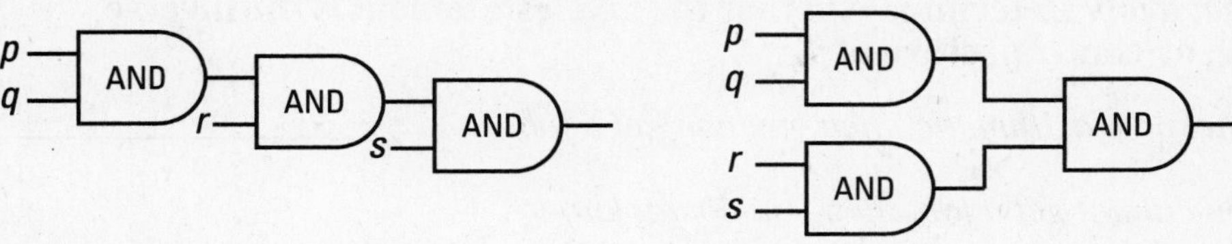

4. Consider the following network.

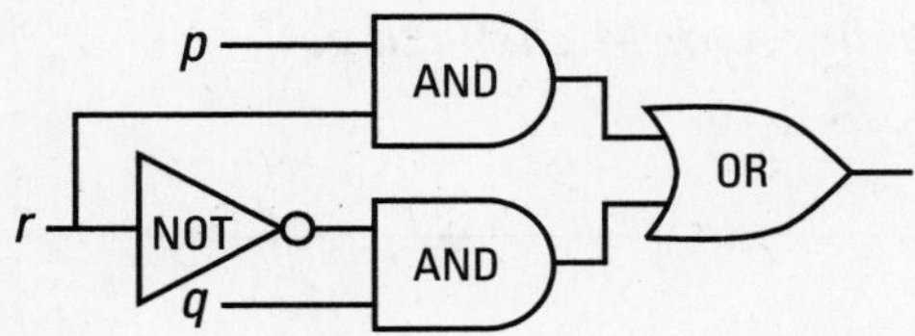

a. Fill in the input-output table below for this network.

p	*q*	*r*	NOT *r*	*p* AND *r*	*q* AND NOT *r*	(*p* AND *r*) OR (*q* AND NOT *r*)
0	0	0				
0	1	0				
1	0	0				
1	1	0				
0	0	1				
0	1	1				
1	0	1				
1	1	1				

b. What effect does input *r* have on the output?

Name ______________________________

LESSON MASTER 1-5

Questions on SPUR Objectives
See pages 71–75 for objectives.

Skills Objective A

In 1–3, let p be the following statement: *If you do not know arithmetic, then you cannot get a job.* Determine whether the given statement is the inverse, converse, or contrapositive of p.

1. *If you know arithmetic, then you can get a job.* ______________

2. *If you cannot get a job, then you do not know arithmetic.* ______________

3. *If you can get a job, then you know arithmetic.* ______________

Skills Objective B

4. Write the following statement as an *if-then* conditional. *Getting a B+ on her final exam is a necessary condition for Michelle to get an A for the quarter.*

____

____

5. Write two *if-then* conditionals contained in the following statement: *For any polynomial $f(x)$, a number c is a solution to $f(x) = 0$ if and only if $(x - c)$ is a factor of $f(x)$.*

____

____

____

Skills Objective C

6. Consider the statement p: $\forall\, x,\ x^2 - 5x + 6 = 0 \Rightarrow x = 3$. Write $\sim p$.

____

7. Write the negation of the following statement as a conditional statement: *There is a substance which is metal and not a good conductor.*

____

Skills Objective D

In 8–11, let $r(x)$: $\frac{1}{x} = \frac{2}{x^2}$ and let $s(x)$: $x^2 = 2x$. Determine whether the given statement is true or false.

8. $\forall$ *real numbers* x, $r(x) \Rightarrow s(x)$.

____

9. $\forall$ *real numbers* x, $\sim r(x) \Rightarrow \sim s(x)$.

____

10. $\forall$ *real numbers* x, $s(x) \Rightarrow r(x)$.

____

11. $\forall$ real numbers x, $\sim s(x) \Rightarrow \sim r(x)$.

____

Name ____________________

▶ **LESSON MASTER 1-5** *page 2*

Properties Objective E

12. Suppose p and $p \Rightarrow q$ are both true statements. What is the truth value of q? ____________

13. Suppose q and $p \Rightarrow q$ are both true statements. What is the truth value of p? ____________

14. *Multiple choice.* Which statement is logically equivalent to $\forall$ *x, if p(x) then q(x)*? ____________

(a) $\exists$ *x such that p(x) and ~q(x).* (b) $\forall$ *x, p(x) or ~q(x).*

(c) $\forall$ *x, ~p(x) or q(x).* (d) $\forall$ *x, p(x) and q(x).*

Uses Objective I

In 15–17, refer to the table below, which shows the types of paints that can be used on different exterior surfaces. Determine whether the given statement is true or false.

	Wood				Masonry			Metal			
	Clapboard	Shutters/trim	Window frames	Natural siding/trim	Brick	Cement/ cinder block	Stucco	Metal siding	Copper surfaces	Galvanized surfaces	Iron surfaces
Latex house	✓	✓	✓		✓	✓	✓	✓		✓	✓
Alkyd house	✓	✓	✓		✓	✓	✓	✓		✓	✓
Cement powder					✓	✓	✓				
Trim		✓		✓				✓		✓	✓
Aluminum			✓		✓	✓	✓	✓		✓	✓

15. $\forall$ *paints p, if p can be used on brick then p can be used on metal siding.* ____________

16. $\forall$ *surfaces s, a latex paint can be used on s if and only if an alkyd paint can be used on s.* ____________

Representations Objective L

17. Complete the truth table for $p \Rightarrow (s \text{ or } r)$.

p	s	r	s or r	p ⇒ (s or r)
F	F	F		
F	F	T		
F	T	F		
F	T	T		
T	F	F		
T	F	T		
T	T	F		
T	T	T		

Name

Questions on SPUR Objectives
See pages 71–75 for objectives.

Properties Objective G

In 1–3, supply the missing premise so that the argument is valid.

1. $s \Rightarrow t$
   ____
   $\therefore \sim s$

2. __________
   $q \Rightarrow r$
   $\therefore n \Rightarrow r$

3. $a \Rightarrow b$
   ____
   $\therefore b$

Properties Objective H

In 4–6, draw a valid conclusion from the given premises and state whether the conclusion is true or false. If the conclusion is false, circle the false premise or premises.

4. *$\forall$ integers $n \geq 1$, if n is not prime then n has a factor less than or equal to $\sqrt{n}$. 101 has no factor less than or equal to $\sqrt{101}$.*

   ____

5. *If a quadrilateral's diagonals are not perpendicular, then it is not a kite. If a quadrilateral is not a kite, then it is not a rhombus.*

   ____

6. *$\forall$ x and y, if x and y are irrational numbers then their product is an irrational number. π and $\frac{1}{\pi}$ are irrational numbers.*

   ____

Uses Objective J

In 7 and 8, tell whether the argument uses the Law of Detachment (modus ponens), the Law of Indirect Reasoning (modus tollens), or the Law of Transitivity.

7. *The movie that wins the Academy Award for "Best Picture" is the most critically acclaimed movie of the year.* Titanic *won the Academy Award for "Best Picture" of 1997. So* Titanic *was the most critically acclaimed movie for that year.*

   ____

8. *If we do not increase federal funding for education, our nation's students will not be prepared for the jobs of the 21st century. And if they are not prepared for the jobs of the 21st century, America will not be able to compete in the global marketplace. America will not be able to compete in the global marketplace, if we do not increase federal funding for education.*

   ____

Name

LESSON MASTER 

Questions on SPUR Objectives
See pages 71–75 for objectives.

In 1–6, tell whether the argument is valid or invalid. Support your answer with a reference to one or more of the following.

I. Law of Detachment
II. Law of Indirect Reasoning
III. Law of Transitivity
IV. Converse Error
V. Inverse Error
VI. Improper Induction

Properties Objective G

1. $\forall x$, *if* $x^2 \le 64$ *then* $x \le 8$.
$9 > 8$
$\therefore 9^2 > 64$

---

2. $\forall x$, *if* $x^2 \le 64$ *then* $x \le 8$.
$(-9)^2 > 64$
$\therefore -9 > 8$

---

3. $\forall x$, *if* $x^2 \le 64$ *then* $x \le 8$.
$-9 \le 8$
$\therefore (-9)^2 \le 64$

---

4. $2^{2^0} + 1 = 3$ *(prime)*, $2^{2^1} + 1 = 5$ *(prime)*, $2^{2^2} + 1 = 17$ *(prime)*,
$2^{2^3} + 1 = 257$ *(prime)*, $2^{2^4} + 1 = 65{,}337$ *(prime)*
$\therefore \forall$ *integers* $n \ge 0$, $2^{2^n} + 1$ *is a prime number.*

Uses Objective J

5. *If Carolyn does not finish her homework, then she will not be allowed to watch television. Carolyn was not allowed to watch television. Therefore, she did not finish her homework.*

---

6. *Mr. Thompson did not commit the crime, if the lab results do not show a match between his DNA and the DNA found at the crime scene. The test results did show a match between Mr. Thompson's DNA and the DNA found at the crime scene, so he must have committed the crime.*

Name ______________________________

LESSON MASTER 1-8

Questions on SPUR Objectives
See pages 71–75 for objectives.

Properties Objective H

In 1 and 2, steps in the solution of an equation are given. Provide the justifications that allow you to conclude the given conditionals.

1. p: $4x - 7 = 2x - 9$
q: $4x = 2x - 2$
r: $4x - 2x = -2$
s: $x(4 - 2) = -2$
t: $2x = -2$
u: $x = -1$

a. $p \Rightarrow q$ ______________________________

b. $r \Rightarrow s$ ______________________________

c. $t \Rightarrow u$ ______________________________

d. $p \Rightarrow u$ ______________________________

2. p: $x^2 + 3x = 10$
q: $x^2 + 3x - 10 = 0$
r: $(x + 5)(x - 2) = 0$
s: $x = -5$ *or* $x = 2$

a. $p \Rightarrow q$ ______________________________

b. $q \Rightarrow r$ ______________________________

c. $r \Rightarrow s$ ______________________________

d. $p \Rightarrow s$ ______________________________

Uses Objective J

3. If it rains today, Andrew will have to drive Amy to work. If Andrew drives Amy to work, he will be late for work. If he is late for work, he will have to reschedule a meeting. If he reschedules his meeting, he won't make it home until late. If he doesn't come home until late, he won't be able to make Amy dinner. If Andrew doesn't make dinner for Amy, Amy must make dinner for Andrew.

a. Who will make dinner if it rains today? ______________

b. What is the weather like if Amy doesn't make dinner for Andrew? ______________

Name ___

LESSON MASTER 2-1

Questions on SPUR Objectives
See pages 142–145 for objectives.

Properties Objective C

1. The table below shows how tornadoes/wind storms are classified using the Fujita Scale. Let r = rank, w = wind speed, d = damage, s = strength, and let f, g, and h be the relations: f: rank → wind speed, g: wind speed → strength, and h: strength → damage.

Rank	Wind Speed	Damage	Strength
0	up to 72 mph	Light	weak
1	73–112 mph	Moderate	weak
2	113–157 mph	Considerable	strong
3	158–206 mph	Severe	strong
4	207–260 mph	Devastating	violent
5	> 261 mph	Incredible	violent

a. Evaluate $f(3)$. ___

b. Evaluate $g(200)$. ___

c. Among f, g, and h, which one is *not* a function? Explain.

___

___

In 2 and 3, a function is given. a. Give a reasonable domain for the function. b. Is the function discrete?

2. $p(x)$ = the number of people in the family of student x in Class A

a. ___ **b.** ___

3. $q(x)$ = the average temperature in a city in month x

a. ___ **b.** ___

In 4 and 5, use interval notation to describe the domain of the real function.

4. $f(x) = \sqrt{x^2 - 3x + 2}$

___

5. $g(z) = \frac{1}{z^3 - 8} + \frac{1}{\sqrt{z - 1}}$

b. ___

6. Suppose the price of regular gasoline is $1.25 per gallon. You want to find the cost if you pump g gallons of gasoline into a tank with a full capacity of 16.5 gallons.

a. Identify a formula for the function mapping g onto the cost. ___

b. Identify the independent variable of this function, and its domain. ___

c. Identify the dependent variable of this function, and its range. ___

Name

LESSON MASTER 2-2

Questions on SPUR Objectives
See pages 142–145 for objectives.

Skills Objective A

1. Let $g(t) = \frac{1 + 8t}{1 + t^2}$. Estimate its range and its maximum and minimum values.

Properties Objective C

2. Let $f(x) = -4x^2 + 8x - 1$.
   a. Find the exact range.
   b. Check your answer to part **a** by using an automatic grapher. Sketch the graph in the screen at the right.

Uses Objective F

3. Fred wants to use a wire to make an isosceles triangle for a decoration. Assume the wire has a length of 6 meters.
   a. Express A, the area of the triangle, as a function of x.
   b. What is the domain of $A(x)$?
   c. Use an automatic grapher to graph $A(x)$. Sketch the graph in the screen at the right.
   d. What is the maximum area of the triangle Fred can make?

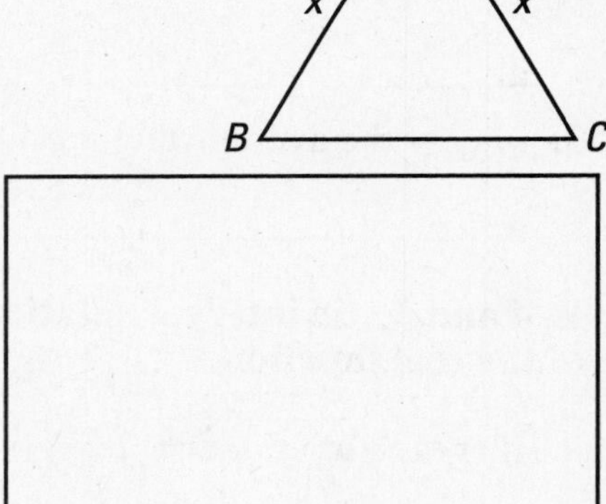

Representations Objective G

4. Sketch a graph of the function f with the following characteristics.
   (a) Domain: (-3, 4]
   (b) Range: [-2, 5]
   (c) Maximum value: $f(0)$; minimum values: $f(-2)$ and $f(4)$

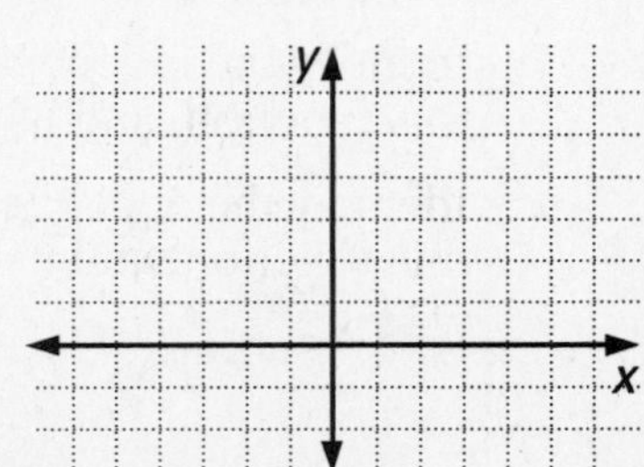

Name

LESSON MASTER 2-3

Questions on SPUR Objectives
See pages 142–145 for objectives.

Skills Objective G

1. The table at the right shows the number of persons below the poverty level in the U.S. between 1975 and 1995. Let $P(x)$ be the number of persons below the poverty level in year x.

Year	Persons Below the Poverty Level (thousands)
1975	25,877
1976	24,975
1977	24,720
1978	24,497
1979	26,072
1980	29,272
1981	31,822
1982	34,398
1983	35,303
1984	33,700
1985	33,064
1986	32,370
1987	32,221
1988	31,745
1989	31,528
1990	33,585
1991	35,708
1992	38,014
1993	39,625
1994	38,059
1995	36,425

a. Find the longest interval over which P is increasing.

____

b. Find the longest interval over which P is decreasing.

____

c. What are the relative minima of P?

____

d. What are the relative maxima of P?

____

e. Solve $P(x) = 35{,}708$.

____

2. Let $f(x) = 2x^2 - x + 15$. Give the interval(s) on which f is

a. decreasing

____

b. increasing

____

Representations Objective G

3. The graph of a function $g(x)$ is given at the right.

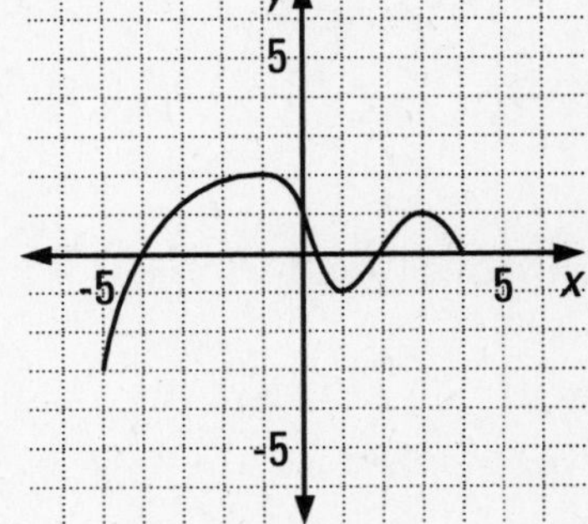

a. Over which intervals is g increasing?

____

b. Find any relative maxima and relative minima of g.

____

____

4. Use an automatic grapher to estimate the relative maximum and relative minimum of the function h with $h(t) = t^3 - 4t^2 + 3t - 4$ on the interval $-1 \le t \le 4$. Sketch the graph in the screen at the right.

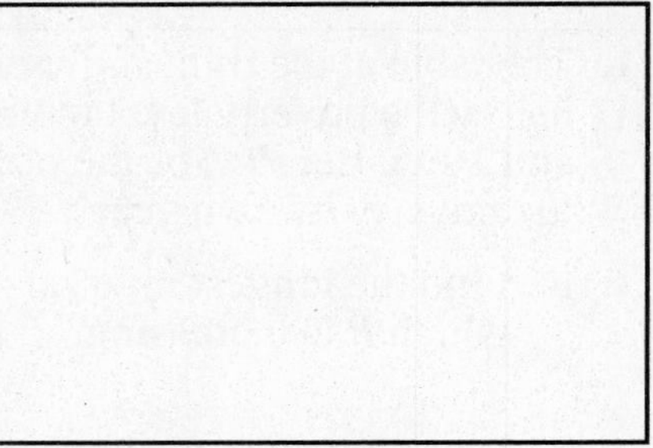

____

____

5. Graph $y = |2x - 1|$ over $-4 \le x \le 4$. Describe all intervals on which the function $x \to y$ is increasing.

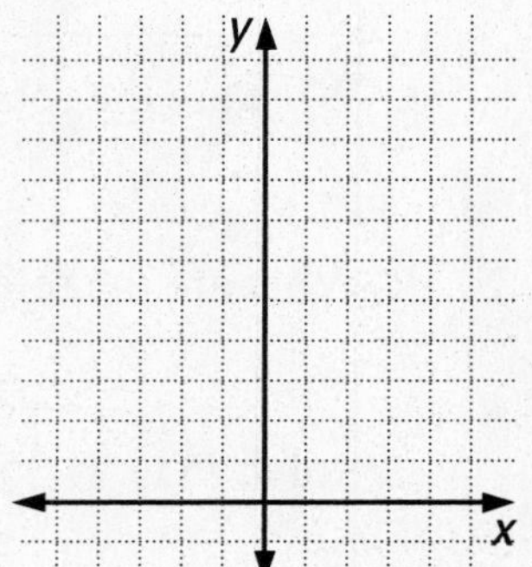

____

Name

LESSON MASTER 2-4

Questions on SPUR Objectives
See pages 142–145 for objectives.

Properties Objective D

1. Consider the function f with $f(x) = \frac{x - 1}{x + 1}$.

a. Complete the table below to give decimal approximations to values of $f(x)$ as x increases.

x	10	100	1,000	10,000	100,000
$f(x)$					

b. What is $\lim_{x \to \infty} f(x)$? __________

c. Write an equation of the horizontal asymptote of f. __________

2. Let $g(x) = 5 + \frac{1}{x^3}$.

a. Find $\lim_{x \to \infty} g(x)$ and $\lim_{x \to -\infty} g(x)$. __________

b. Is g *odd, even,* or *neither*? __________

c. For what values of x is $g(x)$ within 0.001 of the limit? __________

3. If $\varphi(x)$ is an even function and $\lim_{x \to \infty} \varphi(x) = -1$, find $\lim_{x \to -\infty} \varphi(x)$. __________

4. Describe the end behavior of $y = -2x^3$.

____

Representations Objective G

5. The function f is graphed at the right.

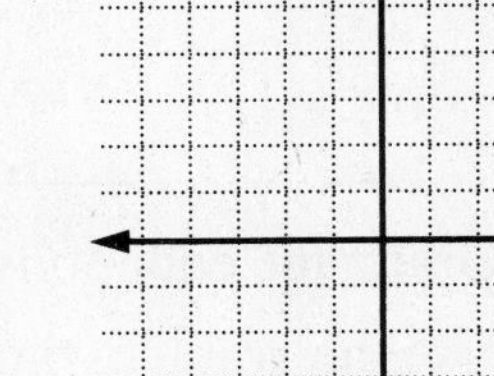

a. Is f *odd, even* or *neither*? __________

b. Describe its end behavior.

____

c. Write the equations of the horizontal asymptotes.

____

6. Sketch the graph of an even function f that has a relative maximum at $x = 2$ and a relative minimum at $x = 1$, with $\lim_{x \to \infty} f(x) = 3$.

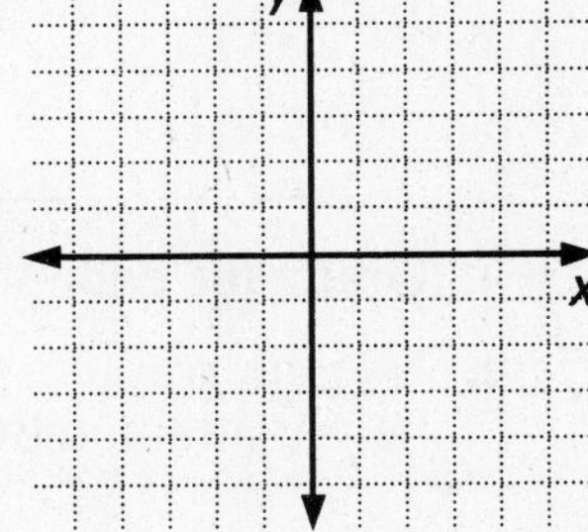

Name

LESSON MASTER 2-5

Questions on SPUR Objectives
See pages 142–145 for objectives.

Representations Objective H

In 1–3, graph the parametric equations.

1. $\begin{cases} x(t) = 2t - 1 \\ y(t) = 2t^2 + 1 \end{cases}$

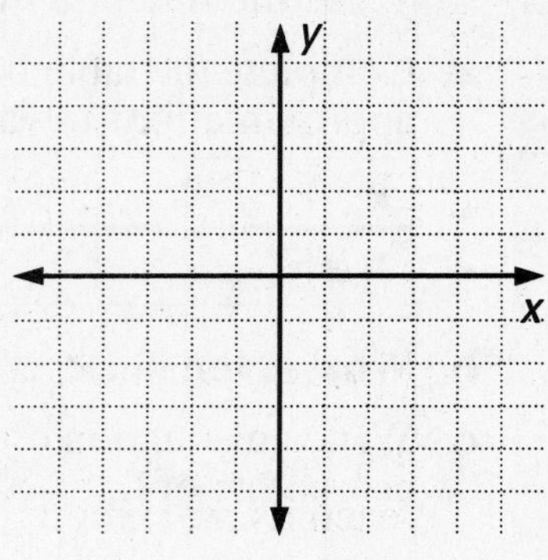

2. $\begin{cases} x(\theta) = \theta + \frac{\pi}{2} \\ y(\theta) = \cos\theta - 1 \end{cases}$

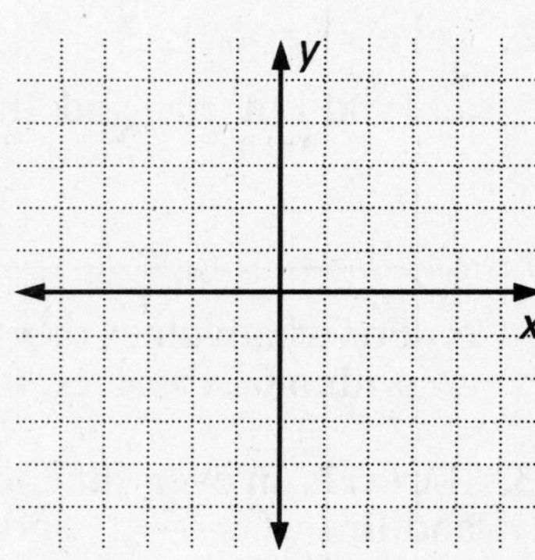

3. $\begin{cases} x(t) = e^t - e^{-t} \\ y(t) = e^t + e^{-t} \end{cases}$ $0 \le t \le 5$

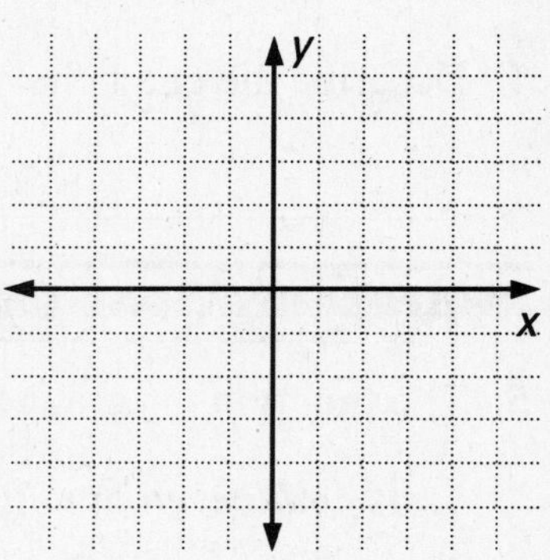

4. Suppose that a ball is thrown with an initial horizontal velocity of 25 ft/sec and an initial vertical velocity of $25\sqrt{3}$ ft/sec, and assume that the only force acting on the object is due to gravity. Let t = time in seconds since ball was thrown.

a. Find the parametric equations for the path of the ball. Assume that the starting point is the origin.

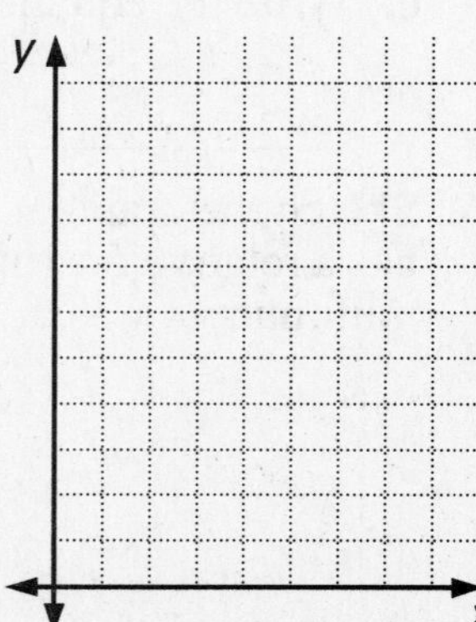

____

b. Graph the equations in the x-y plane.

c. Use the graph to find the maximum height attained by the ball.

____

Name

Questions on SPUR Objectives
See pages 142–145 for objectives.

Properties Objective D

1. Consider the function with equation $y = 2 \sin (3x) - 3$.

   a. Give its domain and range.

   b. What is the fundamental period of the function?

   c. Find its maximum and minimum values.

   d. For how many values of x does the function reach its maximum and minimum values?

   e. Describe the end behavior of the function.

Representations Objective G

In 2–4, a function is given. Tell whether the function is *odd, even,* or *neither.*

2. $f(x) = \cos x$ **3.** $g(x) = \sin x$ **4.** $h(x) = \sin x + \cos x$

5. Consider the function f with $f(x) = -\sin (2x)$ on the interval $0 \le x \le 2\pi$.

   a. Over what intervals is f increasing?

   b. For what values of x does f reach its minimum value?

   c. What is the fundamental period of f?

6. **a.** On the x-y plane, graph the curve defined by the parametric equation

$$\begin{cases} x(t) = \cos t + 1 \\ y(t) = 2 \sin t - 1 \end{cases}.$$

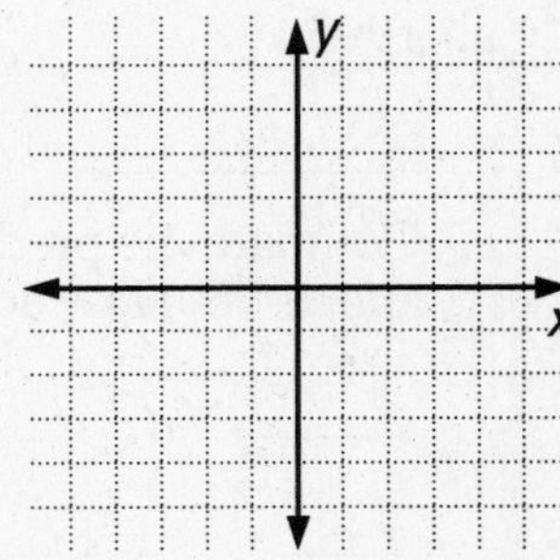

   b. Prove that every point on this curve is on the ellipse with equation $(x - 1)^2 + \frac{(y + 1)^2}{4} = 1$.

Name

LESSON MASTER 2-7

Questions on SPUR Objectives
See pages 142–145 for objectives.

Skills Objective B

In 1 and 2, rewrite the expression without using "+" or "–".

1. 5^{1-x} ____________ **2.** e^{x+y} ____________

Properties Objective D

3. Contrast the end behavior of $f: x \rightarrow 2^x$ with that of $g: x \rightarrow 2^{-x}$.

____

____

Uses Objective E

In 4–6, use the following table, which shows the GDP (gross domestic product) of the U.S. from 1992 to 1996 in billions of dollars.

Year	1992	1993	1994	1995	1996
GDP	6,038.5	6,343.3	6,736.1	7,265.4	7,636.0

4. Find the formula predicting the GDP of the United States x years after 1992, assuming a discrete model and an annual growth rate of 5.1%.

____

5. Calculate the GDP predicted by the formula in Question 4 for

a. 1993. **b.** 1994. **c.** 1995. **d.** 1996.

________ ________ ________ ________

e. Compare the predicted GDP and the actual GDP between 1993 and 1996. How accurate is the formula for the prediction?

____

____

6. Use the formula in Question 4 to predict the GDP of the United States in the year 2000. ____________

Name ______________________________

7. A lake has been polluted by a certain chemical. To have the water safe for use, the concentration of that chemical must be equal to or less than 15% of its present level. If the chemical naturally dissipates so that 3% of it is lost each year, use the Continuous Change Model to find about how many years it will take for the lake water to become usable. ______________

Representations Objective G

8. Let f be defined by $f(x) = ab^x$. For what values of a and b is f a decreasing function?

____

9. Use an automatic grapher to graph $y = e^{\sqrt{x}}$. Sketch the graph at the right. Then analyze the function from its graph.

____

____

____

____

____

____

Name

LESSON MASTER 

Questions on SPUR Objectives
See pages 142–145 for objectives.

Properties Objective D

1. Find $\lim_{n\to\infty} a_n$ if $\begin{cases} a_1 = -5 \\ a_{k+1} = \frac{a_k}{4} \ \forall\, k \geq 1 \end{cases}$. ________

2. Let $\begin{cases} c_1 = 3 \\ c_{k+1} = \frac{1}{3}c_k \ \forall\, k \geq 1 \end{cases}$.

   a. What is the limit of c_n as $n \to \infty$? ________

   b. For what values of n is c_n within 0.001 of the limit? ________

3. Use limit notation to describe and then find the limit of $S_n = \left(-\frac{4}{5}\right)^{2n+1}$ as n increases without bound.

____

Uses Objective E

4. Square $ABCD$ has sides of length a, A_1, B_1, C_1, and D_1 are the midpoints of $\overline{AB}$, $\overline{BC}$, $\overline{CD}$, and $\overline{DA}$, respectively. Also, from $n \geq 2$, A_n, B_n, C_n, and D_n, are the midpoints of $\overline{A_{n-1}B_{n-1}}$, $\overline{B_{n-1}C_{n-1}}$, $\overline{C_{n-1}D_{n-1}}$, and $\overline{D_{n-1}A_{n-1}}$, respectively. Let S_n be the area of square $A_nB_nC_nD_n$.

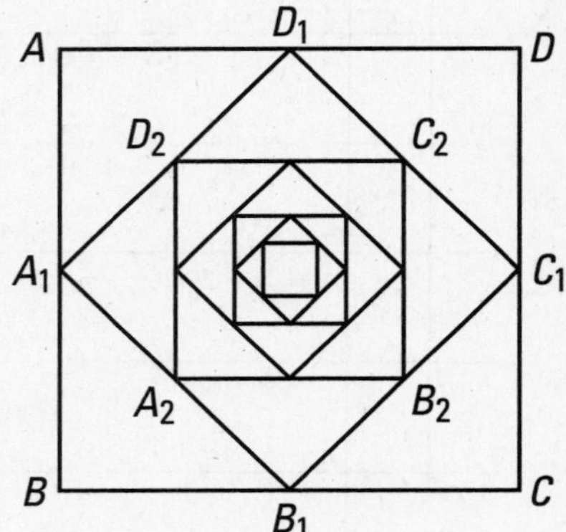

   a. Find S_1.

   ____

   b. Give an equation relating S_n and S_{n-1}. ________

   c. Find $\lim_{x\to\infty} S_n$ and explain what it means.

   ____

   ____

   ____

▶

Name

5. A traveler brought 10 rabbits initially into an unpopulated island. Left undisturbed, the rabbit population will triple each year.

a. Write a difference equation for the sequence P of the rabbit population at the end of the nth year (assuming an unlimited growth model.)

b. Instead of assuming an unlimited growth model, suppose that the island has a support limit of 10,000 rabbits. Modify the difference equation of part **a** to account for this limitation.

Representations Objective G

In 6 and 7, graph the first five terms of the sequence, and find its limit as $n \to \infty$.

6. $a_n = \frac{2n^2 - 1}{n^2}\ \forall n \geq 1$

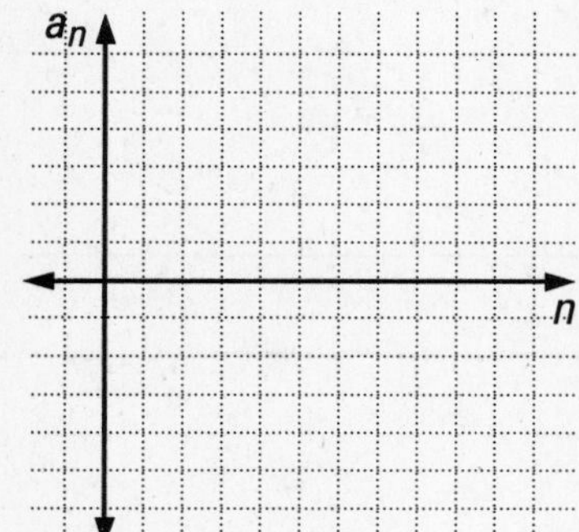

7. $\begin{cases} b_1 = 3 \\ b_{n+1} = 2b_n + 1\ \forall n \geq 1 \end{cases}$

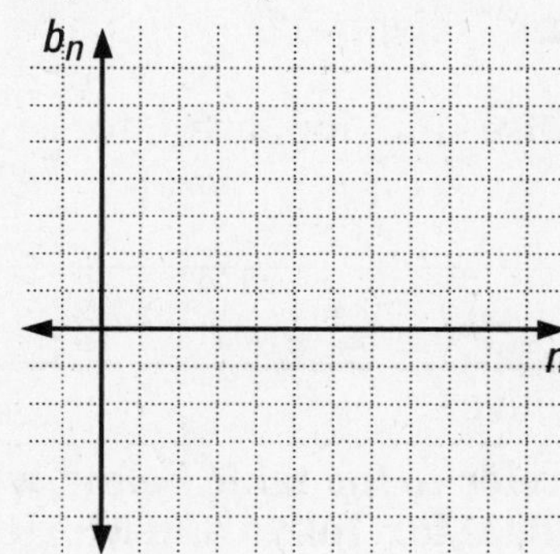

Name ______________________________

LESSON MASTER 

Questions on SPUR Objectives
See pages 142–145 for objectives.

Skills Objective B

1. Evaluate each expression.

a. $\log_2\left(\frac{1}{2}\right)^5$ b. $\log_{10}\sqrt{1{,}000}$ c. $\ln \frac{1}{e^3}$

______ ______ ______

2. Express $\log_a\left(\frac{n^3}{m^2}\right)^{\frac{1}{5}}$ in terms of $\log_a n$ and $\log_a m$.

______

3. Given log 7 = 0.8451 and log 8 = 0.9030. Find

a. log 2. b. log 14. c. log 28.

______ ______ ______

4. Solve for x: $\log_x 169 = 2$ ______

Properties Objective D

5. *True or false.* $\lim_{x \to -\infty} \log_b x = 0$ for any $b > 1$. Justify your answer.

______

Uses Objective E

In 6 and 7, refer to the table below, which gives population data for Tokyo and Mexico City, the world's two most populous urban areas in 1995.

	Population (1995, in thousands)	Annual Growth rate 1990–1995 (percent)
Tokyo, Japan	26,959	1.4%
Mexico City, Mexico	16,562	1.81%

6. Assuming a discrete model, what was the population of each urban area in 1990?

Tokyo ______ Mexico City ______

7. Assume that the annual growth rates in both areas remain constant. In what year will Mexico City's population exceed Tokyo's? ______

 ►

Name

▶ **LESSON MASTER 2-9** *page 2*

Representations Objective G

8. a. Graph the function f with $f(x) = \log_{\frac{1}{2}} x$.

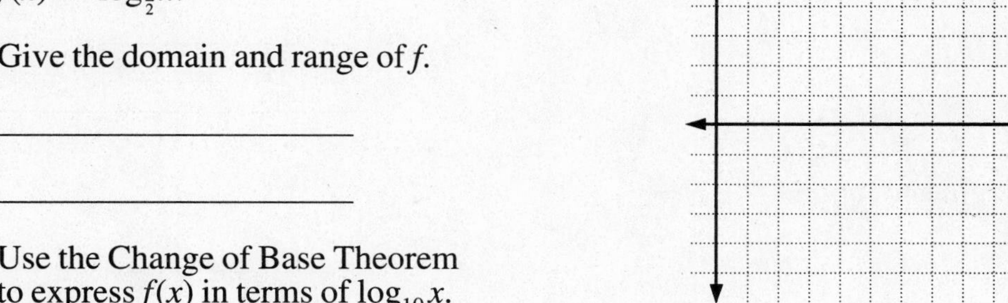

b. Give the domain and range of f.

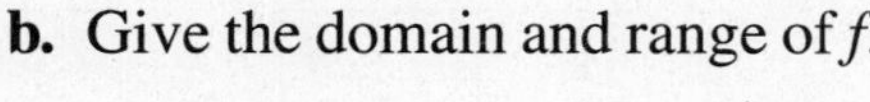

____

____

c. Use the Change of Base Theorem to express $f(x)$ in terms of $\log_{10} x$.

____

d. Describe the interval of x over which f is increasing or decreasing.

____

e. Compare the graph of f to the graph of g where $g(x) = \log_2 x$

____

____

Name

LESSON MASTER 

Questions on SPUR Objectives
See pages 218–221 for objectives.

Skills Objective B

In 1–3, find a formula for $h(x)$ and state the domain for the indicated function h.

1. $f(x) = x$, $g(x) = x + 3$; $h = \frac{f}{g}$

2. $f(x) = 3^x$, $g(x) = 3^{-x}$; $h = f \cdot g$

3. $f(x) = \frac{1}{1 - x}$, $g(x) = \frac{1}{1 + x}$; $h = f - g$

4. $f(x) = \sin x$, $g(x) = \cos x$; $h = \frac{f - g}{f + g}$

Uses Objective I

5. Suppose for a trip to Egypt, a tour organizer charges \$2,200 per person for groups of a minimum of 15 people. For each additional person in the group, however, the organizer reduces the entire group's per-person rate by \$25. The organizer's expenses for the trip included a fixed cost of \$3,000 and a per-person cost of \$1,575.

   a. Write a formula for $P(x)$, the per-person rate for a group of x people.

   b. Write a formula for $R(x)$, the revenues generated from a group of x people.

   c. Write a formula for $E(x)$, the expenses incurred from a group of x people.

   d. How is $I(x)$, the net income generated by the organizer, related to $R(x)$ and $E(x)$?

   e. Write a formula for $I(x)$ in terms of x.

   f. Use an automatic grapher to graph $I(x)$ from part e on a relevant domain and use the graph to determine the group size x for which the organizer receives its maximum net income.

Representations Objective K

6. Let $f(x) = e^{-\frac{x}{3}}$ and $g(x) = \sin(4x)$. On the grid at the right, sketch graphs of the functions f and $f \cdot g$ over the interval $[-2\pi, 2\pi]$.

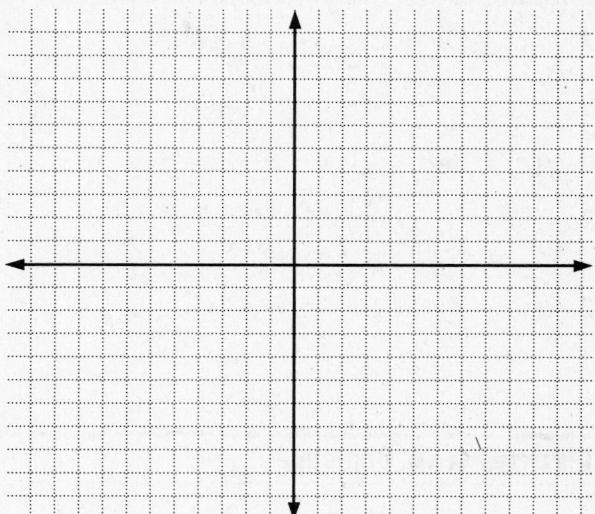

7. The functions f and g are graphed at the right.

a. Sketch the graph of $f + g$.

b. Sketch the graph of $f \cdot g$.

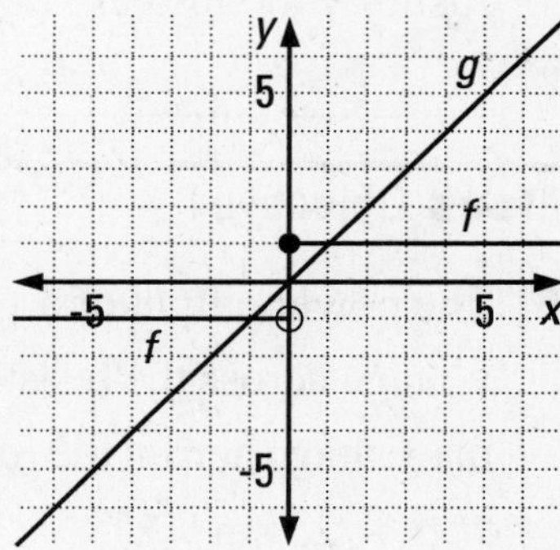

a.

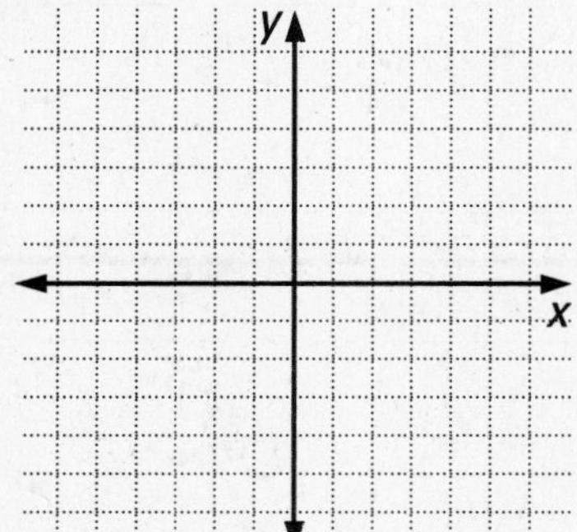

b.

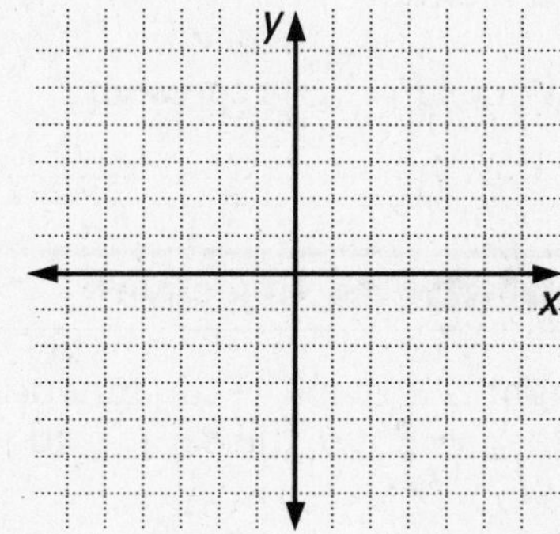

Name

LESSON MASTER 3-2

Questions on SPUR Objectives
See pages 218–221 for objectives.

Skills Objective B

In 1–3, find a formula for $h(x)$ and state the domain for the indicated function h.

1. $f(x) = 3x + 2$, $g(x) = 5x$; $h = g \circ f$

2. $f(x) = \log_3 x$, $g(x) = x^3$; $h = f \circ g$

3. $t(x) = \tan x$, $g(x) = \frac{x - 2}{3}$; $h = t \circ g$

Properties Objective F

4. Are $g: x \rightarrow |x| + 1$ and $h: x \rightarrow |x - 1|$ inverse functions? Justify your answer.

Uses Objective I

5. The power output of a 1 k Ω resistor, as a function of the voltage across the resistor, is given by $P(V) = \frac{V^2}{1000}$. Suppose the voltage across the resistor as a function of time is given by $V(t) = 25 \sin\left(\frac{\pi t}{30}\right)$.

   a. Find a formula for $P(V(t))$.

   b. What does $P(V(t))$ represent?

Representations Objective K

6. At the right is a graph of the function $f: x \rightarrow \ln x + 2$. On the same grid, sketch a graph of f^{-1}.

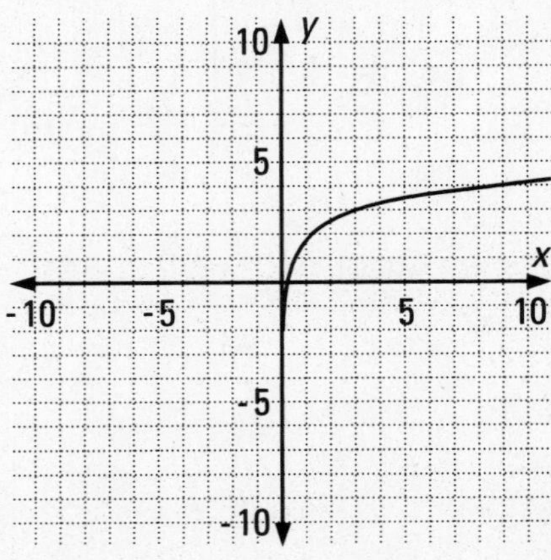

Name

Questions on SPUR Objectives
See pages 218–221 for objectives.

Skills Objective A

In 1–8, find all real solutions.

1. $(2 + y)^2 = (3 + y)^2$

2. $(z - 26)^2 = z^2$

3. $\sqrt{5r + 6} = -r$

4. $\sqrt{2t + 1} + \sqrt{2t - 1} = 10$

5. $e^{2k+2} = e^{4k-3}$

6. $3^{(2x^2+3x)} = \frac{1}{3}$

7. $\frac{1}{a^2 + 2a - 15} = \frac{1}{3 - a}$

8. $\ln(3d + 2) = \ln(2d + 7)$

Properties Objective E

9. Consider the following solution of $\log(x^2 - 18) = \log(-3x + 10)$.

0. $\log(x^2 - 18) = \log(-3x + 10)$
1. $x^2 - 18 = -3x + 10$
2. $x^2 + 3x - 28 = 0$
3. $(x + 7)(x - 4) = 0$
4. $x = -7$ or $x = 4$

a. Are there any nonreversible steps in the solution? If so, where?

b. Are both $x = -7$ and $x = 4$ solutions to the original equation? Why or why not?

Uses Objective H

10. On January 1, 1998, Penny deposited \$5,000 in an account with an annual interest rate of 5%, compounded continuously. One year later, on January 1, 1999, Penny's sister Rupee deposited \$5,000 in an account with an annual interest rate of 7%, also compounded continuously. Give the date on which the balances in Penny's and Rupee's accounts will be equal.

Name

Questions on SPUR Objectives
See pages 218–221 for objectives.

Properties Objective G

1. a. Tell whether the function $f: x \rightarrow \frac{1}{\cos x}$ is continuous on the given interval.

i. $\left[0, \frac{\pi}{4}\right]$ ______

ii. $\left[\frac{\pi}{4}, \frac{3\pi}{4}\right]$ ______

iii. $\left[-\frac{\pi}{4}, 0\right]$ ______

b. For the function of part a, $f\left(\frac{\pi}{4}\right) > 0$ and $f\left(\frac{3\pi}{4}\right) < 0$, yet there is no x in the interval $\left[\frac{\pi}{4}, \frac{3\pi}{4}\right]$ such that $f(x) = 0$. Does this contradict the Intermediate Value Theorem? Why or why not?

______

______

2. *True or false.* If a function g is continuous on the interval [3, 6], $g(3) = 12$, and $g(6) = 19$, then, according to the Intermediate Value Theorem, $12 \le g(4) \le 19$. ______

Uses Objective H

3. On January 1, 1998, Frank deposited \$5,000 in an account with an annual interest rate of 5%, compounded continuously. One year later, on January 1, 1999, Frank's brother Mark deposited \$5,000 in an account with an annual interest rate of 7%, also compounded continuously. Give the date on which Mark's account will have \$10 more than Frank's account. ______

Representations Objective M

4. Consider the equation $e^{-x} \sin x = 1$.

a. *Multiple choice.* In which one of the following intervals must there be a solution to the equation? ______

(a) $\left[\frac{3\pi}{2}, -\pi\right]$ (b) $\left[-\pi, \frac{\pi}{2}\right]$ (c) $\left[\frac{\pi}{2}, 0\right]$ (d) $\left[0, \frac{\pi}{2}\right]$

b. Use an automatic grapher to find an interval of length 0.05 that contains a solution to the equation. ______

Name

Questions on SPUR Objectives
See pages 218–221 for objectives.

Skills Objective D

In 1–8, solve the inequality for all real-number solutions.

1. $-7n + 3 > 38$

2. $\ln z \leq -2$

3. $3^r > 3^{2-r}$

4. $\log_7 (2t + 3) \geq \log_7 (5t - 4)$

5. $k^{1.5} \geq 20$

6. $\sqrt[3]{x - 5} < -2$

7. $(7x - 3.2)^5 \geq (-x + 4.8)^5$

8. $x^3 + 3x^2 + 3x + 1 < 125$

Properties Objective E

9. Consider the following solution of $\frac{1}{x} > \frac{1}{x+1}$.

Conclusion	Justification
0. $\frac{1}{x} > \frac{1}{x+1}$	Given
1. $x < x + 1$	Apply $h(x) = \frac{1}{x}$ to both sides.
2. $0 < 1$	Add $-x$ to both sides.
3. All real values of x are solutions.	

a. The solution is not correct. Give the values of x which are not solutions to the original inequality.

b. The function h in the solution is 1 - 1 and is decreasing on the intervals $(-\infty, 0)$ and $(0, \infty)$, so where is the mistake in the solution?

Name

▶ **LESSON MASTER 3-5** *page 2*

Properties Objective F

In 10 and 11, *true or false*.

10. If a real function f is either increasing or decreasing throughout its entire domain, then the inverse of f is also a function. __________

11. If the inverse of a real function f is also a function, then f is either increasing or decreasing throughout its entire domain. __________

Uses Objective J

12. The atmospheric pressure p (in lb/in^2) as a function of altitude above sea level h (in feet) can be approximated by the formula $p = 14.7e^{-\frac{h}{28,300}}$. For what altitudes is the atmospheric pressure at least 12 lb/in^2? __________

Representations Objective K

13. *Multiple choice.* If f is a real function which is decreasing throughout its entire domain, which of the following could be the graph of f^{-1}? __________

(a)

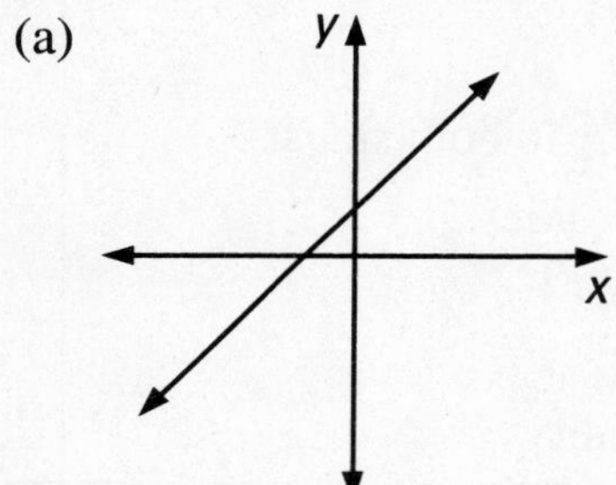

(b)

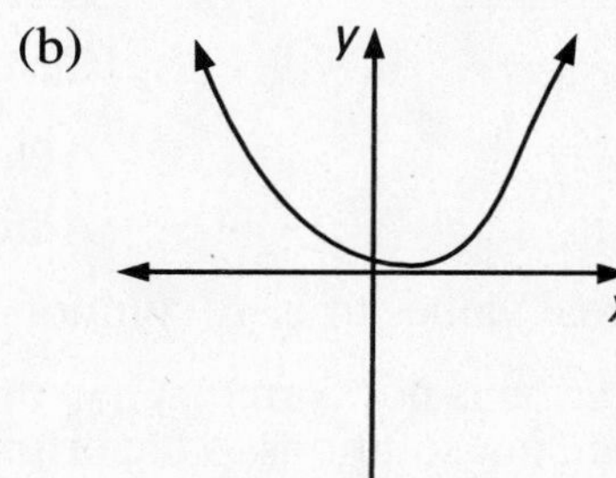

(c)

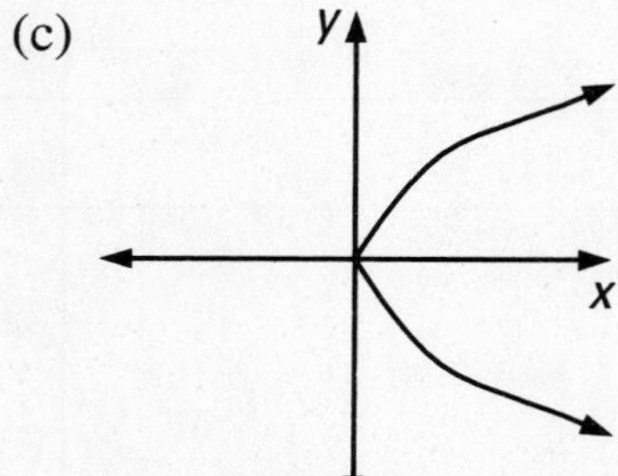

(d)

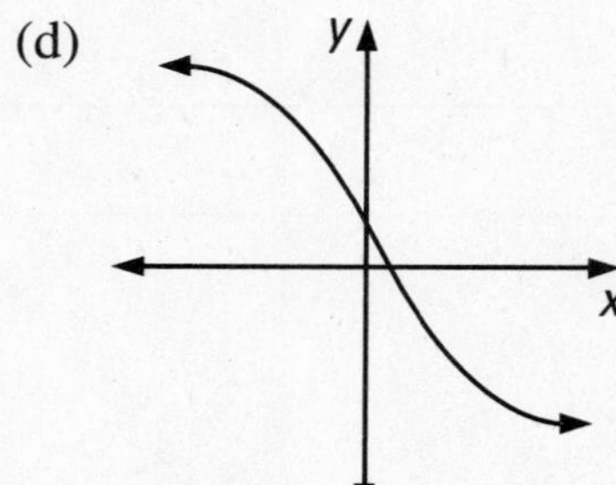

Name

LESSON MASTER **3-6**

Questions on SPUR Objectives
See pages 218–221 for objectives.

Skills Objective C

In 1–4, find all exact zeros of the given function.

1. $f(m) = 3(2^m) - 384$

2. $g(t) = 5^{2t} - 26(5^t) + 25$

3. $k(r) = (\log r)^2 + 0.5 \log r - 0.5$

4. $h(\theta) = \sin^2\theta - \sqrt{3}\sin\theta + \frac{3}{4}$

In 5–8, find all solutions to the given equation.

5. $x^6 + 9x^3 = 2x^3 + 8$

6. $\frac{1}{x^2} + 8 = \frac{6}{x}$

7. $\cos^4 x + \frac{1}{4} = \cos^2 x$

8. $(5^x - 4)^3 + 7 = 5^x + 3$

Uses Objective H

9. Ms. Yuan wishes to invest $2,000 by placing half the money in an insured no-risk certificate of deposit with an annual interest rate of 3.5%, compounded continuously, and the other half in a higher-risk bond fund with an annual interest rate of 7%, also compounded continuously.

   a. Write a formula for $V(t)$, the total value of Ms. Yuan's investment as function of time.

   b. Determine the time it will take Ms. Yuan's initial investment of $2,000 to reach $6,000.

Name

LESSON MASTER 3-7

Questions on SPUR Objectives
See pages 218–221 for objectives.

Skills Objective D

In 1–8, find the exact solution set to each inequality.

1. $\frac{x^2 - 4}{x + 3} < 0$

2. $e^{x^2} > e^{7x+8}$

3. $(7v - 2)(4v - 3) \le 0$

4. $\frac{x^2 - 9}{x} < 0$

5. $t^8 - 4t^6 \ge 0$

6. $\log(c^2 - 9c) \le \log(c - 24)$

7. $(b + 5)(b - 2)(b - 3) > 0$

8. $10^{x^2 - 3x} < 10^{-x-1}$

9. Fill in the blanks to determine when $\frac{x^2 + 5x}{x^2 - 5x + 6} < 0$.

	$(-\infty, -5)$	$(-5, 0)$			
$x + 5$	$-$				
$x - 3$		$-$			$+$
$x - 2$			$-$		
x	$-$	$-$	$+$	$+$	

Name ______________________

LESSON MASTER 

Questions on SPUR Objectives
See pages 218–221 for objectives.

Skills Objective D

In 1–3, solve the inequality.

1. a. $x^2 < 25x$ ______________

b. $(y + 2)^2 < 25(y + 2)$ ______________

2. a. $c^2 > 3c - 2$ ______________

b. $(a - 1)^2 > 3(a - 1) - 2$ ______________

3. a. $v^2 < 16v$ ______________

b. $(4u)^2 < 16(4u)$ ______________

Representations Objective L

4. The circle $x^2 + y^2 = 1$ is transformed by $S_{5,4}$ and then $T_{2,6}$.

a. Find the equation of the image under $S_{5,4}$. ______________

b. Find the equation of the image under the transformation $T \circ S$. ______________

5. From the parametric equations, give an equation relating x and y.

$$\begin{cases} x = 4\cos t - 1 \\ y = \frac{1}{2}\sin t + 2 \end{cases}$$ ______________

Representations Objective M

In 6–8, use an automatic grapher to estimate the zeros of the function.

6. $f(x) = e^{x-3436} - 3$ ______________

7. $g(x) = 3^{\frac{x}{2} - 7}$ ______________

8. $h(x) = \ln(x - 525) + 2$ ______________

Name

LESSON MASTER 3-9

Questions on SPUR Objectives
See pages 218–221 for objectives.

Skills Objective A

In 1–4, solve the equation.

1. $|a + 5| = 3a$ __________

2. $1 = |3x - 2|$ __________

3. $|c^2 - 9| = 7$ __________

4. $|d^3 - 13| = 14$ __________

Skills Objective D

In 5–8, solve the inequality.

5. $|x + 5| \leq 3$ __________

6. $|4t - 5| > t + 1$ __________

7. $4 > |s^2 + 3|$ __________

8. $6 < |x^2 - 5x|$ __________

Uses Objective J

9. A poll is conducted to calculate the approval rating of a politician. The poll results vary from the true amount by at most 5% with a confidence of 90%. The poll finds the approval rating to be 60%.

a. Write the possible values *t* for the 90% confidence interval using a double inequality. __________

b. Describe the possible values *t* for the 90% confidence interval using an absolute value. __________

Name ______________________________

LESSON MASTER 4-1

Questions on SPUR Objectives
See pages 278–281 for objectives.

Skills Objective D

1. Express $(x - 5)(x^2 - 3x + 2) + (x - 5)(x^2 - 1)$ as a product of three polynomials.

____

2. Express $y^8 + 4y^4 - 5$ as a product of four polynomials.

____

Properties Objective F

3. For what values of k is x^k a factor of $a_n x^n + a_{n-1} x^{n-1} + \dots + a_m x^m$, where $0 < m < n$? ______________

In 4 and 5, determine whether the statement is true or false and explain your answer.

4. -4 is a factor of 64 • 77.

____

5. $y + 2$ is a factor of $17y^2 + 37y + 6$.

____

In 6–8, prove the conjecture or give a counterexample to disprove it.

6. 3 is a factor of the sum of any three consecutive integers.

____

____

____

7. 4 is a factor of the sum of any four consecutive integers.

____

____

____

Name ______________________________

LESSON MASTER 4-2

Questions on SPUR Objectives
See pages 278–281 for objectives.

Skills Objective A

In 1 and 2, values for n and d are given. Find the values of q and r as defined in the Quotient-Remainder Theorem for Integers.

1. $n = 61{,}302$, $d = 179$ ______________

2. $n = -173$, $d = 11$ ______________

3. When the polynomial $p(x) = x^5 + 2x^4 + 3x^2 + 3x + 1$ is divided by $x^3 + 1$, the quotient is $x^2 + 2x$.

a. Find the remainder. ______________

b. Write $p(x)$ in the form of the Quotient-Remainder Theorem for Polynomials.

____

Properties Objective H

In 4 and 5, $d > 0$ and $n = q \cdot d + r$ in accordance with the Quotient-Remainder Theorem for Integers.

4. Suppose that q is negative.

a. What can be said about n? ______________

b. What can be said about r? ______________

5. Suppose that q is a factor of n.

a. What can be said about d? ______________

b. What can be said about r? ______________

6. Suppose that $d = 11$ and $r = 9$.

a. Give a possible positive value of n. ______________

b. Give a possible negative value of n. ______________

Name

In 7 and 8, $p(x) = q(x) \cdot d(x) + r(x)$ in accordance with the Quotient-Remainder Theorem for Polynomials.

7. If the degree of $r(x)$ is 10 and the degree of $q(x)$ is 4, what is the minimum possible degree of $p(x)$? ____________

8. If $p(x)$ has lower degree than $d(x)$, what can be said about $q(x)$ and $r(x)$? ____________

Uses Objective K

9. John decides on a Wednesday to leave on a trip exactly 115 days later. On what day of the week will he begin his trip? ____________

10. A market sells a certain bottled soft drink packaged three ways: individually for 70¢ a bottle, in 6-packs for $3.50 per pack, and in cases (four 6-packs per case) for $11 per case. Suppose n bottles are bought using c cases, s 6-packs, and b individual bottles, in such a way that the total cost is minimized.

a. What are the values of c, s, and b if $n = 64$? ____________

b. What are the values of c, s, and b if $n = 100$? ____________

c. Are your answers to parts a and b unique? Explain.

____

____

____

Name ______________________________

LESSON MASTER 

Questions on SPUR Objectives
See pages 278–281 for objectives.

Skills Objective B

In 1 and 2, use long division to find the quotient $q(x)$ and remainder $r(x)$ when $p(x)$ is divided by $d(x)$.

1. $p(x) = x^5 + x^4 - x^3 - 3x^2 - 2x$, $d(x) = x^2 + x + 1$

$q(x) =$ ______________

$r(x) =$ ______________

2. $p(x) = 3x^3 + 7x^2 + 11x + 6$, $d(x) = x + \frac{1}{3}$

$q(x) =$ ______________

$r(x) =$ ______________

3. What is the height of a rectangular box, if the bottom of the box measures $(m + 6)$ inches by $(m + 4)$ inches and the volume of the box in cubic inches is $m^3 + 7m^2 - 6m - 72$? ______________

Properties Objective H

4. Consider the polynomials $p(x) = x^6 - 9x^4 - x^2 + 9$ and $d(x) = x^2 + 1$.

a. Use long division to find the quotient $q(x)$ and remainder $r(x)$ when $p(x)$ is divided by $d(x)$.

$q(x) =$ ______________

$r(x) =$ ______________

b. Divide the quotient found in part b by $x^2 - 9$.

____

c. Using the results of parts a and b, express $p(x)$ as a product of five polynomials.

____

d. Find the values of $p(1)$, $p(-1)$, $p(3)$, $p(-3)$.

$p(1)$ ________ $p(-1)$ ________ $p(3)$ ________ $p(-3)$ ________

5. If $f(x)$ is a polynomial, $f(-3) = 5$, and the quotient is $x^2 + x + 1$ when $f(x)$ is divided by $x + 3$, what is $p(x)$?

____

6. *Multiple choice.* If $p(x)$ is divided by $x + \frac{7}{2}$, the remainder is given by which of the following? ______________

(a) $p(7)$ (b) $p\left(\frac{7}{2}\right)$ (c) $p\left(-\frac{7}{2}\right)$ (d) $p(2)$

Name

4-4

Questions on SPUR Objectives
See pages 278–281 for objectives.

Skills Objective D

1. Factor the polynomial $3x^6 - 39x^4 + 108x^2$ completely over the reals.

____

Skills Objective E

2. a. Show that -1 is a zero of the polynomial $g(x) = 6x^3 - 5x^2 - 46x - 35$.

____

____

b. Find the remaining real zeros of $g(x)$. ______________

3. Given that $x - 4$ is a factor of $p(x) = x^4 - 23x^2 + 18x + 40$ and that -1 is a zero of $p(x)$, find all real zeros of $p(x)$. ______________

4. Given that $t^2 + 1$ is a factor of $f(t) = t^5 - 3t^4 - 39t^3 - 3t^2 - 40t$, find all real zeros of $f(t)$. ______________

Properties Objective H

5. *Multiple choice.* If the graph of the equation $y = p(x)$, where $p(x)$ is a polynomial function, crosses the line $y = b$ five times, which of the following statements is not necessarily correct? ______________

(a) $p(x)$ has degree at least 5.

(b) $p(x)$ has 5 real zeros.

(c) $f(x) = p(x) - b$ has 5 real zeros.

(d) $f(x) = p(x) - b$ has degree at least 5.

6. Suppose that $g(x)$, $h(x)$, and $k(x)$ are all factors of the polynomial $f(x)$. If 5 is a zero of $g(x)$, -5 and 2 are zeros of $h(x)$, and -2 is a zero of $k(x)$, find a polynomial of degree 4 that is a factor of $f(x)$.

____

____

7. Fill in the blanks in the following sentence. If $ax + b$ is a

factor of $p(x)$, then ________ is a zero of $p(x)$, provided

that ________ .

Name

Questions on SPUR Objectives
See pages 278–281 for objectives.

Skills Objective C

1. Name two elements in each of the congruence classes modulo 5.

In 2 and 3, give the smallest positive integer that makes the congruence true.

2. $m \equiv 11 \bmod 5$ ______

3. $x \equiv -9 \pmod{21}$ ______

4. Consider the congruence classes $R_0, R_1, R_2, \ldots R_{10}$ for integers modulo 11.

   a. If you add an element of R_1 to an element of R_{10}, which class contains the sum? ______

   b. If you multiply an element of R_4 and an element of R_7, which class contains the product? ______

Properties Objective G

5. If a "special leap year" is defined as a year divisible by 4 but not divisible by 100, express any special leap year y as a solution to congruence sentences.

6. If $m \equiv 3 \pmod{14}$ and $n \equiv 7 \pmod{14}$, write a congruence statement for

   a. $m - n$

   b. mn.

Uses Objective L

7. Find the last three digits of 11^{12}. ______

8. The first 11 digits of the Universal Product Code (UPC) for a product give information; the last digit is the *Modulo 10 Check Character.* To calculate this check digit, add the values in the even-numbered positions of the first 11 digits starting from right to left. Then multiply this sum by 3, and add the product and the sum of the values in the odd-numbered positions. The check digit is the least number that when added to the above result gives a number that is a multiple of 10. Find the check digit for each number.

   a. 0-212000-15577-? ______

   b. 0-87547-36720-? ______

Name ______________________________

4-6

Questions on SPUR Objectives
See pages 278–281 for objectives.

Representations Objective M

In 1 and 2, find the base-2 representation of the number.

1. 38 ______________ **2.** 111 ______________

In 3–6, find the base-10 representation of the number.

3. 1100011_2 ______________ **4.** 100001_2 ______________

5. 327_8 ______________ **6.** BF21_{16} ______________

7. Express 100 in base n where

a. $n = 2$. ______________ **b.** $n = 5$. ______________

c. $n = 8$. ______________ **d.** $n = 6$. ______________

In 8 and 9, perform the indicated addition and then verify your answer by finding the base 10 representations of the numbers.

8.
$$\begin{array}{r} 101_2 \\ +\,1110_2 \\ \hline \end{array}$$

______________ ______________________

9.
$$\begin{array}{r} 1110110_2 \\ +\,100111_2 \\ \hline \end{array}$$

______________ ______________________

Name

LESSON MASTER 4-7

Questions on SPUR Objectives
See pages 278–281 for objectives.

Skills Objective D

In 1–4, factor completely into prime polynomials over the reals.

1. $6x^2 + 11x - 10$

2. $20t^4 - 31t^2 + 12$

3. $g(x) = 8x^3 + 22x^2 - x - 15$, given that $x + 1$ is a factor of $g(x)$

4. $(x^2 - xy)(x + y - 4) - (x^2 - xy)(x^2 + y - 7)$

Properties Objective I

In 5, write the assumption that you would make to begin the proof of the given statement by contradiction.

5. For any integer n, $\log n^2 > 0$.

6. Consider the statement: *If a and b are real numbers, then* $a^2 + b^2 < 2ab$.

a. To write a proof by contradiction, with what assumption would you start?

b. Complete the proof.

Properties Objective J

In 7 and 8, list the numbers that must be tested as factors to determine whether *n* is prime, then tell whether *n* is prime.

7. $n = 151$

8. $n = 1147$

In 9 and 10, give the standard prime factorization of the number.

9. 160

10. 221,850

Name

Questions on SPUR Objectives
See pages 344–347 for objectives.

Skills Objective B

In 1–4, show that each result is rational by expressing it as the ratio of two integers.

1. $4.3 - 6.2$ ______________

2. $\sqrt{\frac{1}{64}}$ ______________

3. $\frac{12}{7} + \frac{2}{13}$ ______________

4. $\log_9 27$ ______________

Properties Objective F

5. What is wrong with the following argument that π is a rational number? All rational numbers can be written as the ratio of two numbers. $\pi = \frac{\pi}{1}$, π can be written as the ratio of two numbers. Therefore π is rational.

____

____

6. Prove or find a counterexample: The square of any rational number is rational.

____

____

____

Uses Objective I

7. A company hires *N* people to work on a construction project. All but 4 of the people work on Phase I of the project, and all but 6 of the people work on Phase II of the project. The company has a total of \$12,000 budgeted for labor expenses, \$7,000 allocated for Phase I and \$5,000 allocated for Phase II. All workers on a given phase of the project are paid equally. Find an expression in terms of *N* for the wage of a person who works

a. only on Phase I. **b.** only on Phase II. **c.** on both phases.

______________ ______________ ______________

Name ______________________________

LESSON MASTER 5-2

Questions on SPUR Objectives
See pages 344–347 for objectives.

Skills Objective A

In 1 and 2, rewrite the expression in lowest terms.

1. $\dfrac{3x^2 + 9x - 84}{2x^2 + 13x - 7}$ ____________

2. $\dfrac{2y^3 + 4y^2 - 30y}{8y^2 + 64y + 120}$ ____________

In 3 and 4, rewrite the expression as a simple fraction and state any restrictions on the variable.

3. $\dfrac{\frac{1}{7} - \frac{7}{a^2}}{\frac{1}{a} + \frac{1}{3a^2}}$ ____________ ____________

4. $\dfrac{\frac{1}{t} + \frac{t}{4}}{\frac{t^3 - 15}{5t^2}}$ ____________ ____________

In 5–7, write the result as a simple rational expression in lowest terms and state any restrictions on the variable.

5. $\dfrac{2m - 4}{m + 6} \div \dfrac{3m + 8}{m^2 + 4m - 12}$ ____________

____

6. $\dfrac{r^2 + 1}{r^2 - 4r + 4} + \dfrac{r^2 - 7}{r^2 + r - 6}$ ____________

____

7. $\dfrac{s^2 + 10s + 9}{s^2 + 5s + 6} \cdot \dfrac{s^2 - 5s - 14}{s^2 - 5s - 6}$ ____________

____

Uses Objective I

8. At a constant temperature, the pressure P of a real gas varies as a function of its volume V according to the formula $P(V) = \dfrac{RT}{(V - b)} - \dfrac{a}{V^2}$, where R, a, and b are constants and T is the temperature in kelvins.

   Rewrite $P(V)$ as a rational expression. ____________

Name

Questions on SPUR Objectives
See pages 344–347 for objectives.

Skills Objective J

1. Consider the functions $f: x \to \frac{-2}{x^2}$ and $g: x \to \frac{-2}{(x+3)^2} + 6$.

a. State the domain and range of f.

b. Give equations for all asymptotes to the graph of f.

c. State the domain and range of g.

d. What transformation maps the graph of f onto the graph of g?

e. Give equations for all asymptotes to the graph of g.

f. On the grid at the right sketch the graphs of f and g, showing their asymptotes.

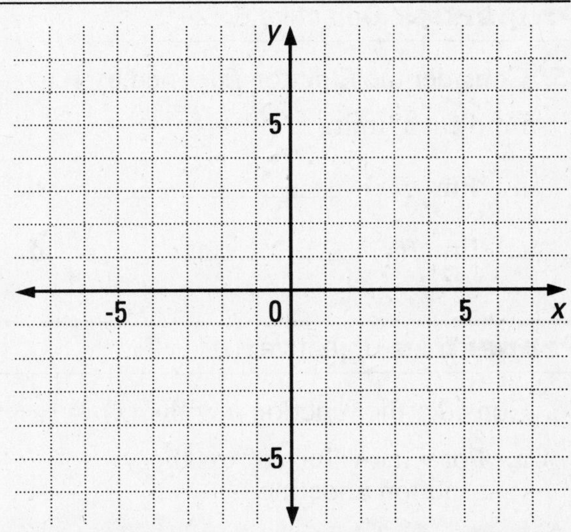

Representations Objective K

In 2 and 3, graph the function defined by the equation. Then use the limit notation to describe all vertical asymptotes.

2. $h(x) = \frac{7}{x - 2}$

3. $k(x) = \frac{1}{3x^4} - 5$

Name

LESSON MASTER 

Questions on SPUR Objectives
See pages 344–347 for objectives.

Skills Objective D

In 1–4, state whether the function defined by the given rule is a rational function. If it is a rational function, determine the values of the independent variable which are excluded from the domain.

1. $f(t) = \dfrac{t + 1}{t^2 + 3t + 2}$ ________________

2. $g(x) = \dfrac{\frac{1}{x^2} - x}{x^2 - 7}$ ________________

3. $h(v) = \dfrac{v^3 + 5v + 13}{v^2 + 5}$ ________________

4. $k(n) = \dfrac{n^2 - 7}{e^n}$ ________________

Properties Objective G

5. Consider the function f defined by $f(x) = \dfrac{x^2 + 5x + 6}{x^2 + x - 6}$. Find each limit.

a. $\lim\limits_{x \to -3^+} f(x)$ ____________ **b.** $\lim\limits_{x \to -3^-} f(x)$ ____________

c. $\lim\limits_{x \to 2^+} f(x)$ ____________ **d.** $\lim\limits_{x \to 2^-} f(x)$ ____________

Properties Objective H

6. Consider the function h with $h(x) = \dfrac{x^2 - 1}{x^3 - x}$.

a. For what values of x is the function undefined? ____________

b. At which of the values in part a is there an essential discontinuity? ____________

c. At which of the values in part a is there a removable discontinuity? ____________

d. Redefine the function at the value(s) in part c so that the discontinuity is removed. ____________

7. Define a function which has a removable discontinuity at $x = 7$ and an essential discontinuity at $x = -2$. ____________

Name

▶ **LESSON MASTER 5-4** *page 2*

8. *True or false.* Suppose f is a rational function having no essential discontinuities with $f(x) = \frac{p(x)}{q(x)}$, where $p(x)$ and $q(x)$ are polynomials over the reals. Then $\forall$ real numbers x, $q(x) = 0 \Rightarrow p(x) = 0$. Justify your answer.

____

____

Representations Objective J

9. a. Graph the rational function $h: x \rightarrow \frac{5x^2 - 8}{x^2 + 1}$.

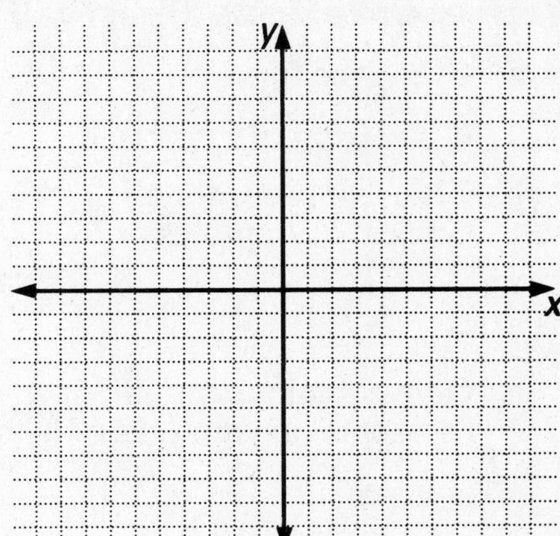

b. Does h have any essential discontinuities? If so, list them.

____

c. Does h have any removable discontinuities? If so, list them.

____

Representations Objective K

10. Suppose a rational function g has the following properties: The domain of g is $\{x: x \neq 0 \text{ and } x \neq 5\}$, $\lim_{x \to 0^-} g(x) = 1$, $\lim_{x \to 0^+} g(x) = 1$, $\lim_{x \to 5^-} g(x) = \infty$, and $\lim_{x \to 5^+} g(x) = -\infty$.

a. Write an equation for a vertical asymptote of g.

____

b. Construct a possible rule for the function of g.

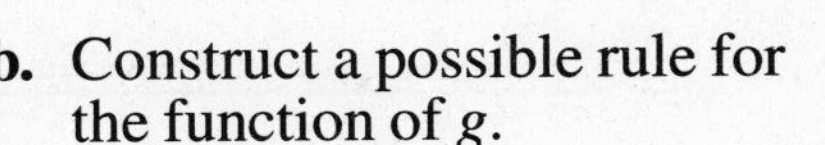

c. Graph the function of part b.

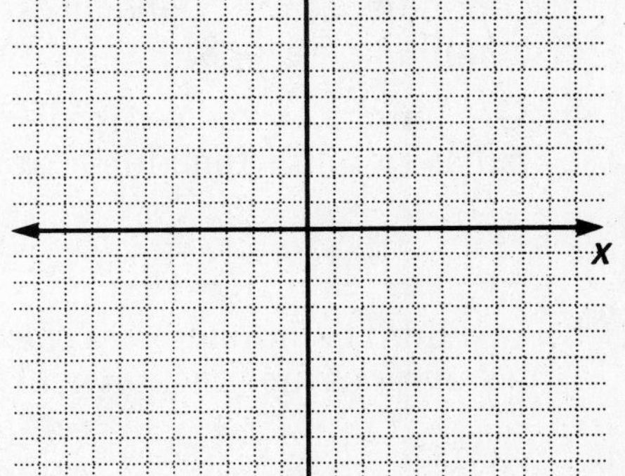

Name

LESSON MASTER 

Questions on SPUR Objectives
See pages 344–347 for objectives.

Properties Objective G

In 1–3, use limit notation to describe the end behavior of the given function.

1. $f(x) = \dfrac{7x^2 - 17}{6x^2 - 5x + 2}$ ________________

2. $g(z) = \dfrac{7z + 1}{9z^3 - 6z + 3}$ ________________

3. $h(t) = \dfrac{4t^3 + 3t^2 + 2t + 1}{t^2 + 2t + 3}$ ________________

Representations Objective J

4. a. Graph the function.

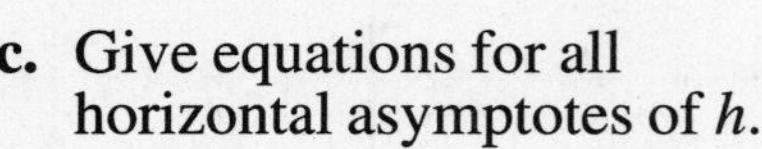

$h: x \to \dfrac{2x^2 - 7x - 1}{7x - 63}$.

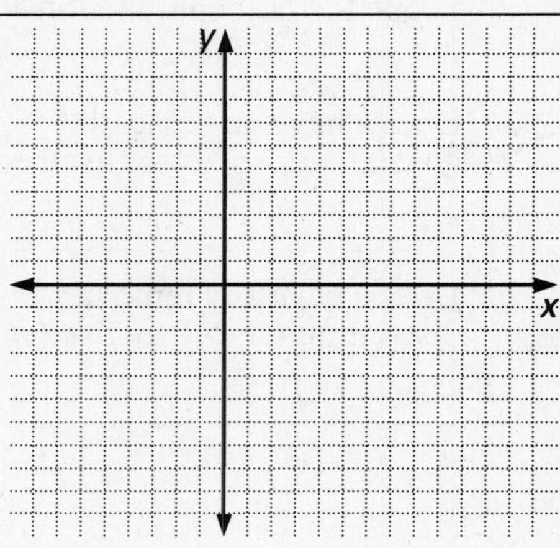

b. Give equations for all vertical asymptotes of *h*.

____

c. Give equations for all horizontal asymptotes of *h*.

____

d. Give equations for all oblique asymptotes of *h*.

____

Representations Objective K

5. The function *k* is graphed at the right, showing its end behavior, a removable discontinuity at $x = 5$, and an essential discontinuity at $x = 8$.

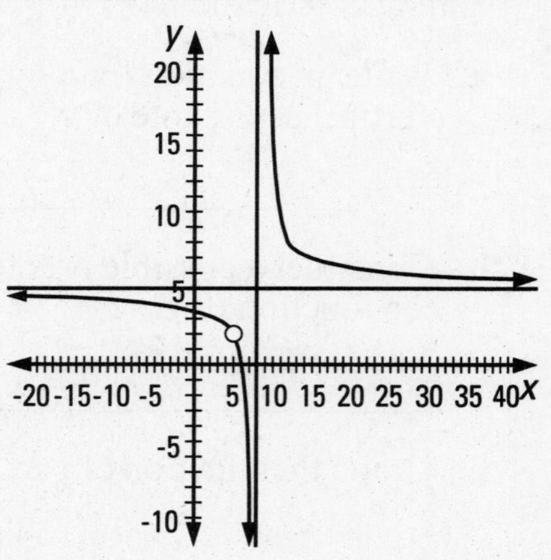

a. Use limit notation to describe the behavior of the function near $x = 5$.

____

b. Use limit notation to describe the behavior of the function near $x = 8$.

____

c. Use limit notation to describe the end behavior of the function.

____

Name ____________________

Questions on SPUR Objectives
See pages 344–347 for objectives.

Skills Objective B

In 1–5, identify each number as rational or irrational. Justify your reasoning.

1. $6 + \sqrt{2}$ ____________________

2. $\sqrt{72}$ ____________________

3. $0.134\overline{134}$ ____________________

4. $\frac{3\pi}{6}$ ____________________

5. $\frac{43e^2}{4e^3}$ ____________________

Skills Objective C

In 6–9, rationalize the denominator.

6. $\frac{7}{3 - \sqrt{2}}$ ____________________

7. $\frac{\sqrt{5}}{7 - \sqrt{10}}$ ____________________

8. $\frac{\sqrt{3} + 2}{\sqrt{5} - 1}$ ____________________

9. $\frac{13}{1 - \sqrt{3}}$ ____________________

Properties Objective F

10. Prove or find a counterexample: The square root of any irrational number is irrational.

____

____

____

____

____

____

Name

LESSON MASTER 5-7

Questions on SPUR Objectives
See pages 344–347 for objectives.

Skills Objective D

In 1 and 2, determine if the function defined by the given rule is a rational function.

1. $f(x) = \frac{1}{\cos x}$ ______

2. $g(x) = \frac{1}{\cot x}$ ______

Properties Objective H

In 3 and 4, a function and its rules are given.

a. List all values of θ at which the function is discontinuous.
b. Tell which discontinuities are removable.

3. $h(\theta) = \frac{1 - 2\cos\theta}{\sin\theta}$

4. $g(\theta) = \frac{1 - \sin^2\theta}{\cos\theta}$

a. ______ b. ______

c. ______ d. ______

Representations Objective K

5. Consider the function $k: x \to \frac{x}{\sin x}$. Use an automatic grapher to graph k.

   a. At what values of x is k undefined? ______

   b. Find $\lim_{x \to 0^-} \frac{x}{\sin x}$. ______

   c. Find $\lim_{x \to 0^+} \frac{x}{\sin x}$. ______

   d. Is 0 a removable or essential discontinuity of the function k? ______

Representations Objective L

In 6–8, use the triangle below to rewrite the trigonometric expression in terms of x.

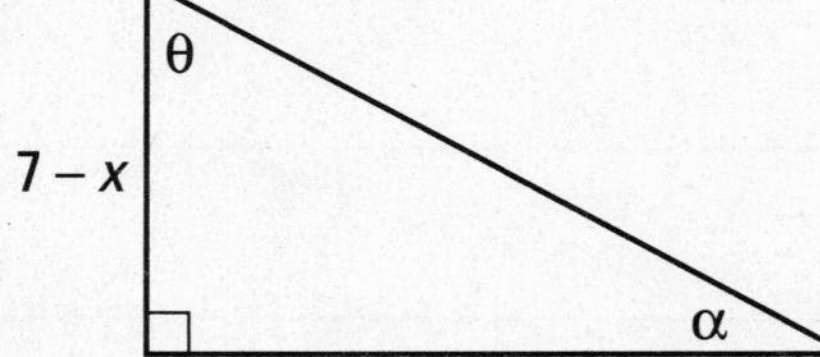

6. $\tan\alpha$ ______

7. $\sec\theta$ ______

8. $\csc\alpha$ ______

Name ______________________________

LESSON MASTER 5-8

Questions on SPUR Objectives
See pages 344–347 for objectives.

Skills Objective E

In 1–4, solve the equation.

1. $\frac{5}{x-2} + \frac{3}{x-1} = 0$ ______________

2. $\frac{7}{y+2} + \frac{4}{y-3} = 3$ ______________

3. $\frac{z}{z+1} - \frac{z}{z+11} = \frac{-1}{(z+1)(z+11)}$ ______________

4. $\frac{t}{t+2} + t = \frac{2-t}{t+2}$ ______________

Uses Objective I

5. A ship's hull was punctured and filled with water before being sealed off. A pump removed water at a steady rate of 5 gallons per minute, but after 75% of the water was removed, the pump slowed. If the water was removed at an average rate of 4 gallons per minute, at what rate was the remaining 25% of the water removed? ______________

6. In an electrical circuit, if two capacitors with capacitances C_1 and C_2 are connected in series, then the equivalent capacitance, C, is found using the equation $\frac{1}{C} = \frac{1}{C_1} + \frac{1}{C_2}$. If C is 8 microfarads less than C_1 and C is two fifths the capacitance of C_2, what are the values of C_1, C_2 and C?

____

Name

LESSON MASTER 6-1

Questions on SPUR Objectives
See pages 401–403 for objectives.

Representations Objective H

In 1–6, use an automatic grapher to conjecture whether or not the equation appears to be an identity. If so, identify the domain of the identity. If not, give a counterexample.

1. $\tan^2\theta - \cot^2\theta = \sec^2\theta - \csc^2\theta$

2. $\csc 2x + \frac{1}{2}\csc x \sec x$

3. $\sec 2x = \sec^2 x - \csc^2 x$

4. $\tan 2x = 2\tan x$

5. $\cot(y - \pi) = \tan\left(\frac{\pi}{2} - y\right)$

6. $\cos^3 x + \sin^3 x = \cos x + \sin x$

7. Use an automatic grapher to determine over what domain $f: x \rightarrow \sin x$, with x in radians, can be approximated by $g: x \rightarrow x - \frac{x^3}{3!} + \frac{x^5}{5!}$ to within 0.01.

8. Explain why it is difficult to use an automatic grapher to determine the domain of the identity $\sin\theta \cot\theta = \cos\theta$.

Name

LESSON MASTER **6-2**

Questions on SPUR Objectives
See pages 401–403 for objectives.

Properties Objective D

In 1–4, prove the identity and specify its domain.

1. $\sec^2 x + \csc^2 x = \sec^2 x \csc^2 x$

2. $\sin^4 x - \cos^4 x = \dfrac{\tan x - \cot x}{\sec x \csc x}$

3. $\tan \theta + \cot \theta = \sec \theta \csc \theta$

4. $\cot 2x \tan 2x = \sin 2x \csc 2x$

5. Fill in the blank to make an identity: $\cos x + \sin x \tan x =$ ____________

Name

Representations Objective H

In 6 and 7, use an automatic grapher to determine whether the equation appears to be an identity. If so, prove it and identify its domain. If not, give a counterexample.

6. $\sin 4x = 4 \sin x$

7. $\cos^4 x + \sin^4 x = 1 - 2 \cos^2 x \sin^2 x$

Name

Questions on SPUR Objectives
See pages 401–403 for objectives.

Representations Objective G

1. How is the graph of $y = 1 + \cos 3x$ related to the graph of $y = \cos x$?

2. Consider the sine wave with the following graph.

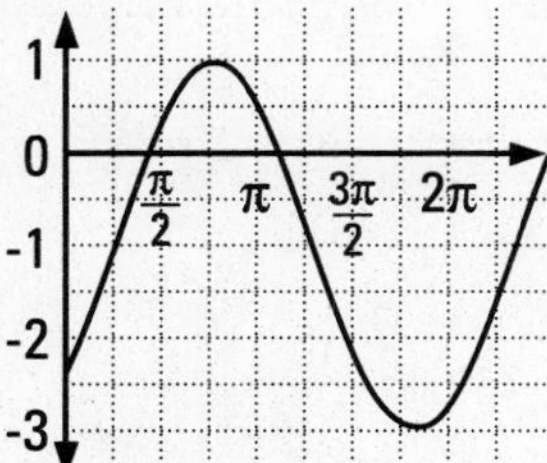

Determine the following.

a. Amplitude ______ **b.** Period ______

c. Phase shift ______ **d.** Vertical Shift ______

e. An equation for the graph ______

3. **a.** Write an equation for the image of $y = \sin x$ under the transformation $T(x, y) = \left(\frac{1}{2}x - \frac{\pi}{3}, 3y - 1\right)$.

b. Give the amplitude, vertical shift, period, and phase shift of the image.

4. a. Write an equation for the image of $y = \sec x$ under the rubberband transformation $(x, y) \rightarrow \left(x + \frac{\pi}{2}, y + 3\right)$.

b. Give the asymptotes and vertical shift of the image.

5. Under what transformation is the graph of $y = 7 \cos\left(5x + \frac{5\pi}{4}\right) - 2$ the image of the graph of $y = \cos x$?

6. a. Write parametric equations for the image of the graph $\begin{cases} x = \cos t \\ y = \sin t \end{cases}$ under the transformation $(x, y) \rightarrow (5x - 2, 3y + 2)$.

b. Write a single equation in x and y for the image graph.

c. What type of figure is the parent graph? What type of figure is the image?

Name

Questions on SPUR Objectives
See pages 401–403 for objectives.

Skills Objective A

1. Suppose $-\pi < \beta < -\frac{\pi}{2} < \alpha < 0$, $\sin \alpha = -\frac{1}{2}$, and $\cos \beta = -\frac{3}{5}$.
Find exact values of the following.

a. $\cos \alpha$ ____________ **b.** $\cos(\alpha + \beta)$ ____________

c. $\sin \beta$ ____________ **d.** $\cos(\alpha - \beta)$ ____________

In 2–5, express the following in terms of rational numbers and radicals.

2. $\cos\left(\frac{\pi}{3} + \frac{\pi}{4}\right)$ ____________ **3.** $\cos \frac{13\pi}{12}$ ____________

4. $\cos \frac{7\pi}{16} \cos \frac{3\pi}{16} + \sin \frac{7\pi}{16} \sin \frac{3\pi}{16}$ **5.** $\cos \frac{\pi}{12}$

____________ ____________

Properties Objective D

In 6–8, prove the identity and state its domain.

6. $\cos(x + 210°) = \frac{-\sqrt{3}\cos x + \sin x}{2}$

7. $\cos(\pi + x + y) = \sin x \sin y - \cos x \cos y$

8. $\cos(A - B)\cos(A + B) = \cos^2 A - \sin^2 B$

Name ______________________________

LESSON MASTER 6-5

Questions on SPUR Objectives
See pages 401–403 for objectives.

Skills Objective A

In 1–4, express in terms of rational numbers and radicals.

1. $\sin \frac{5\pi}{12}$ ______________________

2. $\tan \frac{\pi}{12}$ ______________________

3. $\sin \frac{15\pi}{11} \cos \frac{4\pi}{11} - \cos \frac{15\pi}{11} \sin \frac{4\pi}{11}$

____

4. $\dfrac{\tan \frac{7\pi}{8} - \tan \frac{\pi}{8}}{1 + \tan \frac{7\pi}{8} \tan \frac{\pi}{8}}$

____

5. Given that $\tan \theta = b$, find an expression for $\tan\left(\theta + \frac{\pi}{4}\right)$ and indicate the values of b for which it is defined.

____

6. Suppose that $\frac{\pi}{2} < x < \pi < y < \frac{3\pi}{2}$, $\sin x = \frac{\sqrt{3}}{2}$, and $\cos y = -\frac{4}{5}$. Find exact values of the following.

a. $\cos x$ ______________________

b. $\sin y$ ______________________

c. $\sin (x + y)$ ______________________

d. $\tan (x + y)$ ______________________

Properties Objective D

In 7–8, prove the identity and specify its domain.

7. $\sin (A - B) \sin (A + B) = \sin^2 A - \sin^2 B$

8. $\tan(45° - x) \tan(135° - x) = -1$

Name

Questions on SPUR Objectives
See pages 401–403 for objectives.

Skills Objective A

1. Given that $\cos\theta = \frac{12}{13}$ and $\sin\theta = -\frac{5}{13}$, find exact values of $\cos 2\theta$, $\cos\frac{\theta}{2}$, $\sin 2\theta$, and $\sin\frac{\theta}{2}$.

In 2 and 3, express the following in terms of rational numbers and radicals.

2. $\sin\frac{\pi}{8}$ ____________

3. $\cos 15°$ ____________

4. a. Use the identity for $\sin(\alpha + \beta)$ to find $\sin\frac{5\pi}{12}$. ____________

   b. Use the identity $\cos 2\alpha = 1 - 2\sin^2\alpha$ to find $\sin\frac{5\pi}{12}$. ____________

   c. Show that your answers to parts a and b are equal.

Properties Objective D

5. Prove that $\sin 3x = 3\sin x - 4\sin^3 x$. (Hint: Express $\sin 3x$ in the form $\sin(2x + x)$ and expand.)

Name

In 6–9, prove the identity and specify its domain.

6. $\frac{\sin 2\theta}{\sin \theta} - \frac{\cos 2\theta}{\cos \theta} = \sec \theta$

7. $\left(\sin \frac{\theta}{2} - \cos \frac{\theta}{2}\right)^2 = 1 - \sin \theta$

8. $\tan \frac{1}{2}\theta = \frac{1 - \cos \theta}{\sin \theta}$

9. $\cos (A + B) + \cos (A - B) = 2 \cos A \cos B$

Name ______

LESSON MASTER

Questions on SPUR Objectives
See pages 401–403 for objectives.

Skills Objective B

In 1 and 2, *true or false.*

1. $\forall x$ in the interval $-1 \le x \le 1$, $\cos(\sin^{-1}x) \ge 0$. ______

2. $\forall x$, $\sin(\tan^{-1}x) \ge 0$. ______

In 3–6, give exact values.

3. $\cos^{-1}\left(-\frac{\sqrt{2}}{2}\right)$ ______

4. $\sec\left(\sin^{-1}\left(-\frac{\sqrt{3}}{2}\right)\right)$ ______

5. $\sin^{-1}\left(\sin\frac{5\pi}{4}\right)$ ______

6. $\tan\left(\cos^{-1}\left(\sin\left(-\frac{\pi}{6}\right)\right)\right)$ ______

7. Use $\triangle PQR$ to evaluate each expression.

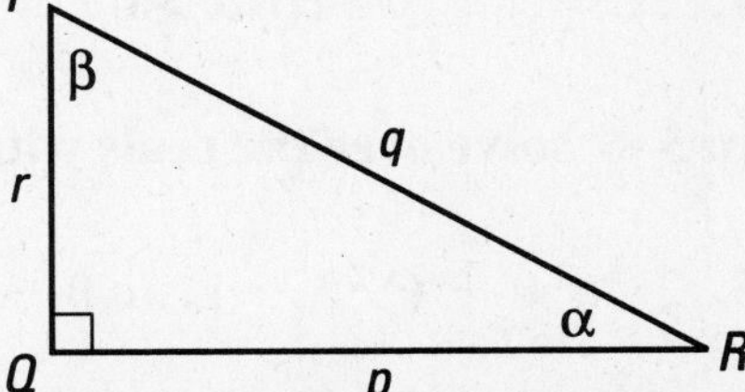

a. $\tan^{-1}\left(\frac{r}{p}\right)$ ______

b. $\csc\left(\cos^{-1}\left(\frac{r}{q}\right)\right)$ ______

Uses Objective E

8. A 24-foot ladder is used to reach the top of an 18-foot wall. If the ladder extends 2 feet beyond the top of the wall, what angle does it make with the horizontal? ______

9. An aircraft is flying eastward at an altitude of 2 miles and a speed of 240 miles per hour. An observer standing directly under the flight path of the aircraft initially spots it overhead and watches it until it is 12 miles east of his position.

a. Express the angle of elevation of the line of sight from the observer to the aircraft as a function of the time in minutes after he initially spots the aircraft. (Assume the observer is at the origin and that east is the positive direction along the horizontal axis.) ______

b. What is the angle of elevation at time $t = 0.5$ minute? ______

Name

LESSON MASTER 6-8

Questions on SPUR Objectives
See pages 401–403 for objectives.

Skills Objective C

In 1–4, solve over the interval $0 \le x \le 2\pi$ without using a calculator.

1. $\cot x \ge 1$

2. $\sec 3x = 2$

3. $2 \sin^2 x = 1 + \cos x$

4. $2 \cos^2 x - \sqrt{3} \cos x > 0$

In 5–6, solve over the reals without using a calculator.

5. $2 \sin^2 \theta + (\sqrt{2} - 1)\sin \theta - \frac{\sqrt{2}}{2} = 0$

6. $\tan 2x = -\sqrt{3}$

Uses Objective F

7. If an object is thrown upward with an initial velocity of v ft/sec and at an angle of θ to the horizontal, the maximum height in feet that it reaches above the starting point is given by $h_{max} = \frac{v^2}{512}(16 \sin \theta - \sin^2\theta)$. If a projectile hurled with an initial velocity of 60 feet per second reaches a maximum height of 56.25 feet above the starting point, at what angle was it thrown?

Representations Objective I

8. a. Use an automatic grapher to approximate to the nearest hundredth all solutions to the equation $\sin x + \cos x = 1.2$ over the inverval $0 \le x \le 2\pi$.

b. Use the results of part a to solve $\sin x + \cos x \ge 1.2$ over the interval $0 \le x \le 2\pi$.

Name

LESSON MASTER 

Questions on SPUR Objectives
See pages 467–469 for objectives.

Skills Objective A

In 1–6, find the first five terms of the sequence defined by the given formula.

1. $a_n = 1 - \left(-\frac{1}{2}\right)^n$

2. $b_n = (1 + n)^{\lceil \frac{n}{3} \rceil}$

3. $\begin{cases} c_1 = 2 \\ c_k = 1 + c_{k-1}^2 \quad \forall\, k \geq 2. \end{cases}$

4. $\begin{cases} s_1 = 2,\ s_2 = -1 \\ s_k = s_{k-2} + ks_{k-1} \quad \forall\, k \geq 3. \end{cases}$

5. $f_n = \lfloor \frac{n}{2} \rfloor \lceil \frac{n}{4} \rceil$

6. $d_n = \tan\left(\frac{(2n + 1)\pi}{4}\right)$

7. In which of the Questions 1–6 are the sequences defined explicitly? __________

Skills Objective B

In 8–11, a sequence is defined recursively.
a. Write the first five terms of the sequence.
b. Conjecture an explicit formula for the sequence that works for the first five terms.

8. $\begin{cases} a_1 = 0 \\ a_k = a_{k-1} + \frac{1}{2} \text{ for } k \geq 2. \end{cases}$

a. __________

b. __________

9. $\begin{cases} a_1 = 1 \\ a_k = \frac{1 - a_{k-1}}{1 + a_{k-1}} \text{ for } k \geq 2. \end{cases}$

a. __________

b. __________

10. $\begin{cases} a_1 = 49 \\ a_k = \frac{1}{7}a_{k-1} \text{ for } k \geq 2. \end{cases}$

a. __________

b. __________

11. $\begin{cases} a_1 = 1,\ a_2 = 3 \\ a_{k+2} = \frac{a_{k+1} + a_k}{2} + 3 \text{ for } k \geq 3. \end{cases}$

a. __________

b. __________

Name

▶ **LESSON MASTER 7-1** *page 2*

Uses Objective H

12. During a period of rapid growth in Haywire County, telegraph lines were run from each town directly to every other town in the county. Let n and l_n be the number of towns and the number of telegraph lines in Haywire County, respectively.

a. Find the first six terms of the sequence $l_1, l_2, l_3, \ldots$. ________________

b. Find a recursive formula for l_n. ________________

c. Conjecture an explicit formula for l_n and check to see whether it gives you the correct recursive formula.

____

____

Representations Objective J

13. a. List the terms generated by the program at the right.

____

```
10 TERM = 2
20 FOR J = 1 TO 5
30 PRINT TERM
40 TERM = TERM * TERM
50 NEXT J
60 END
```

b. Write a recursive formula for the sequence generated by the program. ________________

c. Write an explicit formula for the sequence. ________________

Name

LESSON MASTER 

Questions on SPUR Objectives
See pages 467–469 for objectives.

Skills Objective C

1. If $n = 2$, find $\sum_{k=-n}^{n+1} k^3 - 2k$. __________

In 2–3, use summation notation to express the sum

2. $(-2)^{-2} + (-1)^{-1} + 0^0 + 1^1 + 2^2 + \ldots + n^n$

3. $\frac{m^2}{n^2} + \frac{m}{n} + 1 + \frac{n}{m} + \frac{n^2}{m^2} + \frac{n^3}{m^3}$

__________ __________

4. a. Rewrite the equation $(1 + 1) + (2 + 4) + (3 + 9) + \ldots + (n + n^2) = (1 + 2 + 3 + \ldots + n) + (1 + 4 + 9 + \ldots + n^2)$ using summation notation.

____

b. Show that the equation is true for $n = 6$.

____

Skills Objective D

5. a. Express $\sum_{i=0}^{101}(i + i^3)$ in terms of $\sum_{i=0}^{100}(i + i^3)$. __________

b. Given that $\sum_{i=0}^{100}(i + i^3) = 25{,}507{,}550$, find $\sum_{i=0}^{101}(i + i^3)$. __________

6. Let $S(n)$ be the statement $\sum_{k=1}^{n}(k^2 + 2k) = \frac{n(n + 1)(2n + 7)}{6}$.

a. Find $\sum_{k=1}^{4}(k^2 + 2k)$ and show that $S(4)$ is true.

____

b. Rewrite $\sum_{k=1}^{n+1}(k^2 + 2k)$ in terms of $\sum_{k=1}^{n}(k^2 + 2k)$.

____

c. Use your answers to parts a and b to find $\sum_{k=1}^{5}(k^2 + 2k)$? __________

d. Use the answer to part c to determine if $S(5)$ is true. __________

Name

LESSON MASTER **7-3**

Questions on SPUR Objectives
See pages 467–469 for objectives.

Properties Objective F

1. Prove that the sequence defined by $\begin{cases} s_1 = 1 \\ s_{k+1} = s_k + (k+1)^3 \ \forall\, k \ge 1. \end{cases}$

satisfies the explicity formula $s_n = \frac{1}{4}n^2(n+1)^2$.

2. a. Find an explicit formula for the sequence defined by $\begin{cases} a_1 = 1 \\ a_{k+1} = a_k + (-1)^{k+1} \ \forall\, k \ge 1. \end{cases}$ ______________

b. Use mathematical induction to prove that the formula found in part a is correct.

►

Name

Properties Objective G

3. Let $S(n)$ be the statement: $\sum_{i=0}^{n} 3^i = \frac{1}{2}(3^{n+1} - 1)$. Use mathematical induction to prove that $S(n)$ is true for all positive integers n.

Representations Objective J

4. Consider the program at the right.

```
10 INPUT N
20 SUM = 0
30 FOR I = 1 TO N
40 SUM = SUM + 3
50 PRINT SUM
60 NEXT I
70 END
```

   a. Write a recursive definition for the sequence generated by the program.

   ____

   b. Find an explicit formula for the sequence. ______________________

   c. What modification to the program would you make so that the computer uses the explicit formula, rather than the recursive definition, to generate the sequence?

   ____

Name

LESSON MASTER **7-4**

Questions on SPUR Objectives
See pages 467–469 for objectives.

Properties Objective G

In 1–3, use mathematical induction to prove that the statement is true.

1. For all integers a, a is a factor of $(a + 1)^n - 1$ $\forall$ positive integers n.

2. 2 is a factor of $n^2 + n$ for all positive integers n.

3. 4 is a factor of $n^4 + n^2$ for all positive integers n.

Name

4. Suppose that the functions f and g are such that $f(x)$ and $g(x)$ are both integers whenever x is an integer. Suppose further that the integer is a factor of $f(n)$ when $n \geq 5$ and is a factor of $g(n)$ when $n \geq 9$. For what values of n can you be sure that n is a factor of the given expression?

a. $f(n) + g(n)$ ________________

b. $f(n) \cdot g(n)$ ________________

5. Prove that $x + y$ is a factor of $x^{2n} - y^{2n}$ $\forall$ positive integers n. (Hint: In the inductive step, add and subtract x^2y^{2k}).

Name

LESSON MASTER **7-5**

Questions on SPUR Objectives
See pages 467–469 for objectives.

Properties Objective G

In 1–3, prove the statement using the Principle of Mathematical Induction.

1. For all integers $n \geq 1$, if $0 < a < 1$, then $0 < a^n < 1$.

2. For all integers $p \geq 2$, $4^p > p^2 + 2p + 1$.

3. For all integers $n \geq 1$ and all real θ such that $\cos\theta \neq 0$, $|\sec^n \theta| \geq |\cos^n \theta|$.

4. a. *True or false.* For all integers $n \geq 1$, if $x > y$, then $x^n > y^n$. __________

b. If your answer to part a is "true," give a proof. If your answer is "false," give a counterexample.

►

Name ______________________________

LESSON MASTER 7-6

Questions on SPUR Objectives
See pages 467–469 for objectives.

Skills Objective E

In 1–3, a series is given. a. Find its value when $n = 5$. b. Find its limit as $n \to \infty$.

1. $\sum_{k=0}^{n} \frac{8}{(-2)^k}$

   a. ______________

   b. ______________

2. $\sum_{j=1}^{n} 3(0.7)^j$

   a. ______________

   b. ______________

3. $\sum_{i=1}^{n} (1.5)^i$

   a. ______________

   b. ______________

4. Let s be the sequence defined by $\begin{cases} s_1 = 4 \\ s_{k+1} = s_k \cdot \sin \frac{\pi}{4} \text{ for } k \geq 1. \end{cases}$

   Let S_n be the nth partial sum of the sequence.

   a. Find a formula for S_n. ______________

   b. Find S_5. ______________

   c. Find $\lim_{n \to \infty} S_n$. ______________

5. Give an example of a sequence for which the partial sums, S_n, satisfy $\lim_{n \to \infty} S_n = 3$. ______________

6. Consider the finite geometric series $c + \frac{3}{2}c + \frac{9}{4}c + \ldots + \frac{243}{32}c$.

   a. Use sigma notation to express the series. ______________

   b. If the value of the series is 332.5, find c. ______________

Representations Objective J

7. Consider the computer program at the right.

```
10 TERM = 7
20 SUM = TERM
30 FOR J = 2 TO 10
40 TERM = 3 * (TERM/4)
50 SUM = SUM + TERM
60 NEXT J
70 PRINT SUM
80 END
```

   a. Use summation notation to express the sum that is calculated by the program.

   b. Use the formula for a finite geometric series to find the sum in part a.

   c. What would be the approximate value of the sum if the 10 in line 30 were changed to 1 trillion.

   a. ______________

   b. ______________

   c. ______________

Name

Questions on SPUR Objectives
See pages 467–469 for objectives.

Properties Objective G

1. Let $S(n)$ be a sentence in n. Suppose that $S(1)$ is false. Also suppose that for all integers $k \geq 1$, the assumption that $S(1), S(2), \ldots S(k-1), S(k)$ are all false implies that $S(k+1)$ is also false. What can you conclude? Explain your answer.

In 2–4, use the Strong Form of Mathematical Induction.

2. Let a be the sequence defined by

$$\begin{cases} a_1 = bq \\ a_2 = cq \\ a_{k+1} = da_k + ea_{k-1} \ \forall\, k \geq 2, \end{cases}$$

where $b, c, d, e,$ and q are all integers. Prove that q is a factor of every term of the sequence.

►

Name ______________________________

▶ LESSON MASTER 7-7 *page 2*

3. Let a be the sequence defined by

$$\begin{cases} a_1 = 7q \\ a_2 = 13q^2 \\ a_{k+1} = 4qa_k + 10q^2a_{k-1} \ \forall\ k \geq 2, \end{cases}$$

where q is an integer.

Prove that q^n is a factor of a_n $\forall\ n \geq 1$.

4. Let b be the sequence defined by

$$\begin{cases} b_1 = 1 \\ b_2 = 2 \\ b_{k+1} = k(b_k + b_{k-1}) \ \forall\ k \geq 2. \end{cases}$$

Prove that $b_n = n!$ for all positive integers n.

Name

LESSON MASTER 

Questions on SPUR Objectives
See pages 467–469 for objectives.

Uses Objective I

In 1–3, use the specified algorithm to arrange the given list in increasing order. Show all intermediate steps.

1. 5, 0, -1, 3 (Bubblesort)

2. $\frac{3}{2}$, -2, 1, 3, 2, $\frac{5}{2}$, 0 (Bubblesort)

3. 10, -2, 9, 11, 4, -3, 7 (Quicksort)

4. What is the maximum number of passes needed for the Bubblesort algorithm to arrange a list of n numbers in increasing order?

5. Refer to the description of the Quicksort algorithm on page 452. Suppose that you want to modify the algorithm so that it will arrange a list L of numbers in decreasing order. What change(s) would you make in the algorithm?

Name ______________________________

Questions on SPUR Objectives
See pages 547–549 for objectives.

Skills Objective A

In 1–3, give the real part and the imaginary part of the complex number.

1. $18 - 13i$ real ________ imaginary ________
2. $-i$ real ________ imaginary ________
3. $\sqrt{7}$ real ________ imaginary ________

In 4 and 5, write the complex number as an ordered pair.

4. $7 + 9i$ ________
5. $-i + \sqrt{5}$ ________

In 6 and 7, write the complex number in $a + bi$ form.

6. $(0, -8)$ ________
7. $\left(-\frac{2}{3}, 1\right)$ ________

Skills Objective B

In 8–13, perform the indicated operation and write the answer in $a + bi$ form.

8. $(6 - i) - (10 + 7i)$ ________
9. $(1 + 6i)(3 - 4i)$ ________
10. $\frac{\sqrt{-72}}{3}$ ________
11. $\frac{9 - 2i}{2 + 5i}$ ________
12. $\frac{7i}{2 + 2i} + 1 - 12i$ ________
13. $(-5 + 8i)^2$ ________

In 14 and 15, solve the equation and express the solution in $a + bi$ form.

14. $-5 + 6i = v + 8 - i$ ________
15. $w^2 = -19$ ________

Properties Objective F

16. Verify that $2 - i$ is a solution of $z^2 - 4z + 5 = 0$.

____

____

17. Let $z = a + bi$ and $w = c + di$. Prove that $\overline{z + w} = \overline{z} + \overline{w}$.

____

____

____

18. Prove that the fifth power of any imaginary number is imaginary.

Uses Objective H

19. If the voltage in an AC circuit is $6 - 12i$ volts and the impedance is $2 + 4i$ ohms, find the current.

20. Two AC circuits with impedances of $-5 + 8i$ and $4 - 3i$ ohms are connected in series.

a. Find the total impedance.

b. If the total current is $-\frac{1}{2} - \frac{5}{2}i$ amps, find the voltage.

Representations Objective I

21. a. On the grid at the right, graph $EFGH$, where $E = 3 + i$, $F = -1 - i$, $G = -2 - 3i$, and $H = 2 - i$.

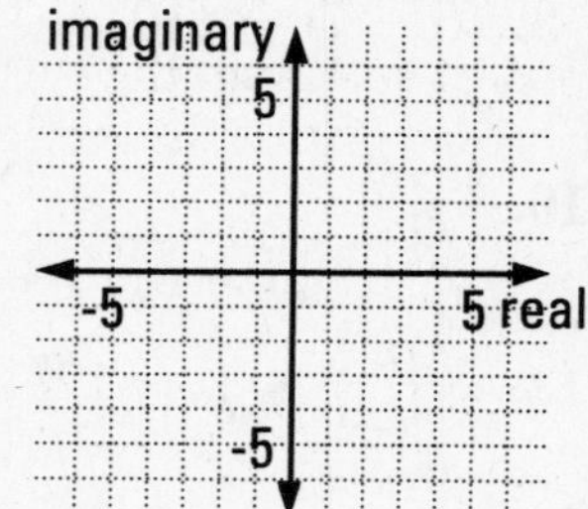

b. Show that $EFGH$ is a parallelogram.

22. Let $A = 1 + 2i$, $B = 5i$, and $C = -4$, and let $f(z) = (1 - i)z$. On the grid at the right, graph $\triangle ABC$ and $\triangle A'B'C'$, where $A' = f(A)$, $B' = f(B)$, and $C' = f(C)$. Label the vertices.

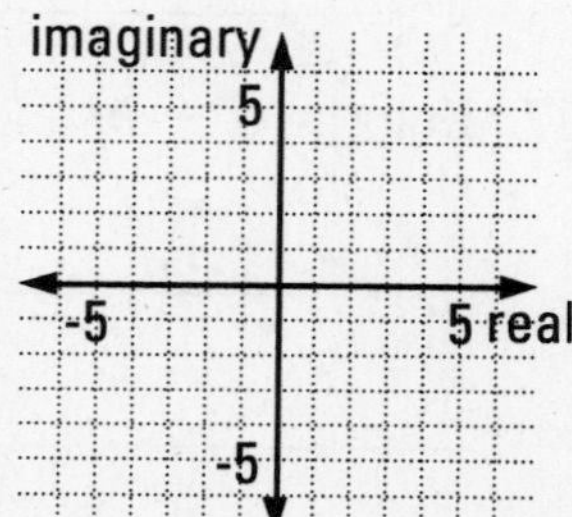

Name

LESSON MASTER 8-2

Questions on SPUR Objectives
See pages 547–549 for objectives.

Skills Objective C

In 1 and 2, find the rectangular coordinates for the point *P* whose polar coordinates are given.

1. [4, 300°] ____________ **2.** $\left[3\sqrt{2}, -\frac{3\pi}{4}\right]$ ____________

In 3 and 4, give one pair of polar coordinates for the (*x*, *y*) pair.

3. (-4, 5) ____________ **4.** $\left(-\sqrt{3}, 1\right)$ ____________

5. If $P = \left[r, \frac{5\pi}{3}\right] = (4, y)$, $r =$ ________ and $y =$ ________

6. Suppose $P = \left[6, \frac{7\pi}{4}\right]$. Give a different polar representation $[r, \theta]$ for *P* satisfying the given conditions.

a. $r = 6$ ________ **b.** $r = -6$ ________ **c.** $\theta < 0$ ________

Representations Objective I

7. Plot and label the following points on the polar grid at the right.

a. $A = \left[3, \frac{\pi}{2}\right]$ **b.** $B = [-2, -120°]$

c. $C = \left[-4, -\frac{\pi}{6}\right]$ **d.** $D = [0, \pi]$

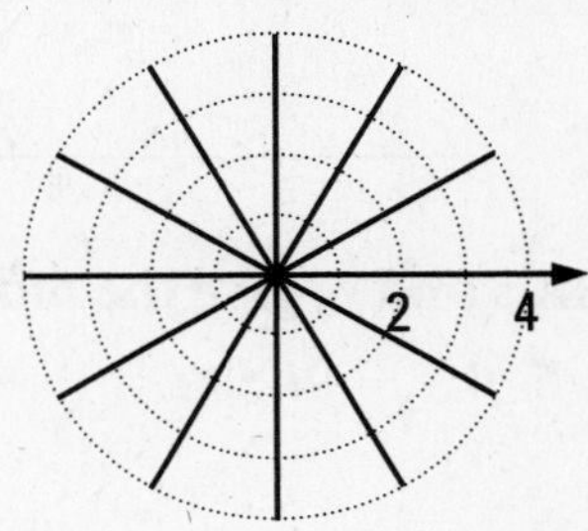

8. Give two polar representations of the point *P* graphed below.

____

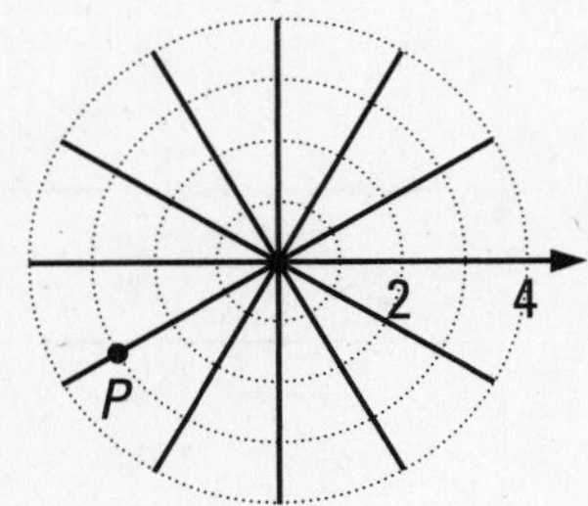

9. On the polar grid below, sketch all solutions to these equations.

a. $r = 2.5$ **b.** $\theta = -\frac{5\pi}{4}$

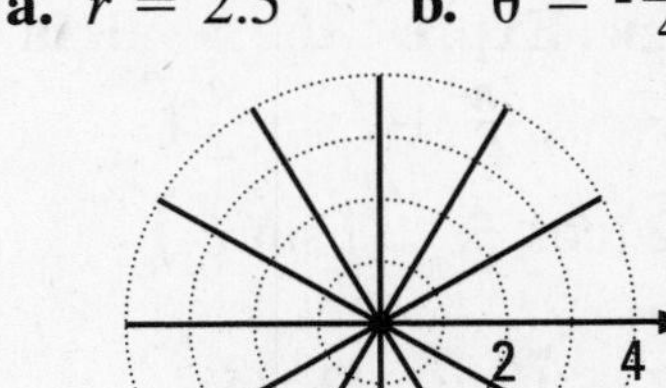

Name

LESSON MASTER 8-3

Questions on SPUR Objectives
See pages 547–549 for objectives.

Skills Objective A

In 1–4, the complex number is written in binomial, rectangular, polar, or trigonometric form. Write it in the other three forms.

1. $-4 + 2i$

2. $[1.4, 80°]$

3. $\frac{\sqrt{2}}{2}$

4. $3\left(\cos -\frac{\pi}{3} + i \sin -\frac{\pi}{3}\right)$

In 5 and 6, give the modulus and an argument θ for the complex number.

5. $12 - 9i$

6. $\sqrt{3}c + ci$ where $c > 0$

Skills Objective B

In 7–9, find *zw*. Express the result in the form of the given numbers.

7. $z = \sqrt{5}\left(\cos \frac{3\pi}{4} + i \sin \frac{3\pi}{4}\right)$,
$w = \sqrt{2}\left(\cos \frac{\pi}{12} + i \sin \frac{\pi}{12}\right)$

8. $z = [4, 125°]$, $w = [3, 35°]$

9. Find z so that $z \cdot [12, 20°] = [6, 170]$.

Properties Objective F

10. Let $z = [r, \theta]$. If z is multiplied by $w = [s, \phi]$, describe the changes to z.

11. Use polar coordinates to show that the square of any imaginary number is a real number.

____

____

Representations Objective I

12. Let $A = -1 + 4i$, $B = -3 - 2i$, and $C = 1 - 2i$.

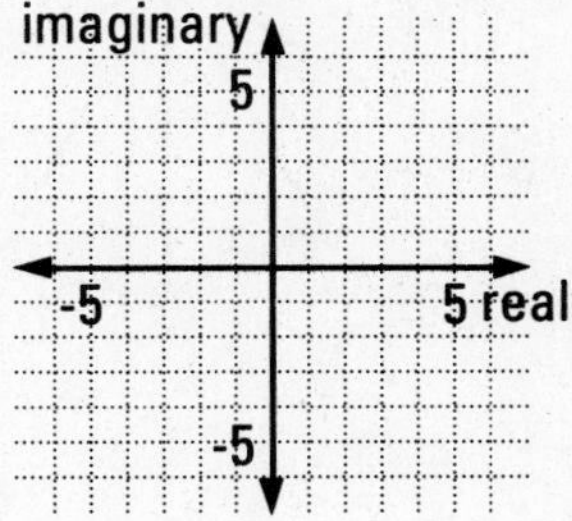

a. Sketch $\triangle ABC$ in the complex plane.

b. What kind of triangle is $\triangle ABC$? ______________

c. Prove your answer to part b.

____

____

13. Refer to the multiplication illustrated at the right. Give w in polar form.

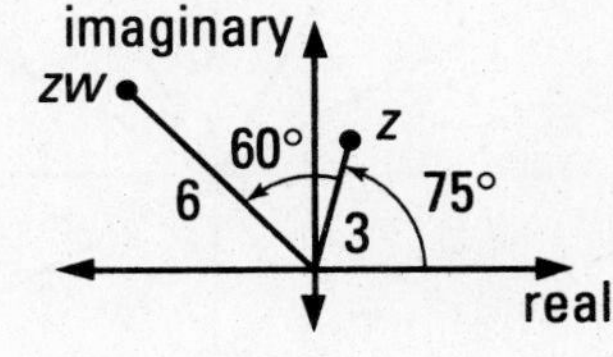

____

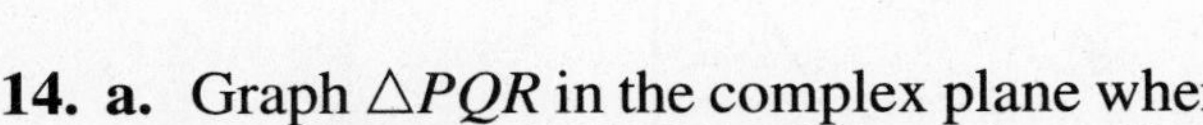

14. a. Graph $\triangle PQR$ in the complex plane where $P = 1 + i$, $Q = -2$, and $R = -1 - 2i$.

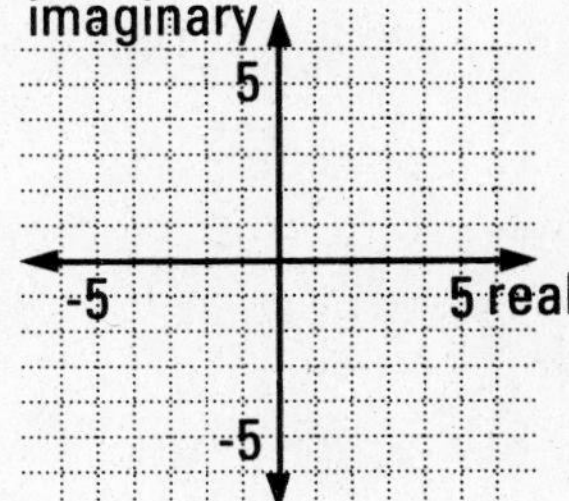

b. Multiply each vertex by $z = 2 + i$ and graph the result as $\triangle P'Q'R'$.

c. Find the ratio of similitude of $\triangle P'Q'R'$ to $\triangle PQR$ and relate it to the Geometric Multiplication Theorem.

____

____

d. How does the argument of R' compare to that of R? Use the Geometric Multiplication Theorem to explain your answer.

____

____

Name

LESSON MASTER 8-4

Questions on SPUR Objectives
See pages 547–549 for objectives.

Representations Objective J

In 1–4, sketch the graph of the polar equation and identify the type of curve obtained.

1. $\theta = -120°$ ______________

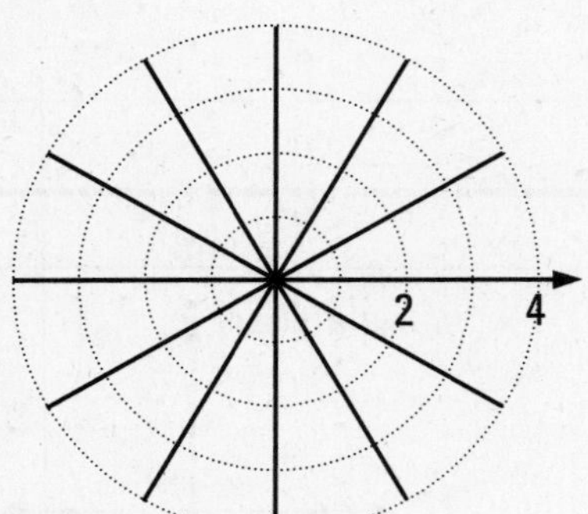

2. $r = \frac{7}{2}$ ______________

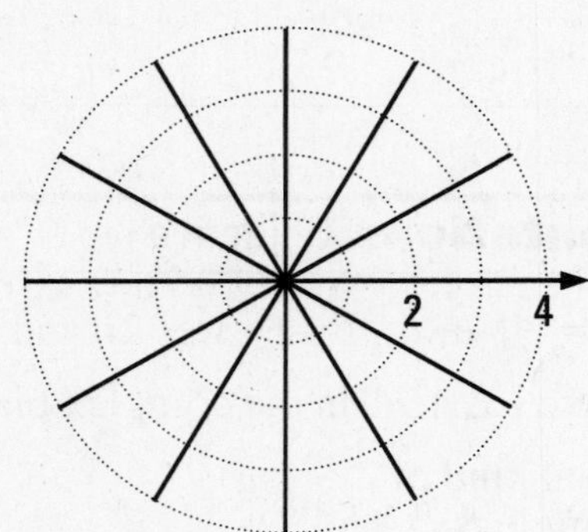

3. $r = 3 + 3 \sin \theta$ ______________

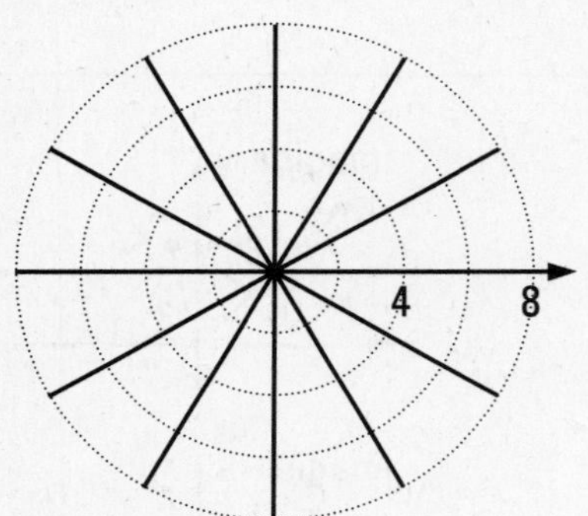

4. $r \cos \theta = -4$ ______________

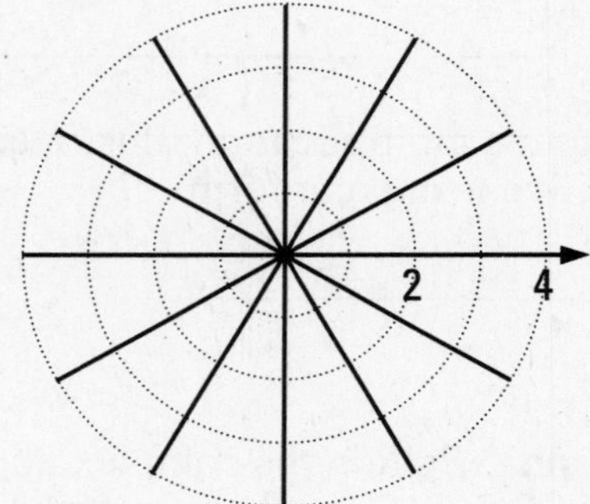

►

Name ____

▶ LESSON MASTER 8-4 *page 2*

5. a. Sketch the rectangular graph of the equation $r = 2 \cos \theta - 1$ $0 \le \theta \le 2\pi$.

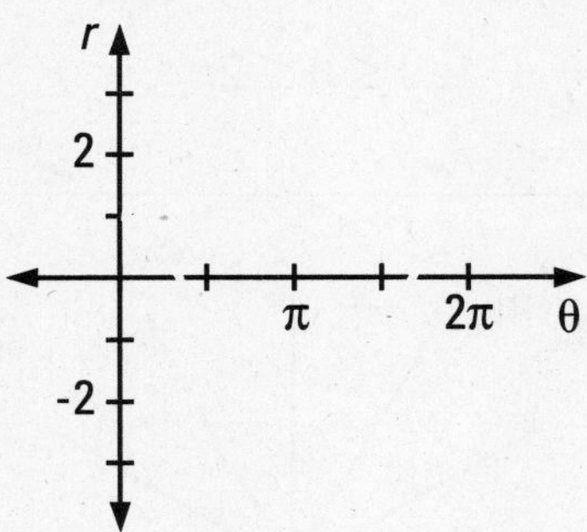

b. Use the rectangular graph in part a to sketch its polar graph.

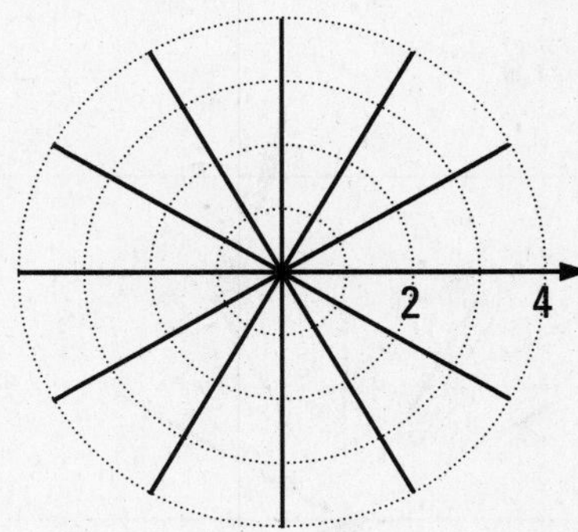

c. Identify the type of curve in part b. ______________________

6. a. Sketch the graph of $r = 3 \sin \theta$.

b. Prove that the graph is a circle and find its center and radius.

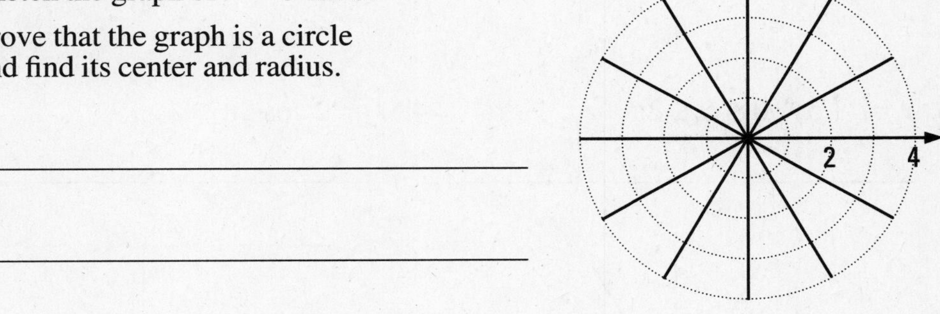

____

____

____

____

____

____

____

7. Describe the polar graph of $r = k \cos \theta$.

____

Name

LESSON MASTER 8-5

Questions on SPUR Objectives
See pages 547–549 for objectives.

Skills Objective J

In 1–4, sketch the graph of the polar equation and identify the type of curve obtained.

1. $r = 3 \sin 4\theta$

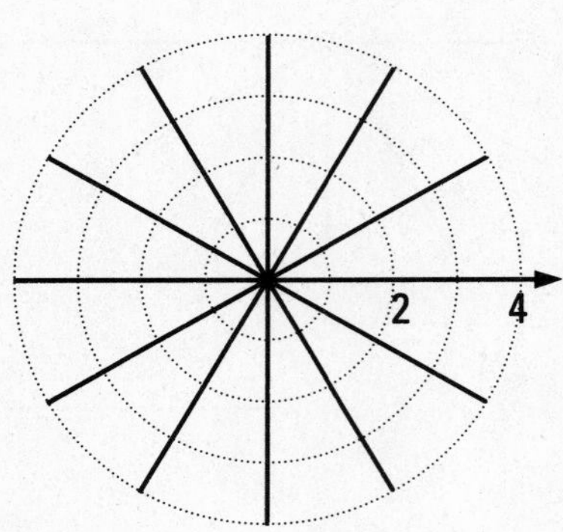

2. $r = 2\theta + 1, 0 \le \theta \le 2\pi$

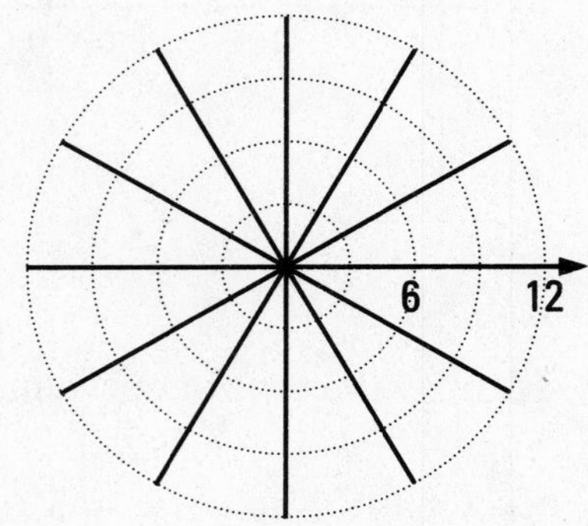

3. $r = (1.5)^{\theta}, 0 \le \theta \le 2\pi$

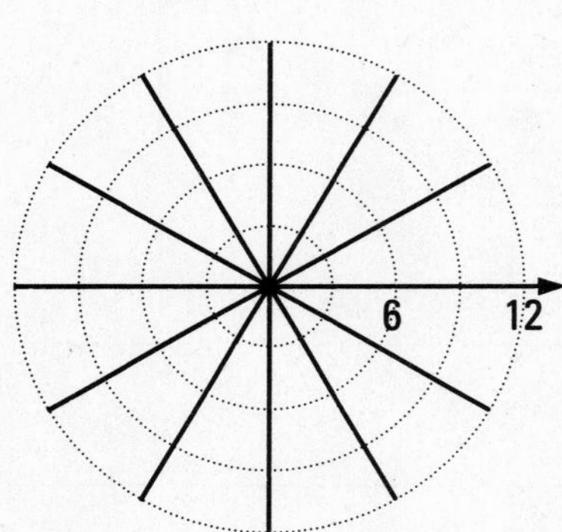

4. $r = 2 \cos 2\theta$

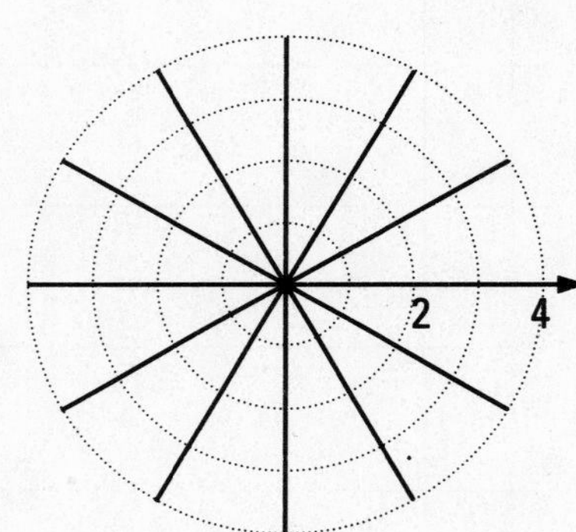

Name ____________________

▶ LESSON MASTER 8-5 *page 2*

5. a. Graph the curve $r = 4 \cos 3\theta$.

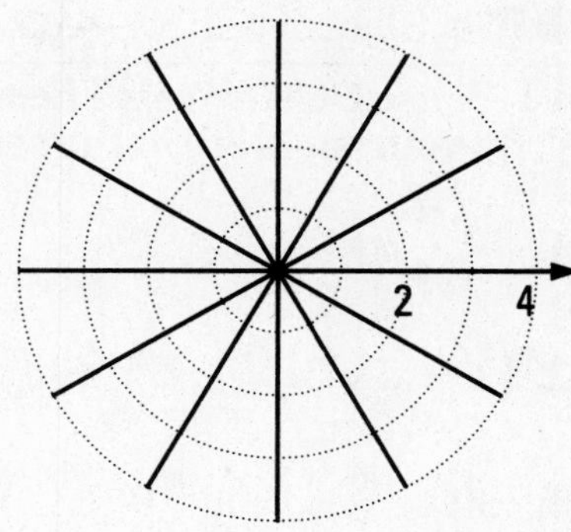

b. Describe its reflection symmetry.

____

c. Prove that your answer to part b is correct.

____

____

____

____

6. a. Write a polar equation for a 4-leafed rose with leaves of length 3.5 that is symmetric over the line $\theta = \frac{\pi}{2}$.

____

b. Graph this curve.

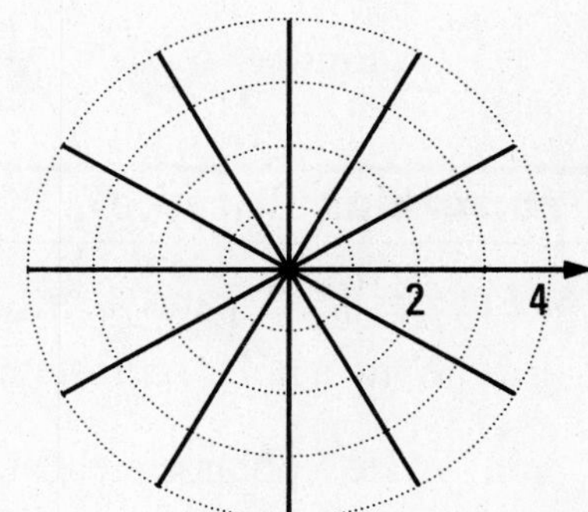

7. Consider the polar graph of the equation $r = a \cos n\theta$.

a. If n is a positive even integer, how many leaves does the curve have? ____________________

b. If n is a positive odd integer, how many leaves does the curve have? ____________________

c. What is the length of each petal? ____________________

Name ______

LESSON MASTER

Questions on SPUR Objectives
See pages 547–549 for objectives.

Skills Objective D

In 1–3, use DeMoivre's Theorem to compute the power. Write your answers in the same form as the base.

1. $\left[-4, \frac{\pi}{4}\right]^6$ ______

2. $(2 - 2\sqrt{3}i)^{11}$ ______

3. $\left[3\left(\cos\frac{\pi}{3} + i\sin\frac{\pi}{3}\right)\right]^5$ ______

In 4 and 5, write the answer in $a + bi$ form.

4. A third root of a certain complex number z is $5(\cos 150° + i \sin 150°)$. Find z. ______

5. An eighth root of a certain complex number w is $\left[-1, \frac{\pi}{2}\right]$. Find w. ______

Properties Objective F

6. Let $z = [2, 8°]$ and $w = [3, 10°]$.

a. Write a polar representation of z^3. ______

b. Write a polar representation of w^3. ______

c. Verify that $(z \cdot w)^3 = z^3 \cdot w^3$.

______

______

______

______

7. Let $z = [r, \theta]$. Prove that $(z^m)^n = z^{mn}$ for all positive integers m and n.

______

______

______

Name

Representations Objective K

8. Give the polar coordinates of z^1, z^2, z^3, z^4, and z^5, where the first four are graphed at the right.

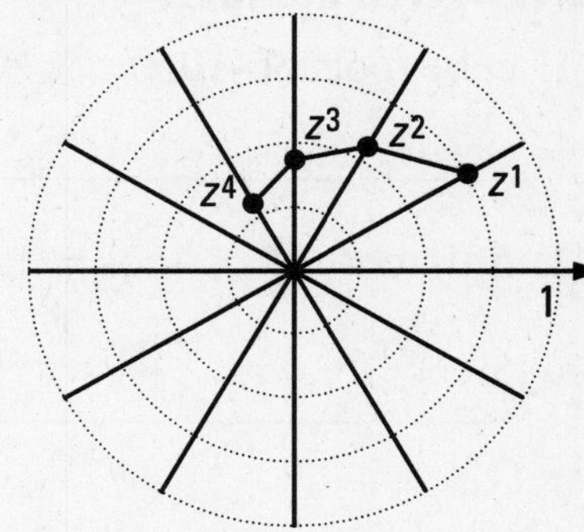

z^1 = ______________________

z^2 = ______________________

z^3 = ______________________

z^4 = ______________________

z^5 = ______________________

9. a. Graph w^1, w^2, w^3, w^4, w^5, and w^6 when $w = 1.25\left(\cos \frac{\pi}{4} + i \sin \frac{\pi}{4}\right)$.

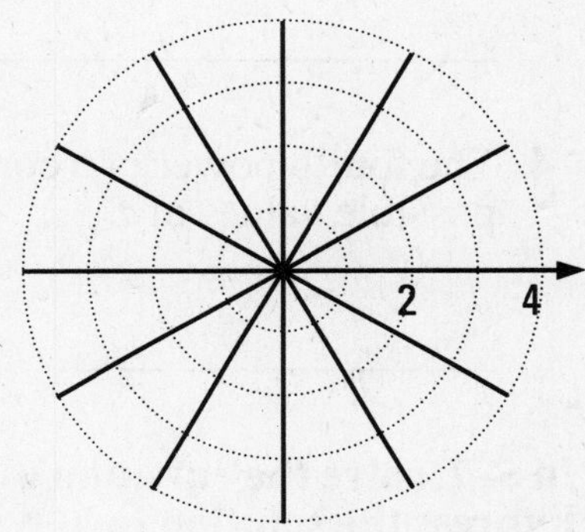

b. Are the points for this sequence of numbers getting closer to or farther from the origin?

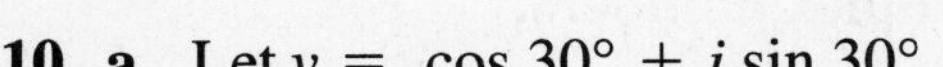

10. a. Let $v = \cos 30° + i \sin 30°$.

b. What is the value of $|v|$?

____

c. Graph the first eight points of the sequence of successive powers of v.

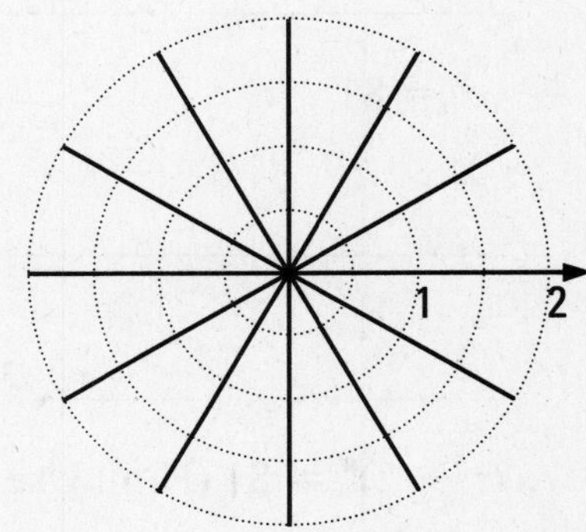

d. Is this sequence periodic? If so, how often do the terms repeat?

____

Name ______________________

LESSON MASTER 

Questions on SPUR Objectives
See pages 547–549 for objectives.

Skills Objective D

In 1–3, find the roots. Write your answer in the same form as the given number.

1. cube roots of $-1000i$

____

2. fifth roots of $243\left(\cos\frac{\pi}{2} + i\sin\frac{\pi}{2}\right)$

____

____

____

3. sixth roots of [64, 300°]

____

____

4. The fourth power of a complex number z is -1. Find all possible values of z.

____

In 5–7, solve the equation over the set of complex numbers. Express the solution in $a + bi$ form.

5. $m^3 = -27$

____

6. $w^8 = 81$

____

____

7. $(z + 2)^8 = 81$ (Hint: Use your answer to Question 6.)

____

____

►

Name

8. A sixth root of a complex number z is $\sqrt{3}(\cos 85° + \sin 85°)$.

a. Find z. ______________________

b. Find the other sixth roots.

____

____

____

____

Representations Objective K

9. Graph the cube roots of -27 on a complex plane. (Refer to Question 5.)

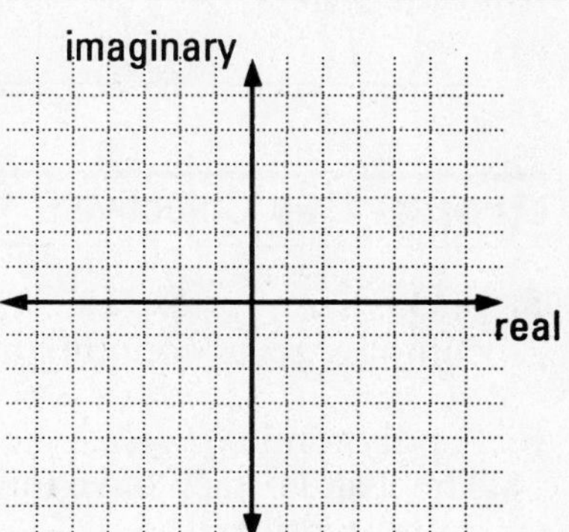

10. a. The fifth roots of $243\left(\cos \frac{\pi}{2} + i \sin \frac{\pi}{2}\right)$ form the vertices of what figure? (Refer to Question 2.) ______________________

b. Graph the figure on a polar grid.

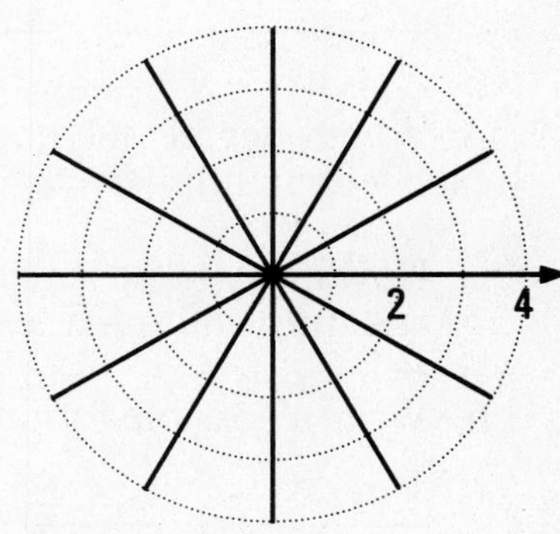

Name ______________________________

LESSON MASTER 

Questions on SPUR Objectives
See pages 547–549 for objectives.

Skills Objective E

In 1–3, a polynomial is given. a. Find all zeros of the polynomial. b. Give the multiplicities of the zeros.

1. $f(x) = (x + 3)^5(2x - 1)(x^2 + 1)$

a. ______________________ **b.** ______________________

2. $g(t) = t^5 + 2t^3 - 3t$

a. ______________________ **b.** ______________________

3. $h(x) = x^4 - 8x^3 + 20x^2 - 32x + 64$ given that $2i$ is a zero of $h(x)$.

a. ______________________ **b.** ______________________

4. Find a polynomial of degree 4 that has zeros 5, -5, i and $-i$.

____

Properties Objective G

5. $p(x) = -2x^9 + 5x^6 + 7x^3 - 12$ has exactly __?__ complex zeros counting multiplicities. ______________

6. A polynomial $f(x)$ has the following zeros: 3, 1, 0, $2i$, and $-2i$. The 3 and 0 each have multiplicity 2, and the other zeros have multiplicity 1.

a. What is the degree of $f(x)$? ______________

b. Write a possible formula for $f(x)$ in factored form.

____

7. An eighth-degree polynomial $q(x)$ has at least 2 simple zeros each with multiplicity 2.

a. How many more zeros does $q(x)$ have, counting multiplicities? ______________

b. Write a possible formula for $f(x)$ in factored form.

____

____

____

____

Name

LESSON MASTER 8-9

Questions on SPUR Objectives
See pages 547–549 for objectives.

Skills Objective E

1. Two of the zeros of the polynomial $p(x) = x^4 - 6x^3 + 11x^2 - 6x + 10$ are $3 - i$ and i. Find the remaining zeros of $p(x)$.

2. If i is a zero of the polynomial $f(y) = 4y^4 - 8y^3 + 9y^2 - 8y + 5$, find the remaining zeros of p(y)

3. If $1 - i$ and $4i$ are zeros of a fourth degree polynomial $q(x)$ with real coefficients, give a possible formula for $q(x)$.

4. Find a polynomial $g(x)$ of smallest degree with real coefficients that has zeros $5 + i$ and 0.

Properties Objective G

5. If $2i$ is a zero of $h(x) = x^2 - 4xi - 4$, is $-2i$ necessarily the other zero? Explain.

6. Does there exist a polynomial $p(z)$ with real coefficients which has exactly three zeros: $5i$, $-5i$, and $3 + 2i$? Justify your answer.

7. What is the smallest possible degree of a polynomial $f(x)$ with real coefficients if $-2 - 2i$, $-1 + i$, and 6 are zeros of $f(x)$?

8. Suppose $p(x)$ is a polynomial with real coefficients such that $p(x) = (x - 1 - 3i)q(x)$ where $q(x)$ is a polynomial. Give a factor of $q(x)$.

9. Prove: If a polynomial with real coefficients has a nonreal zero z with multiplicity 2, then the degree of polynomial is at least 4.

Name

LESSON MASTER 

Questions on SPUR Objectives
See pages 596–599 for objectives.

Skills Objective A

1. Find the average rate of change in $q(x) = x^2 + 12$ from $x = -1$ to $x = 4$. ______

2. Find the average rate of change in $g(n) = 3n^3 - n^2 + 6$ over the interval $-2 \le n \le 2$. ______

3. Let $f(x) = 2x^2 + 3x$. Find the average rate of change in f over the given interval.

a. From x to $x + \Delta x$ ______

b. From 2 to 2.1 ______

c. From 2 to 2.01 ______

Uses Objective D

4. A stone is thrown upward from a height of 2 meters with an initial velocity of 8 meters per second. If only the effect of gravity is considered, then the stone's height in meters after t seconds is given by the equation $h(t) = -4.9t^2 + 8t + 2$.

a. Find a formula for the average velocity from $t = 1$ to $t = 1 + \Delta t$. ______

b. Use your answer in part a to find the average from $t = 1$ to $t = 3\frac{1}{2}$. ______

Representations Objective G

5. Refer to the graph of g at the right. Find the average rate of change in g over each interval.

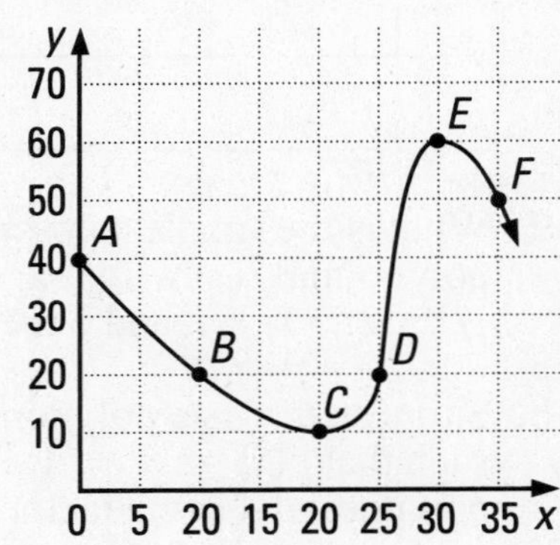

a. C to E ______

b. $0 \le x \le 35$ ______

Over what interval does the average rate of change in g have the given value?

c. 0  **d.** $-\frac{3}{2}$ 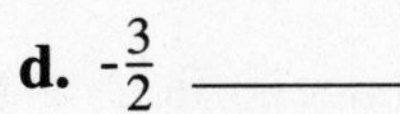

6. Suppose $P = (3, 7)$ and $Q = (9, a)$ are points on the graph of the function h. If the average rate of change in h from $x = 3$ to $x = 9$ is $-\frac{5}{3}$, find a. ______

Name

Questions on SPUR Objectives
See pages 596–599 for objectives.

Skills Objective B

In 1–3, find the derivative of the function at the given value of *x*.

1. $f(x) = 3x^2 + 4; x = 2$

2. $g(x) = -12x + 8; x = .5$

3. $h(x) = 22; x = 7$

4. Let $f(x) = -2x^2 + x - 3$

a. Compute $f'(0)$.

b. Compute $f'(3)$.

Uses Objective D

5. The typical number of mosquitoes $m(r)$ in hundreds of thousands in a certain county during the month of June is approximated by $m(r) = 8r - r^2$, where r is the average total rainfall for the month in inches.

a. Find the derivative of m when $r = 2$.

b. What does your answer to part a mean?

Uses Objective E

6. The height h in feet of a small rocket t seconds after launch is approximated by $h(t) = 320t - 16t^2$.

a. Find the instantaneous velocity at time $t = 5$.

b. Find the instantaneous velocity at time $t = 14$.

c. Find the instantaneous velocity at time $t = 10$.

d. At what time does the rocket reach its maximum height?

Name

7. A pebble is dropped from a cliff 60 feet high. The height of the pebble in feet above the ground at time t seconds is given by $h(t) = -16t^2 + 60$.

   a. Find the instantaneous velocity of the pebble at time $t = 0.5$ second. ______

   b. At what time does the pebble hit the ground? ______

   c. Find the instantaneous velocity of the ball at the moment just before it hits the ground. ______

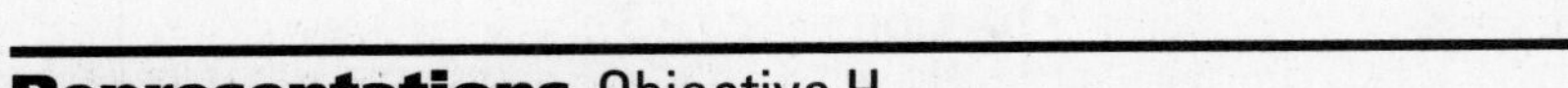

Representations Objective H

8. Refer to the graph of f at the right. Give a value of x for which $f'(x)$ is

   a. positive. ______

   b. negative. ______

   c. zero. ______

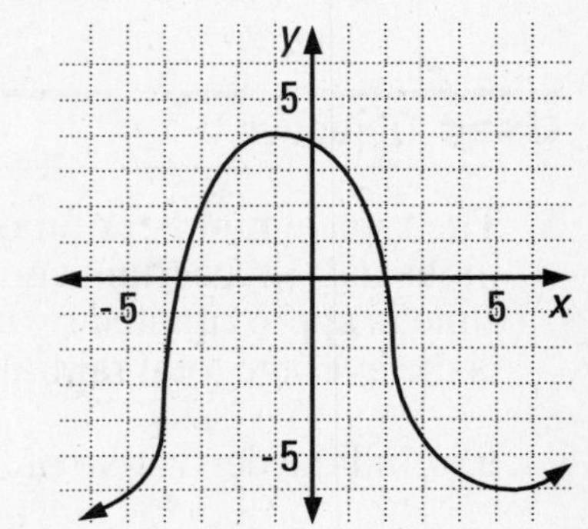

9. Refer to the graph of g at the right. Estimate g' for each value of x given below.

   a. $x = -4$ ______

   b. $x = -1$ ______

   c. $x = 4$ ______

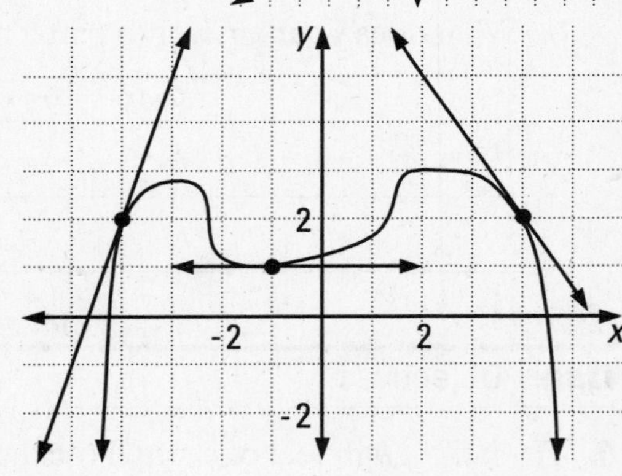

Name

LESSON MASTER 9-3

Questions on SPUR Objectives
See pages 596–599 for objectives.

Skills Objective B

In 1–4, find the derivative of the function whose formula is given.

1. $f(y) = 7y^2$

2. $g(x) = 7x^2 - 3x$

3. $p(v) = -4.5v$

4. $q(x) = 94$

Uses Objective D

5. If $800 is invested at an interest rate of 7.5% compounded continuously, the amount in the account after t years is $A(t) = 800e^{0.075t}$ dollars. The derivative of A is $A' = 60e^{0.075t}$.

   a. Find the amount in the account after 5 years.

   b. Find $A'(5)$.

   c. What does your answer to part b mean?

6. A certain flashlight is pointed directly at a wall. The area A in square inches of the illuminated area is $A(d) = \pi d^2 + 2\pi d + \pi$ where d is the flashlight's distance in inches from the wall.

   a. Find the illuminated area at $d = 3$ inches.

   b. Find the derivative of $A(d)$.

   c. Find the instantaneous rate of change of the illuminated area when $d = 3$ inches.

   d. Find the illuminated area at $d = 6$ inches.

   e. Calculate $A'(6)$.

   f. What does your answer to part e mean?

Name

Uses Objective E

7. A particle moves so that the distance s traveled in meters at time t seconds is given by $s(t) = t^2 + 5t - 4$.

a. Find the average velocity between 3 and 4 seconds. __________

b. Find the instantaneous velocity of the particle at time $t = 8$. __________

c. What is the initial velocity of the particle (that is, at time $t = 0$ seconds)? __________

Representations Objective H

8. The function j is graphed at the right.

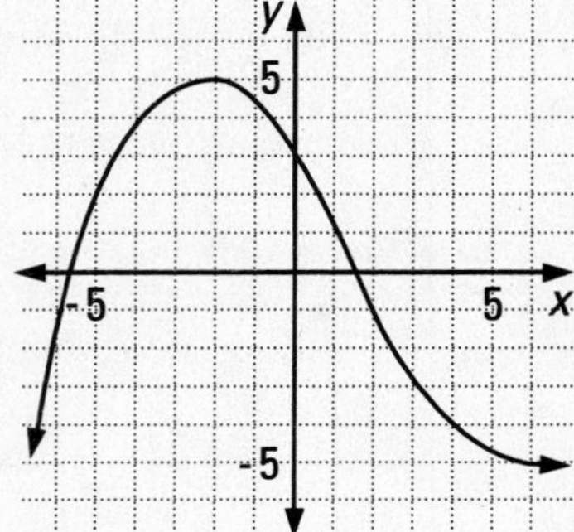

a. Estimate the values of $j'(x)$ when $x = -5, -3, -2, 0, 1, 3$ and 5.

____

____

____

____

b. Use the information from part a and the graph of j to sketch a graph of j'.

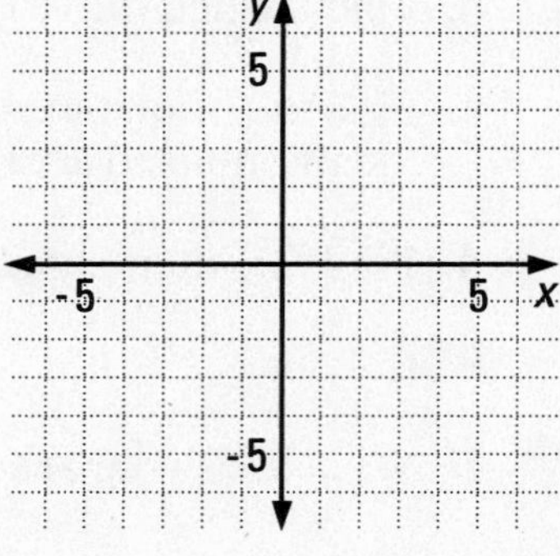

Name

LESSON MASTER 

Questions on SPUR Objectives
See pages 596–599 for objectives.

Skills Objective D

1. A bowl of hot soup is placed on a table to cool. The temperature in degrees Celsius of the object after t minutes is given by $C(t) = 65e^{-0.198t} + 20$. For this function, $C' = -12.87e^{-0.198t}$ and $C'' = 2.56e^{-0.198t}$.

a. In what units is $C'(t)$? ____________

b. In what units is $C''(t)$? ____________

c. How fast is the temperature changing at time $t = 4$ minutes? ____________

d. How fast is the rate of cooling changing at time $t = 4$ minutes? ____________

e. Is the change in the rate of cooling at $t = 7$ minutes greater or less than at $t = 4$ minutes? ____________

Uses Objective E

2. A particle moves horizontally so that its position in feet to the right of the starting point at time t seconds is given by $f(t) = -t^2 + 5t + 6$.

a. At time $t = 8$ seconds, is the particle moving to the right, to the left, or stationary? ____________

b. What is the speed of the object at time $t = 8$ seconds? ____________

c. What is the acceleration of the object at time $t = 8$ seconds? ____________

d. Is the acceleration increasing, decreasing, or staying the same at time $t = 8$ seconds? ____________

3. A ball is thrown directly upward. Its height h in meters after t seconds is given by the equation $h(t) = -4.9t^2 + 28t + 2$.

a. Find the instantaneous velocity at each time.

i. 0 seconds ____________ **ii.** 3 seconds ____________

b. Find the instantaneous acceleration at each time.

i. 0 seconds ____________ **ii.** 3 seconds ____________

Name

LESSON MASTER

Questions on SPUR Objectives
See pages 596–599 for objectives.

Skills Objective C

1. Suppose g is a function such that $g(x) = -\frac{2}{3}x^3 + 5x^2 - 12x$. Then $g'(x) = -2x^2 + 10x - 12$. Use the first derivative to find each.

 a. The interval(s) on which g is increasing. ______

 b. The interval(s) on which g is decreasing. ______

 c. The points at which g may have a relative maximum or minimum. ______

2. Suppose $f(x) = 3x^5 + 3x$. Then $f'(x) = 15x^4 + 3$. Is f increasing or decreasing on the set of all real numbers? Explain your answer.

______

______

Uses Objective F

3. A rectangular pen adjacent to a shed is to be enclosed with 40 feet of fencing. What should the dimensions of the pen be in order to maximize the area? ______

Representations Objective I

4. Consider the function f graphed at the right.

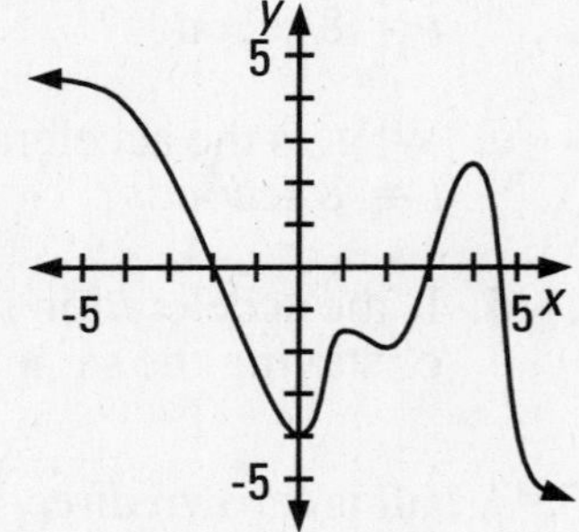

 a. On what interval(s) is $f'(x)$ positive?

 ______

 b. On what interval(s) is $f'(x)$ negative?

 ______

 c. For what values of x is $f'(x) = 0$?

 ______

5. The derivative h' of a function h is graphed at the right. Describe the values of x where

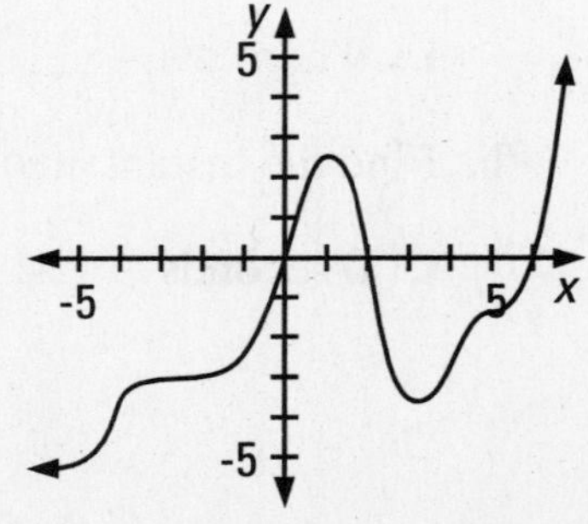

 a. h is increasing. ______

 b. h is decreasing. ______

 c. h has a relative maximum or minimum. ______

Name ____

LESSON MASTER 

Questions on SPUR Objectives
See pages 653–655 for objectives.

Skills Objective A

In 1–8, describe the essential features of the problem in the question. You do not have to answer the question.

1. Mrs. Kerrigan returned from a trip to Spain with 12 different souvenirs. She wants to give one to each of her three children. In how many different ways can she do this?

____

2. The combination lock on a briefcase has three dial wheels with the digits from 0 through 5 on each wheel. How many different lock combinations are possible?

____

3. A social committee of five members is to be chosen from the 44-member Student Council. In how many ways can the committee be formed?

____

4. The school store has construction paper in eight different colors. Angelo needs to buy five sheets for an art project. How many different selections are possible?

____

5. How many integers from 100 to 999 have at least one digit that is a zero?

____

6. How many different 3-letter code words, such as *SOS*, can be made from the letters *A, B, G, M, O, S, T, X*?

____

7. Harriet wants to hang 7 skirts and 13 blouses on a rod in her closet. How many different arrangements are possible if she keeps the skirts together and the blouses together?

____

8. How many different ways can 5 cards be chosen from a deck of 52 cards?

____

Name ______________________________

LESSON MASTER 

Questions on SPUR Objectives
See pages 653–655 for objectives.

Uses Objective F

1. A vendor sells belts in *s* different sizes, *c* different colors, and *w* different widths. How many different kinds of belts are available? ______________

2. Can Doreen wear a different outfit every day of the year if she chooses from 10 pairs of slacks, 12 blouses, and 3 pairs of shoes? ______________

3. **a.** How many integers from 100 to 999 have at least one digit that is a zero? ______________

   b. If one of the integers in part a is chosen at random, what is the probability that its first and last digits are the same? ______________

4. How many different 5-letter code words can be made from the letters *C, E, G, M, R, S, U,* and *W* satisfying the indicated condition?

   a. The letters can be repeated. ______________

   b. The letters cannot be repeated. ______________

   c. The first letter must be *E* and the last must be *S*, with no repetition allowed. ______________

5. How many *c*-letter codes can be created from *l* different letters if the letters can be repeated? ______________

6. How many different license plates can be made if three letters are to be followed by four digits, but the letters *I* and *O* are not allowed? ______________

7. In the computer program below, how many numbers does line 50 ask to be printed? ______________

```
10  FOR I = 0 TO 5
20  FOR J = 1 TO 4
30  FOR K = 2 TO 9
40  SUM = I + J + K
50  PRINT SUM
60  NEXT K
70  NEXT J
80  NEXT I
90  END
```

Representations Objective I

8. a. Fran and Bob are planning to play a game that has four game pieces: a ship, a plane, a car, and a train engine. Each player must choose one piece. Draw a possibility tree to show the number of different ways Fran and Bob can pick their pieces.

b. In how many of these ways does Bob pick the car? ____________

9. For the conference championship, the Darts will play the Jolts in a series of games. The first team to win either three games in all or two games in a row is the champion. Draw a possibility tree to show the possible outcomes.

Name

Questions on SPUR Objectives
See pages 653–655 for objectives.

Skills Objective B

In 1–4, evaluate the expression.

1. $P(11, 9)$ ______ **2.** $P(20, 3)$ ______

3. ${}_7P_4$ ______ **4.** $0!$ ______

5. Find a so that $P(22, a) = \frac{22!}{15!}$ ______

Skills Objective D

6. If $n! = n \cdot 18!$, what is n? ______

7. a. Verify that $P(9, 8) = P(9, 9) = 9!$.

______

______

b. Generalize the results from part a.

______

Skills Objective F

6. Each year Clyborn High School has a sock hop, a junior prom, and a senior prom. In how many ways can these three school dances be scheduled from a set of fourteen available Saturdays? ______

7. A photographer is arranging three sets of triplets in a row. If each set of triplets is not to be separated, in how many ways can the nine people be arranged? ______

8. Using the digits from 0 to 9, how many 4-digit personal identification numbers (PIN) are possible under the given conditions?

a. The digits can repeat. ______

b. The digits cannot repeat. ______

c. The first digit must be odd, the rest even, and repetition is allowed. ______

d. The first digit must be odd, the rest even, and repetition is not allowed. ______

Name ______________________________

Questions on SPUR Objectives
See pages 653–655 for objectives.

Skills Objective B

In 1–4, evaluate the expression.

1. $C(15, 6)$ ____________ **2.** $C(9, 9)$ ____________

3. ${}_{10}C_5$ ____________ **4.** $\binom{7}{3}$ ____________

5. Find a and b so that $C(a, 5) = \frac{11!}{b!5!}$ ____________

6. Find j and k so that $C(6, 4) \cdot 4! = P(j, k)$. ____________

Skills Objective D

7. Show that $C(n, r) \cdot r! = P(n, r)$

____

8. a. Verify that $C(10, 3) = C(10, 7)$.

____

b. Generalize the results from part a.

____

Skills Objective G

9. The high school band has been rehearsing seven pieces. The band director needs to select two of them for an audition tape. In how many ways can this choice be made? ____________

10. At a family party, 18 people need to be seated at two tables, a table for eight and a table for ten. In how many ways can the table assignments be made? ____________

11. Rigio's deluxe pizza offers any three toppings from a choice of nine. Armando's deluxe pizza allows any four toppings from a choice of eight. Which pizzeria offers the greater number of different possible deluxe pizzas? ____________

12. Lorna needs to pack 5 blouses and 4 pairs of slacks for a vacation. She has 14 blouses and 8 pairs of slacks to choose from. In how many different ways can she choose her clothes for the trip? ____________

Name

Questions on SPUR Objectives
See pages 653–655 for objectives.

Skills Objective C

1. a. What combination yields the coefficient of x^9y^{13} in the expansion of $(x + y)^{22}$? ________

   b. What is this coefficient? ________

2. What is the coefficient of xy^7 in the expansion of $(x + 4y)^8$? ________

3. Write the following expression as the power of a binomial:

   $\sum_{k=0}^{6} \binom{6}{k}(4x)^{6-k}y^k$. ________

In 4–6, expand using the Binomial Theorem.

4. $(x + y)^5$

5. $(2a - 5b)^4$

6. $(x + 5)^7$

7. Find the sixth power of $(1 + i)$. ________

8. Find the tenth term of $(x + y)^{18}$. ________

9. Find the first term of $(3x - y)^{10}$. ________

10. Find the last term of $(-2x + y)^5$. ________

11. The coefficients of which terms of the expansion of $(x + y)^{12}$ are the same?

Name

Questions on SPUR Objectives
See pages 653–655 for objectives.

Properties Objective E

1. What combination yields the number of 5-element subsets that can be formed from a set with 9 elements? ________

2. How is ${}_{10}C_7 + {}_{10}C_8 + {}_{10}C_9 + {}_{10}C_{10}$ related to the number of subsets that can be formed from a set?

____

____

____

Uses Objective G

3. In how many ways is it possible to obtain at least three heads in 11 tosses of a coin? ________

4. In how many ways is it possible to obtain at least six tails in eight tosses of a coin? ________

5. A pizzeria offers ten different pizza toppings. In how many different ways can a pizza be topped if at least one topping is used? ________

Uses Objective H

6. A long multiple-choice text is designed so that each of the choices, *A*, *B*, *C*, and *D*, is the correct answer 25% of the time. A computer randomly assigns the correct answer to *A*, *B*, *C*, and *D* in each question. What is the probability that in the first ten questions *A* is the correct answer for five questions? ________

7. In a board game, a player must roll a 1 or a 2 on a die to attain a bonus. In five rolls of a fair die, what is the probability that the player will roll a 1 or a 2 at least once? ________

8. A cereal manufacturer has packaged a small toy in 8% of its boxes of cereal. Assuming that the boxes are randomly distributed to the stores, what is the probability that a purchase of four boxes will result in

   a. exactly four toys? ________

   b. no toys? ________

   c. at least one toy? ________

   d. at least two toys? ________

Name

LESSON MASTER 10-7

Questions on SPUR Objectives
See pages 653–655 for objectives.

Skills Objective G

In 1–3, give the number of different terms in each expansion.

1. $(x + y + z)^8$

2. $(w + x + y + z)^6$

3. $(2a - 5b + 3c - d + 8)^{12}$

4. In how many different ways can six passengers be distributed among the cars of a four-car commuter train?

5. Benny's Bagels offers seven different varieties. How many different half-dozen selections can be made?

6. Suppose a die is tossed ten times. An outcome is defined as a certain number of occurrences of each number. For example, one possible outcome is two 1s, zero 2s, two 3s, four 4s, one 5, and one 6. How many different outcomes are possible in the ten tosses?

7. How many different solutions (a, b, c) are there to the equation $a + b + c = 15$ for which a, b, and c are all nonnegative integers?

8. How many positive integers less than 1000 have digits whose sum is 12?

9. a. How many positive integers less than 10,000 have digits whose sum is 18?

b. How many of the numbers in part a begin with a 4?

c. How many of the numbers in part a have exactly one 9?

10. For Homecoming, a royal court of eight students was elected from the student body at large. The court was made up of one freshman, three sophomores, one junior, and three seniors. If each possible court is defined to be the number of freshmen, sophomores, juniors, and seniors that were elected, how many *other* different courts were possible?

Name

LESSON MASTER 

Questions on SPUR Objectives
See pages 713–717 for objectives.

Uses Objective E

1. Suppose the process of producing a high school musical involves the tasks listed in the table below.

Task	Description	Time Required (days)	Prerequisite Tasks
A	Choose musical	2	none
B	Negotiate royalty agreement	5	A
C	Hold cast tryouts	3	A
D	Hold orchestra auditions	1	A
E	Design set and costumes	5	A
F	Rehearse cast (without orchestra)	20	C
G	Rehearse orchestra (without cast)	15	D
H	Construct set, sew costumes	25	E
I	Rehearse cast with orchestra	10	F, G
J	Perform technical rehearsal	2	H, I
K	Perform dress rehearsal	1	J
L	Perform musical	4	B, K

a. Sketch a digraph to represent the process.

b. What is the minimal time required for producing the musical through the last performance? ________________

2. In Brickton, 84% of the adult residents own their own homes and the rest rent. 58% of the homeowners favor a tax increase to pay for alley paving, while 18% of the renters favor this increase.

a. Draw a probability tree to represent this situation.

b. What percent of adult residents who favor the tax increase to pay for alley paving? ____________

c. If there are 17,400 adult residents, how many do not favor this tax increase? ____________

d. If a randomly selected adult resident favors this tax increase, what is the probability that the resident is a renter? ____________

Uses Objective G

3. The segments of the grid at the right represent the streets of a section of a city, and the vertices represent the intersections.

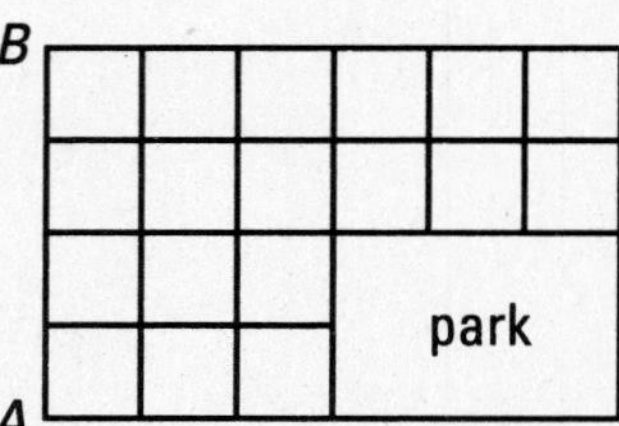

a. On the grid, draw a path that allows an ice cream truck to begin at *A* and end at *B* and visit each intersection exactly once.

b. Is such a path possible that begins and ends at *A*? If so, draw it on the second grid.

____

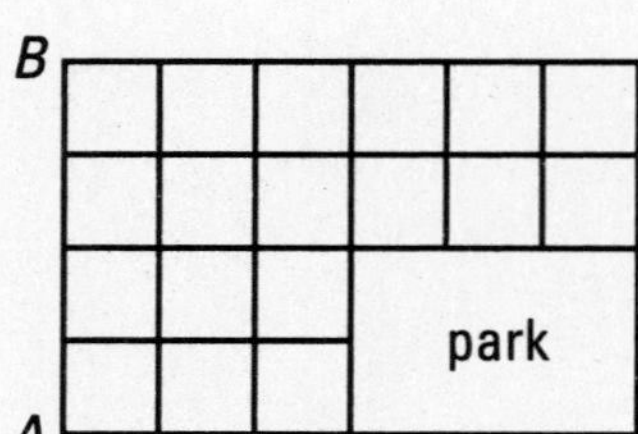

Name

LESSON MASTER 11-2

Questions on SPUR Objectives
See pages 713–717 for objectives.

Skills Objective A

In 1–4, draw a graph with the specified characteristics.

1. three vertices and four edges

2. two vertices, a loop, and three parallel edges

3. three edges and four vertices, one of which is isolated

4. four vertices, four edges, and a crossing

5. Draw the graph G defined as follows:

(1) set of vertices: $\{v_1, v_2, v_3, v_4\}$

(2) set of edges: $\{e_1, e_2, e_3, e_4, e_5\}$

(3) edge-endpoint function:

edge	endpoints
e_1	$\{v_1, v_2\}$
e_2	$\{v_1, v_2\}$
e_3	$\{v_2, v_4\}$
e_4	$\{v_4\}$
e_5	$\{v_4\}$

Properties Objective B

6. **a.** What is a *simple graph*?

b. Is the graph in Question 5 simple? Explain your answer.

Name

7. Use the graph at the right.

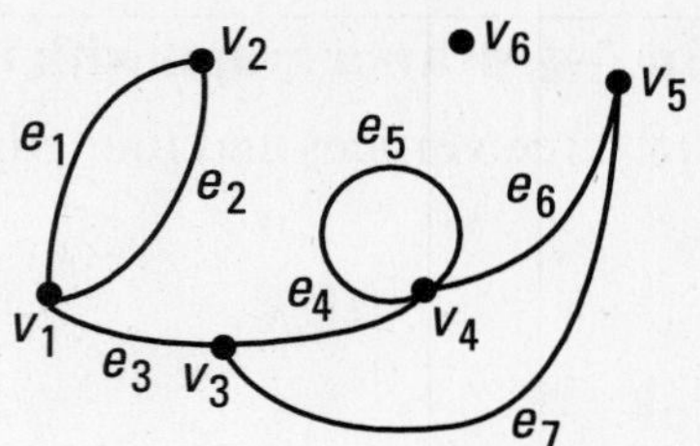

a. Identify any loops.

____

b. Identify any isolated vertices.

____

c. Identify all vertices adjacent to v_5.

____

d. Identify all edges adjacent to e_3.

____

e. At the right, give the edge-endpoint function table for the graph.

edge	endpoints

Representations Objective I

8. Write the adjacency matrix for the directed graph below.

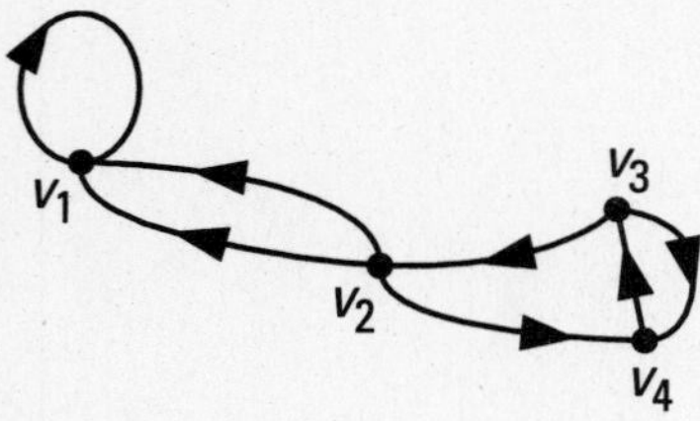

9. Draw an undirected graph with the following adjacency matrix.

$$\begin{matrix} & v_1 & v_3 & v_3 \\ \begin{matrix} v_1 \\ v_2 \\ v_3 \end{matrix} & \multicolumn{3}{c}{\begin{bmatrix} 0 & 1 & 0 \\ 1 & 0 & 2 \\ 0 & 2 & 1 \end{bmatrix}} \end{matrix}$$

10. In the adjacency matrix for a simple graph, no element can be greater than what number? ______________________

Name

LESSON MASTER 

Questions on SPUR Objectives
See pages 713–717 for objectives.

Skills Objective A

1. Draw a simple graph with five vertices of degrees 1, 2, 3, 3, and 3.

2. Draw a graph with three vertices of degrees 1, 6, and 1.

Properties Objective B

3. Refer to the graph at the right.

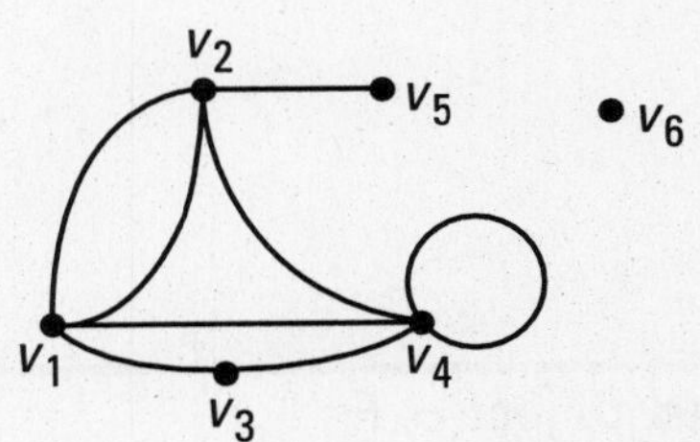

a. Give the degree of each vertex.

____

____

b. Give the total degree of the graph.

____

4. A graph has five edges. What is its total degree? ______________

5. *True or false.* The degree of any vertex is even. ______________

6. *True or false.* The total degree of any graph is even. ______________

7. *True or false.* Every graph has an odd number of vertices with even degree. ______________

8. *True or false.* Every graph has an even number of vertices with odd degree. ______________

Properties Objective C

In 9 and 10, either draw a graph with the given properties, or explain why no such graph exists.

9. a simple graph with three vertices of degrees 1, 4, and 1

10. a graph with six vertices of degrees 2, 2, 3, 3, 4, and 4

Uses Objective F

11. The Scholastic Bowl in each of five schools is scheduled to play every other team exactly once.

a. At the right, draw a graph to represent this situation.

b. How many different pairings result?

____

12. At a bake-off, 19 contestants have baked their special cookie recipes. Is it possible for each contestant to sample the cookies of exactly five other contestants? Explain.

____

____

____

____

____

Name

LESSON MASTER 11-4

Questions on SPUR Objectives
See pages 713–717 for objectives.

Properties Objective B

1. Refer to the graph at the right. Describe, if possible.

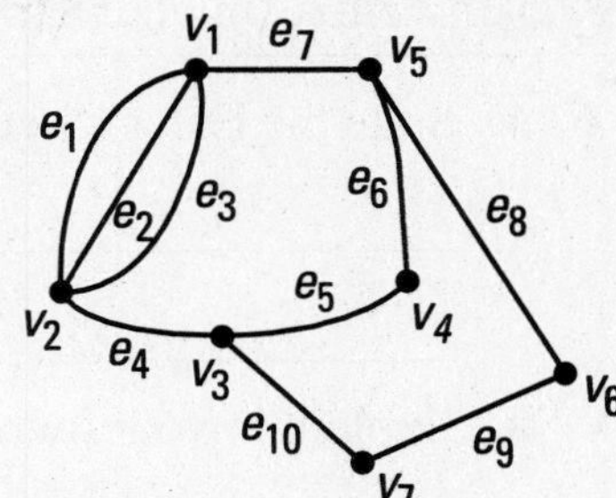

   a. a walk from v_2 to v_5 that is not a path.

   ____

   b. a path from v_2 to v_6

   ____

   c. a circuit starting at v_7 ______________________________

   d. an Euler circuit ______________________________

In 2–4, determine whether or not the graph is connected.

2. 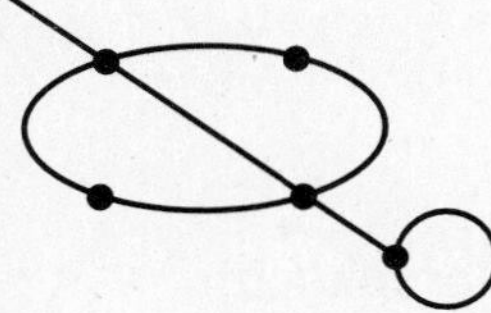

____

3. 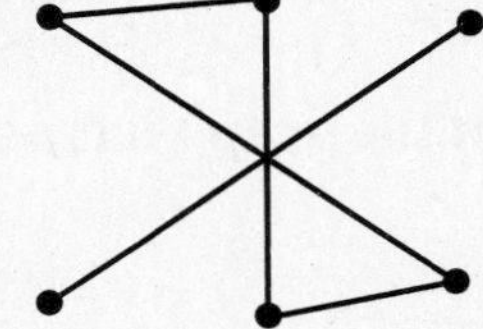

____

4. 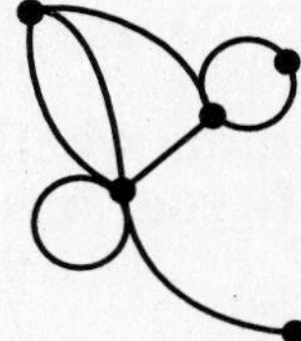

____

5. Consider the graph at the right.

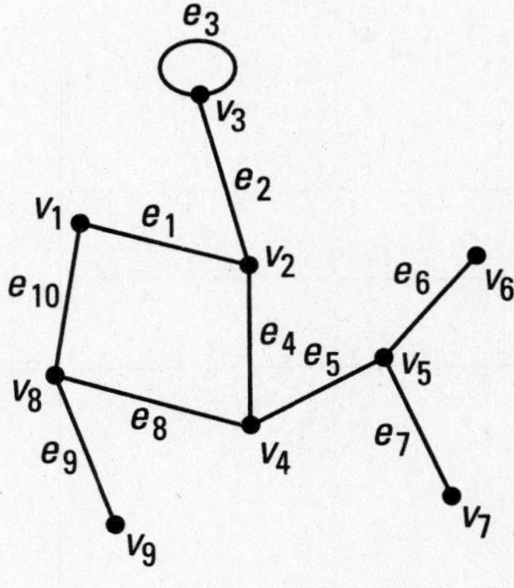

   a. If e_4 is removed, would the graph remain connected?

   ____

   b. Give each edge whose removal (by itself) would keep the graph connected.

   ____

   c. What is the maximum number of edges that can be removed simultaneously while keeping the graph connected? ______________

Name

▶ **LESSON MASTER 11-4** *page 2*

Properties Objective D

6. **a.** State the Euler Circuit Theorem.

b. Explain in your own words why the Euler Circuit Theorem is reasonable.

In 7–9, determine whether or not the graph has an Euler circuit. Justify your answer.

7.

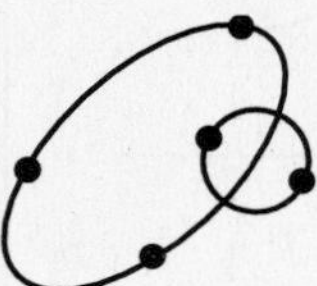

8.

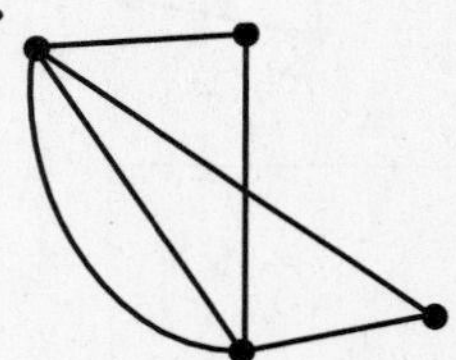

9. the graph with adjacency matrix

$$\begin{array}{c} \\ v_1 \\ v_2 \\ v_3 \end{array} \begin{array}{c} \begin{array}{ccc} v_1 & v_2 & v_3 \end{array} \\ \begin{bmatrix} 0 & 0 & 4 \\ 0 & 0 & 2 \\ 4 & 2 & 1 \end{bmatrix} \end{array}$$

Properties Objective G

10. Suppose a camp counselor wants to check "lights out" at each cabin. Is it possible for her to start and end at her own cabin, *C*, and visit every cabin using each path given in the map exactly once? If so, draw the possible route on the map. If not, explain why.

2 1 3 C 4 5

Name

LESSON MASTER

Questions on SPUR Objectives
See pages 713–717 for objectives.

Properties Objective B

1. Consider the graph at the right.

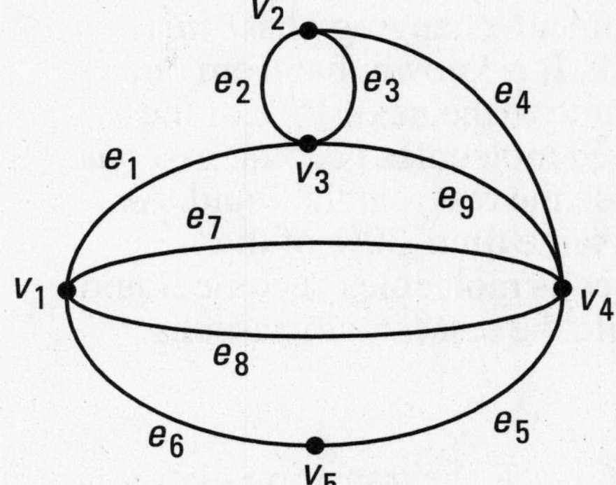

a. List all the different walks of length 2 from v_1 to v_2.

b. List three different walks of length 4 from v_4 to v_1.

Representations Objective J

2. The adjacency matrix for a directed graph is $A = \begin{matrix} & v_1 & v_2 & v_3 & v_4 \\ v_1 & 0 & 1 & 0 & 0 \\ v_2 & 0 & 0 & 1 & 1 \\ v_3 & 0 & 2 & 0 & 1 \\ v_4 & 1 & 0 & 1 & 1 \end{matrix}$.

Use the fact that $A^4 = \begin{bmatrix} 2 & 3 & 4 & 5 \\ 5 & 10 & 8 & 12 \\ 6 & 9 & 13 & 16 \\ 6 & 12 & 9 & 14 \end{bmatrix}$ to answer the following.

a. How many walks of length 1 are there from v_3 to v_2?

b. How many walks of length 4 are there from v_3 to v_2?

c. How many walks of length 4 are there from v_4 to v_4?

d. What does the 8 in A^4 indicate?

3. a. Give the adjacency matrix for the graph at the right.

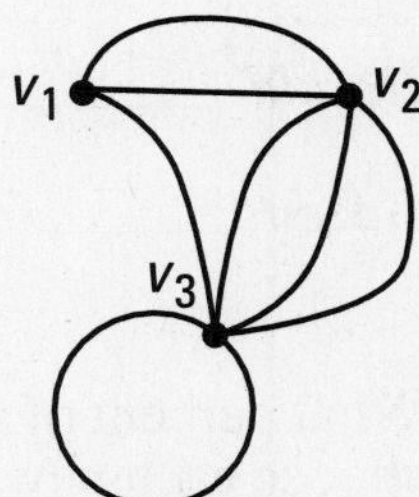

b. How many walks of length 3 are there from v_1 to v_3?

c. How many walks of length 3 start at v_2?

Name

LESSON MASTER 11-6

Questions on SPUR Objectives
See pages 713–717 for objectives.

Uses Objective H

1. In a laboratory, molecules of a liquid are changing phase in a flask. It is known that from one minute to the next, 15% of the liquid molecules become gaseous, while the rest remain liquid. At the same time, 30% of the gaseous molecules become liquid while the rest remain gaseous.

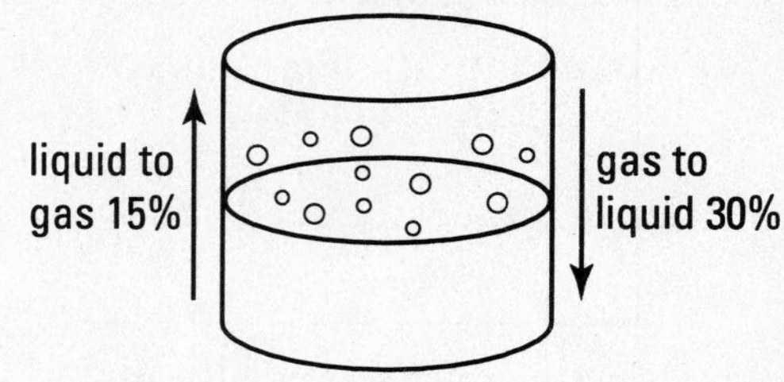

   a. Give T, the transition matrix for this situation. ____________

   b. After sufficient time, the substance will reach equilibrium so that the percent that is liquid and the percent that is gaseous become constant. Estimate these percents by calculating T^{10}.

   ____

   c. Find the exact percents by solving a system of equations.

   ____

2. A large city has three major newspapers, the *Times,* the *Herald,* and the *Gazette.* A survey of readers who buy their newspapers at newsstands revealed they switched newspapers daily according to the directed graph below.

   a. Suppose that today 38% of the readers chose the *Times,* 45% chose the *Herald,* and 28% chose the *Gazette.* Based on the model, what percent of the readers would choose each newspaper tomorrow?

   Times ____________

   Herald ____________

   Gazette ____________

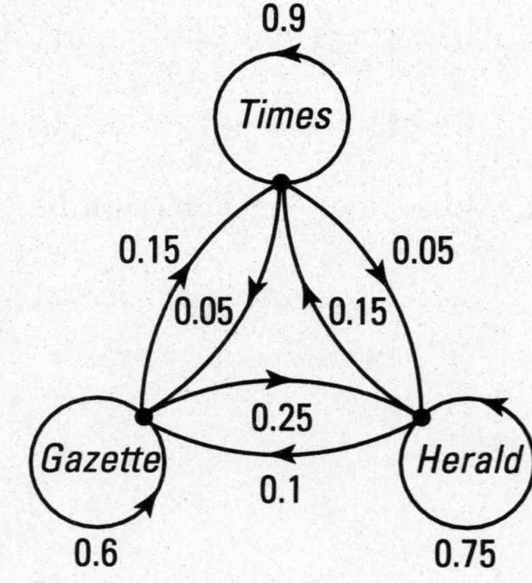

   b. What percent of the readers would eventually choose each newspaper after a long period of time?

   Time ____________ *Herald* ____________ *Gazette* ____________

Name

LESSON MASTER 12-1

Questions on SPUR Objectives
See pages 778–781 for objectives.

Skills Objective A

In 1–3, find the magnitude and direction of the given vector.

1. (-3, 7) ______________ **2.** (-0.8, -0.6) ______________

3. the arrow joining (2, -2) to (4, 9) ______________

4. Find all possible directions for a vector whose x-component is half its y-component. ______________

5. Find a polar representation of the vector (5, -1) ______________

Uses Objective G

6. A plane's velocity is represented by [600, 120°], where the magnitude is measured in miles per hour and the direction is in degrees counterclockwise from due east.

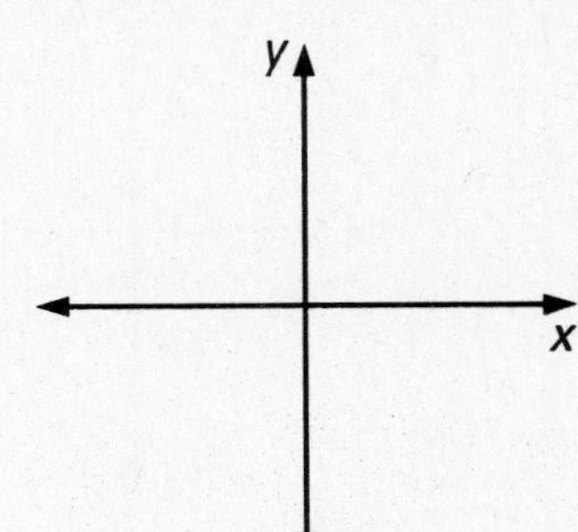

a. Sketch a vector for the velocity.

b. Give the vector in component form.

____

c. Interpret the components.

____

____

7. A monkey is swinging from the end of a 24-foot rope. Its angle with the horizontal is 50°. Assume the rope is taut.

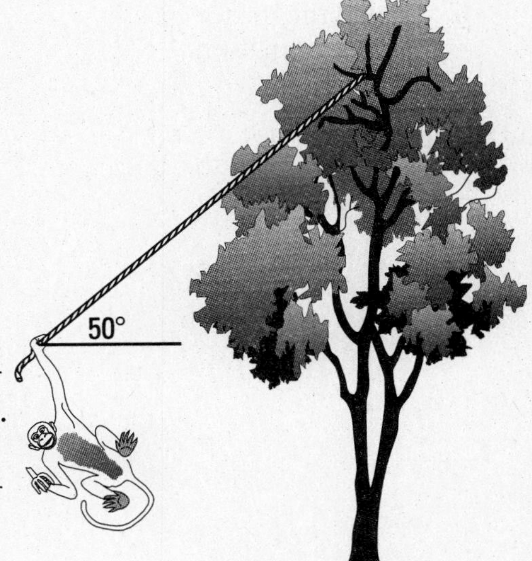

a. Write a polar representation for the monkey's position, using the rope's knot on the tree branch as the origin.

____

b. Compute a component representation.

____

c. Interpret the components.

____

____

Name

► **LESSON MASTER 12-1** *page 2*

Representations Objective I

8. Suppose $P = (4, -1)$ and $Q = (x, y)$ are points. in a plan. If $\overrightarrow{PQ} = \left[8, \frac{\pi}{6}\right]$ find the coordinates of Q. __________

9. a. Find the component representation of [7, 330°].

____

b. Sketch the vector.

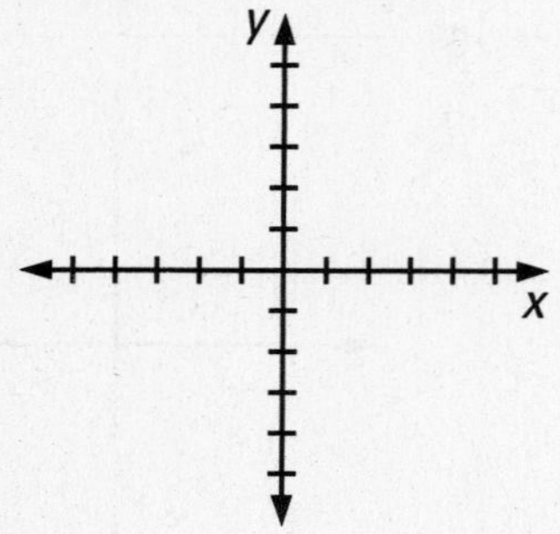

10. a. Give the endpoint of a vector with polar representation [2, -90°] and initial endpoint (3, 1).

____

b. Sketch the vector.

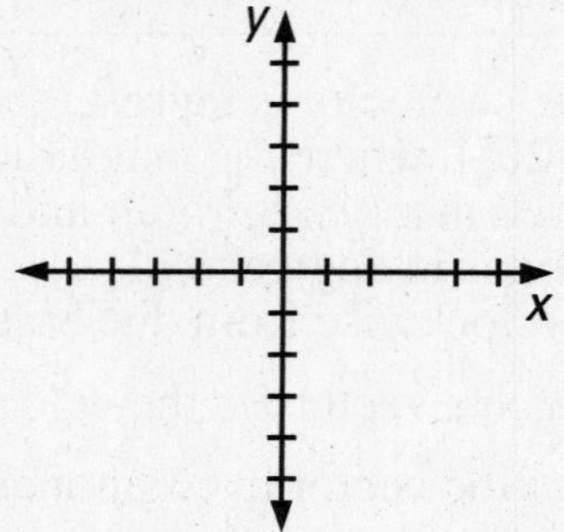

11. a. Find the component representation of the vector shown at the right.

____

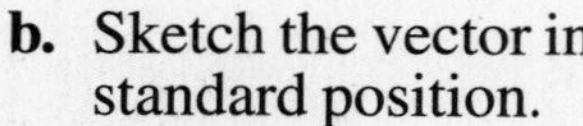

b. Sketch the vector in standard position.

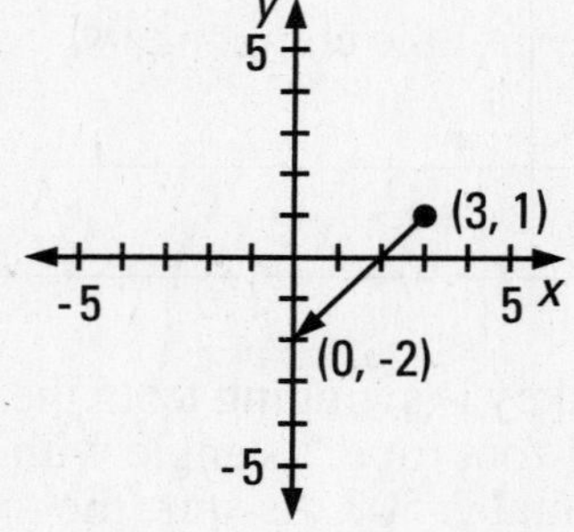

Name ______________________________

LESSON MASTER 

Questions on SPUR Objectives
See pages 778–781 for objectives.

Skills Objective B

In 1–4, let $\vec{u} = (-2, -5)$, $\vec{v} = (4, 1)$, and $\vec{w} = (-6, 0)$. Find the sum or difference.

1. $\vec{u} + \vec{w}$ ____________ **2.** $\vec{u} - \vec{v}$ ____________

3. $-\vec{u}$ ____________ **4.** $\vec{w} - \vec{v} + \vec{u}$ ____________

In 5 and 6, let $\vec{s} = [4, 75°]$ and $\vec{t} = [1, 20°]$. Compute and express the answer in its polar representation.

5. $\vec{s} + \vec{t}$ ____________ **6.** $\vec{s} - \vec{t}$ ____________

Properties Objective E

7. Prove that if $\vec{v} + \vec{u} = \vec{v} + \vec{w}$, then $\vec{u} = \vec{w}$.

8. Show that $\vec{v} = (\cos 50°, 5 \sin 50°)$ is the opposite of $\vec{w} = (5 \cos 230°, 5 \sin 230°)$.

Name ______________________________

Uses Objective H

9. Two children push a friend on a sled with the forces shown at the right.

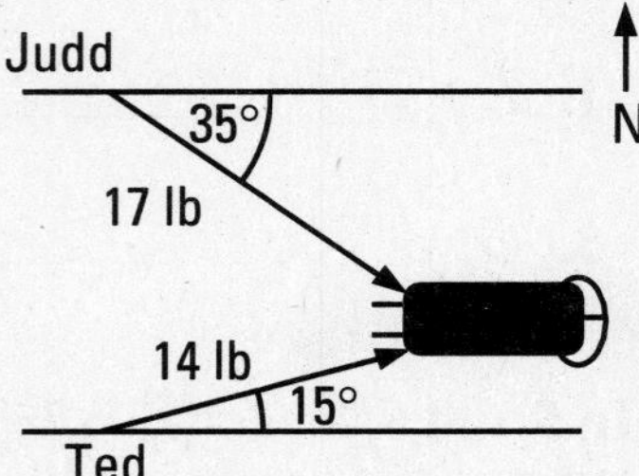

a. Give the resultant force in polar form.

____

b. Interpret your answer to part a.

____

____

c. Which child is exerting more forward force? How much more? ______________________________

10. Relative to the water, a boat is moving with a speed of 25 mph in the direction 10° north of east. Due to the current which is moving 5° north of west, the boat is actually heading north relative to the land.

a. Find the speed of the current. ______________________________

b. Find the speed of the boat moving north. ______________________________

Representations Objective J

11. The vectors $\vec{u}$ and $\vec{v}$ are shown at the right. Sketch the following.

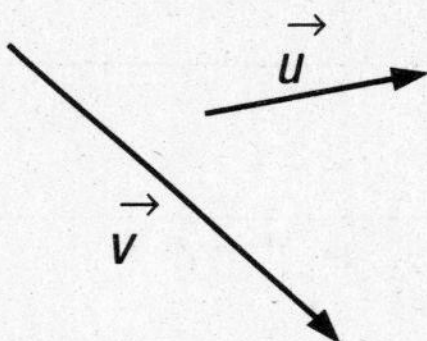

a. $\vec{u} + \vec{v}$

b. $-\vec{u}$

c. $\vec{v} - \vec{u}$

Name

Questions on SPUR Objectives
See pages 778–781 for objectives.

Skills Objective B

In 1–4, let $\vec{u} = (-4, 12)$, and $\vec{v} = (-6, 1)$, and compute.

1. $\frac{2}{3}\vec{u}$ ____________ **2.** $5\vec{v}$ ____________

3. $\frac{2}{3}\vec{u} + 5\vec{v}$ ____________ **4.** $3\vec{u} - 4\vec{v}$ ____________

Properties Objective E

5. Show that $\vec{v} = (-2, 5)$ and $\vec{w} = (12, -30)$ are parallel.

____

6. Show that the line passing through (-2, -2) and (0, 8) is parallel to the vector $\vec{v} = (-1, -5)$.

____

____

Properties Objective F

In 7–9, is the given vector parallel to $\vec{u} = (12, 2)$?

7. $\vec{v} = \left(-4, -\frac{2}{3}\right)$ ____________

8. $\vec{w} = (-24, 4)$ ____________

9. $\vec{n} = (12, 2)$ ____________

10. Are $\vec{u} = [2, 40°]$ and $\vec{v} = [3, 220°]$ parallel? ____________

Representations Objective I

11. Sketch $\vec{v} = (-2, -5)$ and $-2\vec{v}$ on the grid at the right.

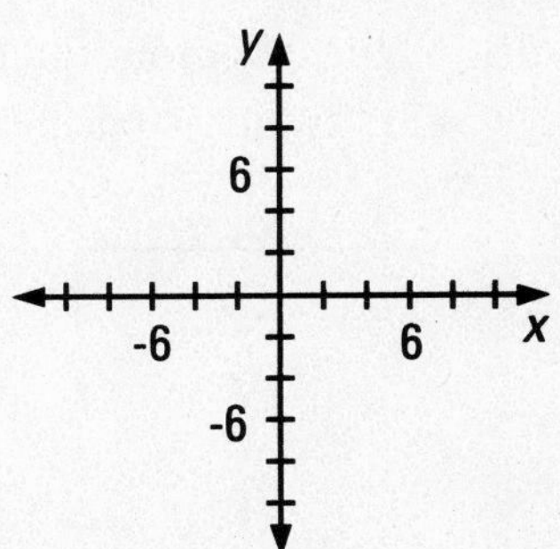

Name

▶ **LESSON MASTER 12-3** *page 2*

12. a. Give the endpoint of a vector $\vec{u}$ which has polar representation [4, 120°] and starts at (3, -6). ____________

b. Give the endpoint of the vector $3\vec{u}$ if it starts at (2, -2). ____________

c. Sketch both vectors on the grid at the right.

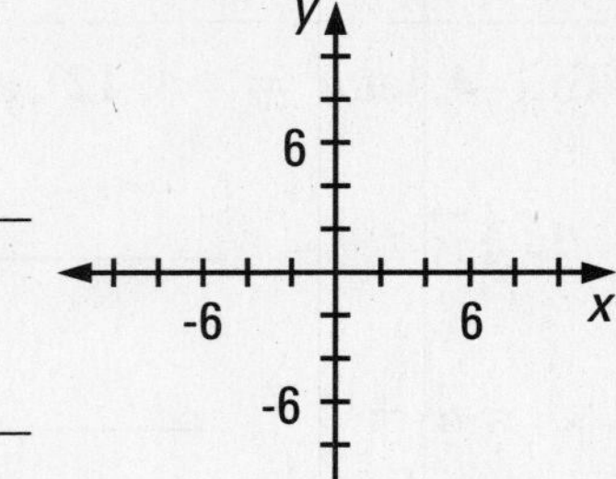

Representations Objective J

13. Given the vectors $\vec{u}$ and $\vec{v}$ shown at the right. Sketch the following.

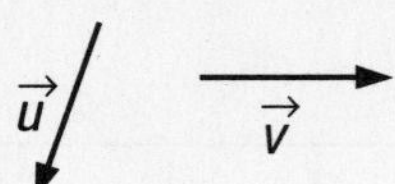

a. $3\vec{u}$

b. $-2\vec{v}$

c. $3\vec{u} - 2\vec{v}$

Representations Objective L

14. a. Find parametric equations of the line through (-1, 4) that is parallel to the vector $\vec{w} = (1, 6)$.

____

b. Graph the line on the grid at the right.

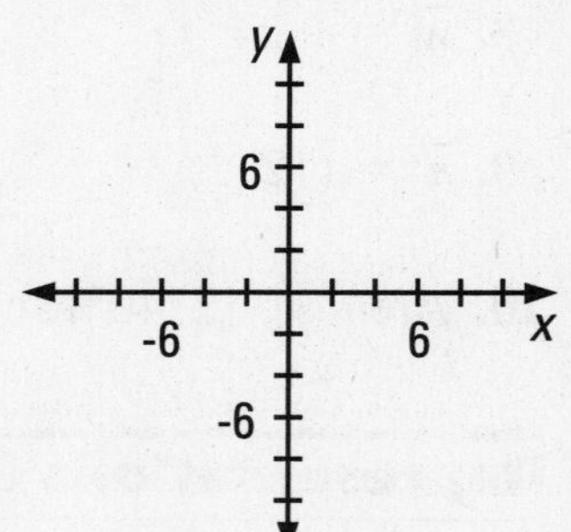

15. Write a vector equation for the line through (3, -2) that is parallel to the vector $\vec{u} = (5, -5)$.

____

Name

LESSON MASTER 

Questions on SPUR Objectives
See pages 778–781 for objectives.

Skills Objective B

In 1–4, let $\vec{u} = (3, 8)$, $\vec{v} = (4, -2)$ and $\vec{w} = (-7, 6)$, and compute.

1. $\vec{v} \cdot \vec{w}$ __________

2. $\vec{u} \cdot \vec{u}$ __________

3. $\vec{u} \cdot (\vec{v} \cdot \vec{w})$ __________

4. $(\vec{v} - \vec{w}) \cdot (\vec{u} + \vec{v})$ __________

Skills Objective D

In 5–8, find the measure of the angle between the two vectors.

5. (-3, -3) and (1, 2) __________

6. (4, 6) and (2, 7) __________

7. (-5, 0) and (0, -12) __________

8. [4, 94°] and [19, 211°] __________

Properties Objective E

9. Show that $\vec{v} = (-4, 7)$ and $\vec{w} = (-12, -9)$ are not orthogonal.

____

____

10. If $\vec{u}$ and $\vec{v}$ are perpendicular vectors, prove that for all nonzero real numbers j and k, $j\vec{u}$ and $k\vec{v}$ are perpendicular.

____

____

____

____

____

____

Name ______________________________

▶ **LESSON MASTER 12-4** *page 2*

Properties Objective F

In 11–13, determine whether $\vec{u}$ and $\vec{v}$ are perpendicular, parallel, or neither.

11. $\vec{u} = (7, 7)$, $\vec{v} = (-3, 8)$ ______________

12. $\vec{u} = (4, -10)$, $\vec{v} = (-5, -2)$ ______________

13. $\vec{u} = (3, -5)$, $\vec{v} = (12, -20)$ ______________

14. Find x so that the vectors $\vec{u} = (10, -12)$and $\vec{v} = (x, 5)$ are orthogonal. ______________

15. Find all plane vectors with length $10\sqrt{2}$ that are orthogonal to $\vec{w} = (1, -7)$. ______________

Representations Objective L

In 16 and 17, let $\vec{v} = (-2, 9)$. Write a vector equation for the line through $P = (1, 4)$ that is

16. parallel to $\vec{v}$. ______________

17. perpendicular to $\vec{v}$. ______________

Name

Questions on SPUR Objectives
See pages 778–781 for objectives.

Representations Objective M

1. Which plane is described by the equation $z = 0$? ______

2. Write an equation for the plane that is parallel to the xz-plane and is 8 units in the negative direction from the origin. ______

3. Let M be the plane parallel to the yz-plane that is 5 units in the positive direction from the yz-plane. Give a system of two linear equations that describes the intersection of M and the xy-plane. ______

4. Write an equation for the sphere with radius 12 and center (-2, 5, 0).

______

5. Find the center and radius of the sphere with equation $x^2 + y^2 + z^2 - 6x + 2z = 10$.

______

6. **a.** Sketch $P = (3, 0, -1)$ and $Q = (1, 2, 4)$ in the three-dimensional coordinate system at the right.

   b. Write an equation for the sphere with center P and radius PQ.

   ______

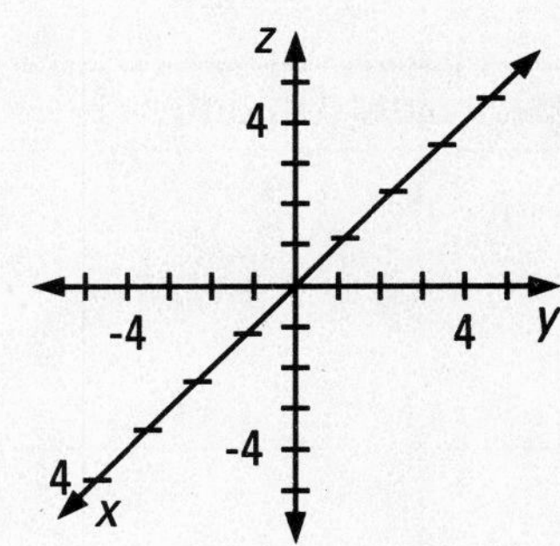

7. Write a system of two linear equations that describes the line parallel to the z-axis passing throught the point (5, 8, -4). ______

Name ______________________________

LESSON MASTER 

Questions on SPUR Objectives
See pages 778–781 for objectives.

Skills Objective C

In 1–6, let $\vec{u} = (3, -2, 1)$, and $\vec{v} = (-4, 4, 5)$, and compute.

1. $\vec{u} + \vec{v}$ ______________

2. $-8\vec{v}$ ______________

3. $|\vec{u}|$ ______________

4. $\vec{u} \cdot \vec{v}$ ______________

5. $5\vec{u} - 3\vec{v}$ ______________

6. $\vec{u} \times \vec{v}$ ______________

7. Find a vector orthogonal to both $\vec{r} = (1, 1, 3)$ and $\vec{s} = (-2, 0, 6)$. ______________

Skills Objective D

In 8–10, find the measure of the angle between the two vectors.

8. $\vec{u} = (2, 3, 4)$, $\vec{v} = (-6, 0, 3)$ ______________

9. $\vec{u} = (0, -1, 7)$, $\vec{v} = (8, -2, -2)$ ______________

10. $\vec{u} = (3, 6, -5)$, $\vec{v} = (-6, -12, 10)$ ______________

Properties Objective E

11. Prove that if $\vec{u}$, $\vec{v}$, and $\vec{w}$ are vectors in 3-space, then $\vec{u} \cdot (\vec{v} + \vec{w}) = \vec{u} \cdot \vec{v} + \vec{u} \cdot \vec{w}$.

____

____

____

____

____

____

____

Name ______________________________

▶ **LESSON MASTER 12-6** *page 2*

Properties Objective F

In 12–14, determine whether $\vec{u}$ and $\vec{v}$ are perpendicular, parallel, or neither.

12. $\vec{u} = (2, 8, 3)$, $\vec{v} = (-1, 6, 4)$ ______________

13. $\vec{u} = (1, 4, -1)$, $\vec{v} = (1, -0.5, -1)$ ______________

14. $\vec{u} = (-8, -6, -2)$, $\vec{v} = \left(\frac{1}{3}, \frac{1}{4}, \frac{1}{12}\right)$ ______________

15. Let $\vec{u} = (-2, y, 4)$ and $\vec{w} = (4, y - 5, -7)$. If are $\vec{u}$ and $\vec{w}$ orthogonal, find y. ______________

Representations Objective K

In 16 and 17, let $\vec{u} = (1, 4, 0)$ and $\vec{v} = (3, -2, 6)$. Use the three-dimensional coordinate system at the right.

16. Sketch the vectors $\vec{u}$ and $\vec{v}$.

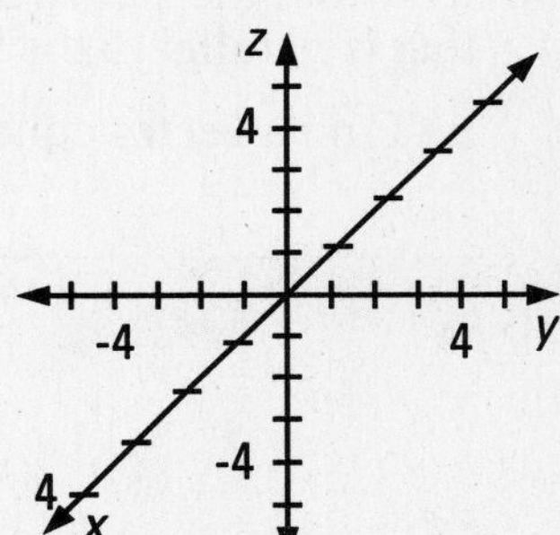

17. Find $\vec{u} - \vec{v}$.

____

18. Sketch the vector $\vec{u} - \vec{v}$ in standard. position.

Name

LESSON MASTER **12-7**

Questions on SPUR Objectives
See pages 778–781 for objectives.

Representations Objective M

1. Let ℓ be a line passing through the two points (8, 3, -5) and (-7, -3, 1). Describe ℓ with

 a. a vector equation.

 b. parametric equations.

2. Find a vector equation for the line through (-2, 5, -1) that is perpendicular to the plane given by $2x - 3y - 4z = 12$.

3. Find a vector perpendicular to the plane defined by the equation $x - 5y + 10z = 20$.

4. Consider the line in 3-space through the point (4, -2, -2) that is parallel to the vector (7, 5, -2).

 a. Find a vector equation for the line.

 b. Find parametric equations for the line.

 c. Find a point other than (4, -2, -2) that lies on the line.

5. Find an equation for the plane that is perpendicular to $\vec{u} = (2, 16, -10)$ and contains the point (3, -5, 0).

6. Show that the planes defined by the equations $2x + y - 4z = 5$ and $-x + 2y + 3z = 8$ are not parallel.

Name ____

7. a. Find the intercepts of the plane defined by the equation $2x - 5y + z = 10$.

____

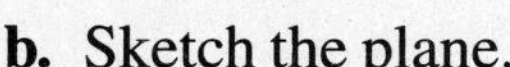

b. Sketch the plane.

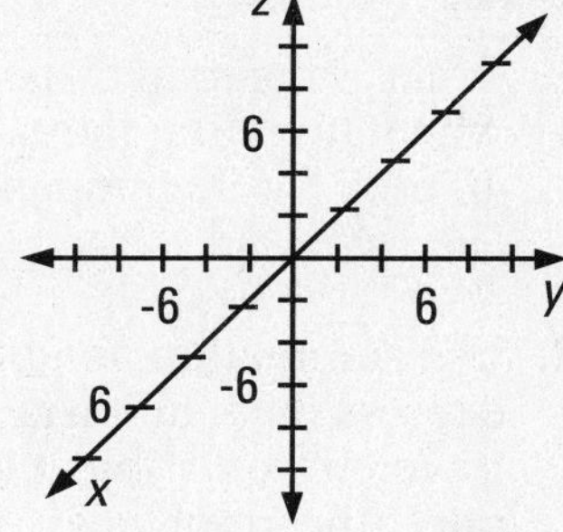

8. Let M be the plane defined by the equation $6x - 4y + 3z = 12$.

a. Sketch M.

b. Show that (3, 0, -2) is a point on the plane.

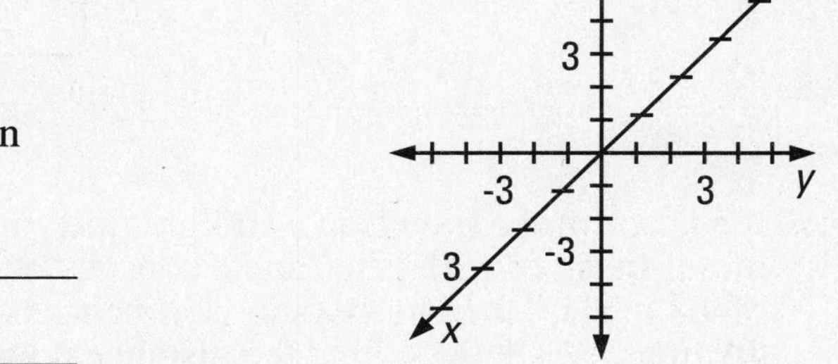

____

____

____

____

____

c. Show that the vector $\vec{u} = (-3, 2, -1.5)$ is perpendicular to M.

____

____

____

____

d. Find equation for the plane N that is parallel to M and passes through (3, -1, 4).

____

Name

LESSON MASTER 

Questions on SPUR Objectives
See pages 836–839 for objectives.

Uses Objective D

1. What is the total distance traveled by a tour bus which travels at the rate of 55 mph for 2.5 hours, 40 mph for 30 minutes, and 25 mph for 15 minutes? ________

2. Use summation notation to express the total distance traveled by an object whose rate-time graph is given at the right.

____

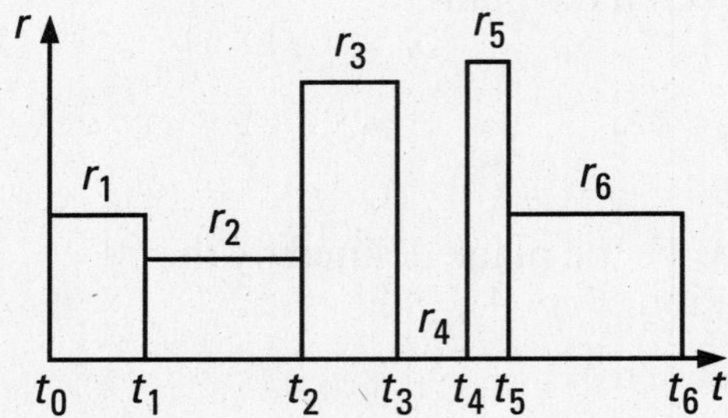

3. If a space probe travels in a straight line with an initial speed of 120 m/sec and a constant acceleration of 9.8 m/sec^2, then its velocity at time t seconds is given by $120 + 9.8t$. Find the distance it will have traveled in 8 seconds. ________

Uses Objective F

4. The rate-time graph below shows the speed of a truck during a trucker's 8-hour work day. Estimate the distance the trucker traveled.

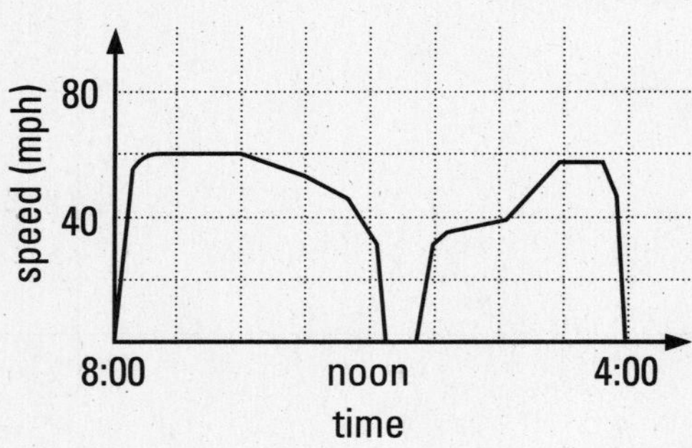

____

5. The rate-time graph below depicts a cyclist riding from home to work. From the graph, estimate the distance to work.

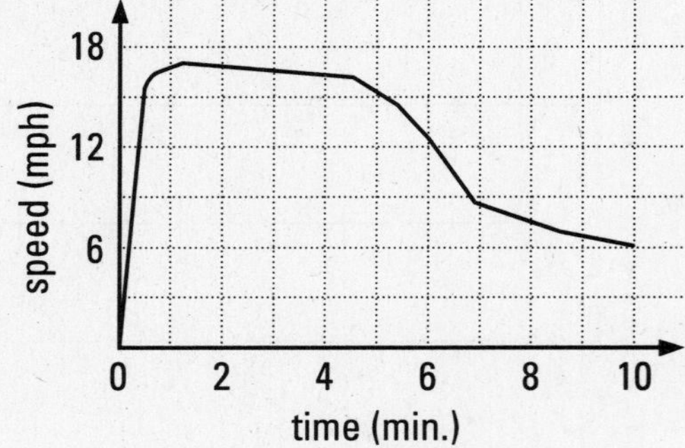

____

Name

Questions on SPUR Objectives
See pages 836–839 for objectives.

Skills Objective A

1. Consider the function f with $f(x) = x^3 + 2$ over the interval from 0 to 10. Let z_i be the rightmost endpoint of the ith subinterval. Evaluate $\sum_{i=1}^{5} f(z_i)\Delta x$. ________

2. For the function g with $g(x) = 2x^3 - 3$, calculate the Riemann sum over the interval $0 \le x \le 2$ for $\Delta x = 0.25$ when

   a. z_i = the left endpoint of the ith subinterval. ________

   b. z_i = the right endpoint of the ith subinterval. ________

3. a. Let $h(x) = \frac{1}{2} \sin x$. Evaluate the Riemann sum $\sum_{i=1}^{n} h(z_i)\Delta x$ over the interval from 0 to $\frac{\pi}{2}$ when z_i is the right endpoint of the ith subinterval, the subintervals are of equal width, and n has the given value.

   i. $n = 4$ ________ ii. $n = 8$ ________ iii. $n = 16$ ________

   b. Which value of n provides an answer that is nearest the area under the graph of h? Why?

   ____

   ____

   c. To what value might you expect the Riemann sum to converge as n increases? ________

3. Use a computer or programmable calculator to evaluate the Riemann sum for the function f with $f(x) = x^2(\cos 2x - \sin x)$ over the interval from 0 to π when z_i is the right endpoint of the ith subinterval of equal width and n has the given value.

   a. $n = 10$ ________ b. $n = 50$ ________

   c. $n = 100$ ________ d. $n = 500$ ________

Name

Uses Objective D

5. The graph below indicates the velocity of a Krazy Car along a track at an amusement park during a 2-minute ride.

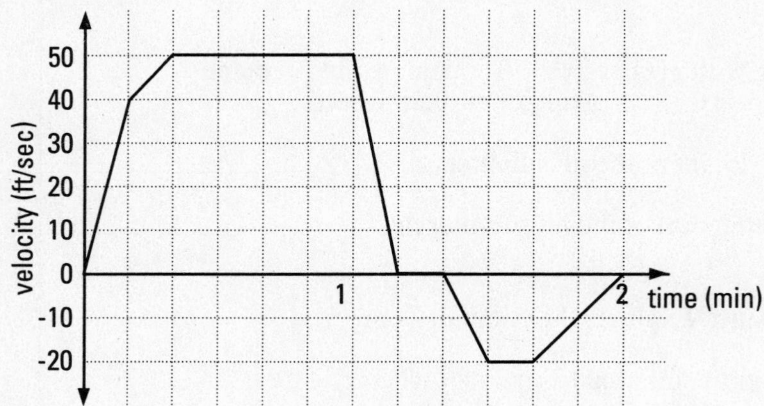

a. How far did the car travel in the first 2 minutes? ____________

b. At the end of the ride, what is the car's distance along the track from its position at the start of the ride? ____________

6. A runner accelerates from 14 ft/sec to 18 ft/sec during the last 5 seconds of a race. The runner's velocity *t* seconds after beginning to accelerate is given by $v(t) = 0.16t^2 + 14$. Estimate the distance the runner runs during these 5 seconds using a Riemann sum with 5 subintervals of equal width and

a. z_i = the left endpoint of the *i*th subinterval. ____________

b. z_i = the right endpoint of the *i*th subinterval. ____________

7. Which of the answers in Question 6 is closer to the exact distance? Why? (Hint: Sketch the velocity-time graph.)

____

____

____

____

____

Name ______________________________

LESSON MASTER 13-3

Questions on SPUR Objectives
See pages 836–839 for objectives.

Skills Objective B

In 1–4, find the exact value of the definite integral.

1. $\int_{-4}^{4} 10\,dx$ ____________

2. $\int_{3}^{7} -x\,dx$ ____________

3. $\int_{0}^{2} (3x + 5)\,dx$ ____________

4. $\int_{0}^{8} \sqrt{64 - x^2}\,dx$ ____________

5. Estimate the value of $\int_{5}^{8} \sqrt{64 - x^2}\,dx$ to the nearest hundredth. ____________

Representations Objective G

In 6–9, consider the shaded region. a. Express the area of the shaded region using integral notation. b. Tell whether the value of the integral appears to be positive or negative.

6.

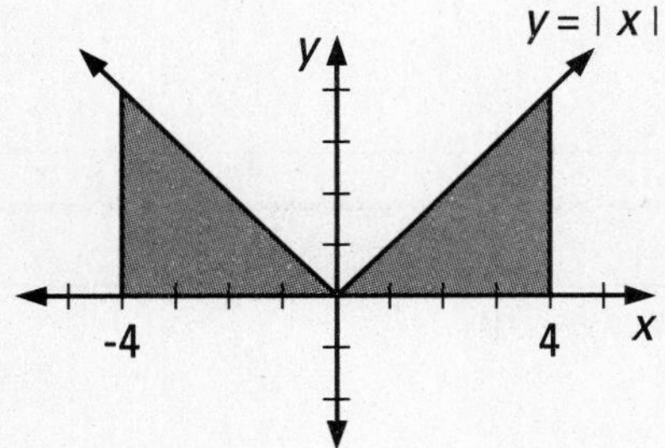

a. ______________________

b. ______________________

7.

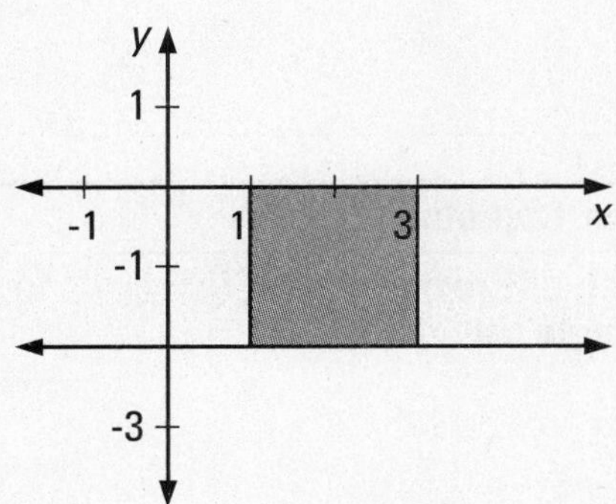

a. ______________________

b. ______________________

8.

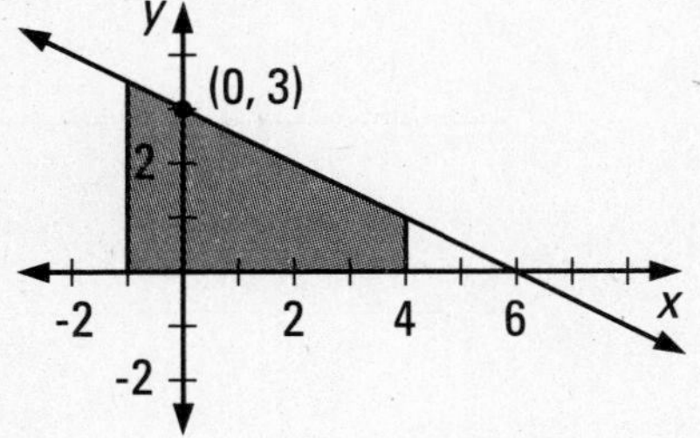

a. ______________________

b. ______________________

9.

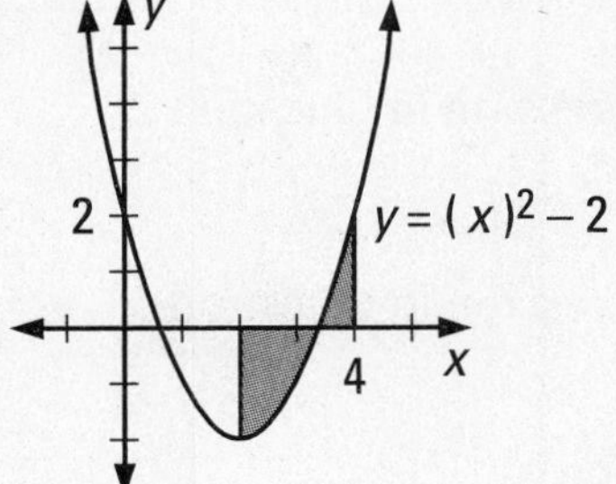

a. ______________________

b. ______________________

Name

Questions on SPUR Objectives
See pages 836–839 for objectives.

Skills Objective B

In 1–6, evaluate the definite integrals.

1. $\int_1^6 4(x + 3)\, dx$

2. $\int_4^7 (x - 2)\, dx + \int_2^4 (x - 2)\, dx$

3. $\int_0^{10} 2x\, dx - \int_0^5 2x\, dx$

4. $\int_0^8 5x\, dx + \int_0^8 (3x - 1)\, dx$

5. $\int_a^b 9\, dx + \int_b^c 9\, dx$

6. $\int_a^b -3x\, dx + \int_a^b 7x\, dx$

Skills Objective C

In 7–12, use properties of integrals to write the expression as a single integral.

7. $\int_0^4 x^3\, dx + \int_0^4 8x\, dx$

8. $\int_0^9 (x + 5)\, dx + 6\int_0^9 x\, dx$

9. $\int_0^2 (x - 3)\, dx + \int_2^5 (x - 3)\, dx$

10. the expression in Question 3

11. the expression in Question 5

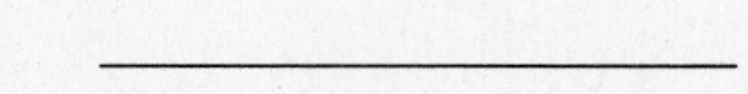

12. the expression in Question 6

Name

▶ **LESSON MASTER 13-4** *page 2*

Uses Objective E

13. A city's two new elevated storage tanks are being filled with water from underground wells. Let $f(t)$ and $g(t)$ represent the rate of water flow (in thousands of gallons per hour) into the two tanks at time t in hours. The table below gives the rates for the first 12 hours.

a. Use integral notation in two different ways to write the total amount of water in the tanks after 12 hours.

t	$f(t)$	$g(t)$
0	1.5	1.6
2	1.4	2.0
4	2.3	2.1
6	1.8	2.2
8	1.5	1.8
10	1.8	1.0
12	2.0	1.4

____

____

b. Approximate the value of your answer to part a by evaluating a Riemann sum, first using the left endpoint for each subinterval and then using the right endpoint.

______________________ ______________________

Representations Objective H

In 14 and 15, express the area of each shaded region using integral notation and find its value.

6.

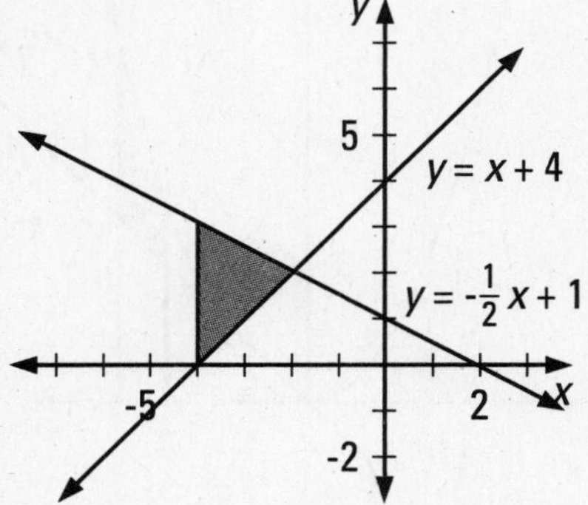

7.

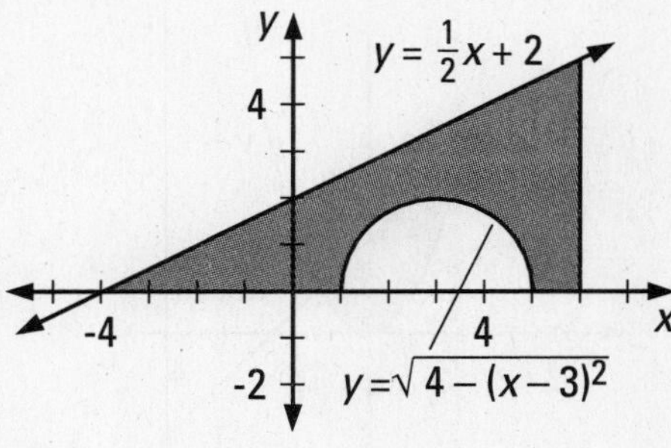

a. ______________________ **a.** ______________________

b. ______________________ **b.** ______________________

Name

LESSON MASTER 13-5

Questions on SPUR Objectives
See pages 836–839 for objectives.

Skills Objective B

In 1–4, evaluate the integral.

1. $\int_0^{12} x^2\,dx$

2. $\int_0^{20} x^2\,dx - \int_{10}^{20} x^2\,dx$

3. $\int_{-6}^{4} (x^2 + 5)\,dx$

4. $\int_3^{8} (x^2 + 3x + 4)\,dx$

Uses Objective D

5. Suppose a car accelerates from 0 to 72 ft/sec in 6 seconds so that its velocity $v(t)$ in this time interval in ft/sec after t seconds is given by $v(t) = -2(t - 6)^2 + 72$. What is the total distance traveled in these 6 seconds?

Representations Objective H

In 6 and 7, express the area of the shaded region using integral notation and find its value.

6.

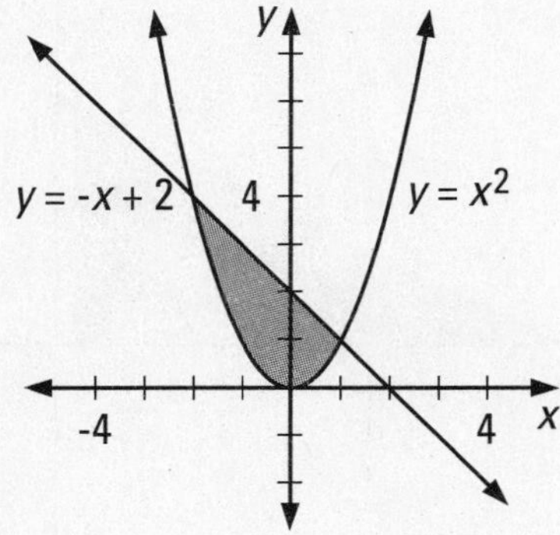

7.

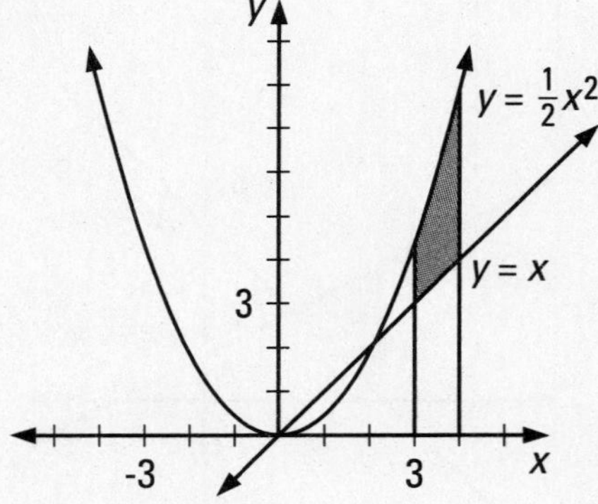

6. a. ______

b. ______

7. a. ______

b. ______

Name

LESSON MASTER 

Questions on SPUR Objectives
See pages 836–839 for objectives.

Uses Objective E

1. The parabolic cross-section of a trough is 3 meters wide and 2 meters high. If the trough is 3 meters long, what is its volume?

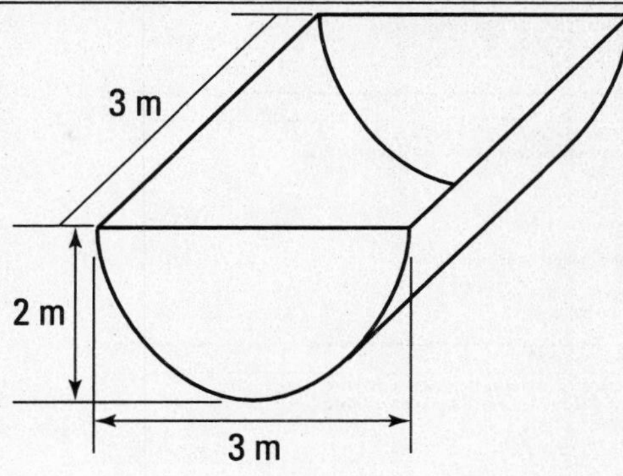

____

2. Suppose a flower pot is formed by rotating the line with equation $y = \frac{1}{4}x + 2$ from $x = 0$ to $x = 8$ around the x-axis, where all coordinates are in inches. How much dirt, in cubic inches, is required to completely fill the pot? ______________________

Representations Objective I

In 3 and 4, a region is described. a. Sketch a graph of the region. b. Calculate the volume of the solid generated when the region is revolved about the x-axis.

3. The region bounded by the x-axis, the y-axis, and the line $y = -\frac{2}{3}x + 3$.

a.

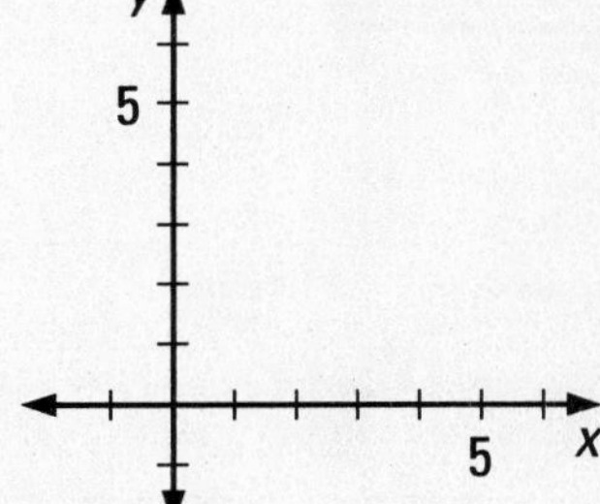

b. ______________________

4. The region bounded by the x-axis and by the lines $x = 1$, $x = 4$, and $y = 5 - \frac{x}{2}$.

a.

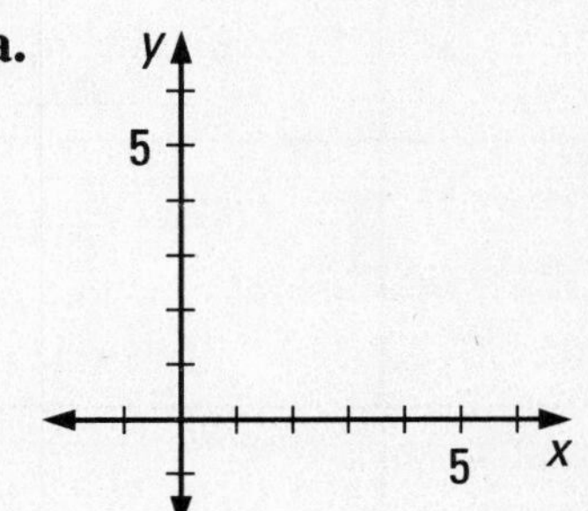

b. 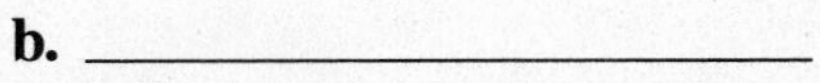

Name

LESSON MASTER 1-1 — **Questions on SPUR Objectives** See pages 71–75 for objectives.

Skills Objective A

1. Is the following statement universal, existential, or neither? *Some integers are prime.* existential

Skills Objective B

2. Rewrite the following statement using universal and existential quantifiers.
Every number is greater than some number.
$\forall x$ in R, $\exists y$ such that $x > y$

Skills Objective D

In 3–6, let $p(x)$ be the sentence $6x^2 - 7x + 2 \le 0$. Determine whether the given statement is true or false.

3. $p(0.68)$ False
4. $\exists$ *an integer x such that p(x).* False
5. $\exists$ *a rational number x such that p(x).* True
6. $\forall$ *real numbers x such that* $0.58 \le x \le 0.62$, $p(x)$. True

Properties Objective E

In 7 and 8, determine whether the given sentence is a statement. If it is a statement, determine whether it is true or false.

7. $\frac{x}{x} = 1$ not a statement
8. $\forall x, \frac{x}{x} = 1$ statement, false

Properties Objective F

9. Given $\forall x, x \ne 1$, $1 + x^1 + x^2 + x^3 + \ldots + x^n = \frac{1 - x^{n+1}}{1 - x}$, use the Law of Substitution to prove that $\forall k, k \ne 1$ and $k \ne 0$, $1 + k^{-1} + k^{-2} + k^{-3} + \ldots + k^{-n} = \frac{k - k^{-n}}{k - 1}$.

Substitute k^{-1} for x. Then, if $k^{-1} \ne x$, $x \ne 1$ and
$1 + (k^{-1})^1 + (k^{-1})^2 + (k^{-1})^3 + \ldots + (k^{-1})^n =$
$1 + k^{-1} + k^{-2} + k^{-3} + \ldots + k^{-n} =$
$\frac{1 - (k^{-1})^{n+1}}{1 - k^{-1}} = \frac{1 - k^{-n-1}}{1 - k^{-1}} \cdot \frac{k}{k} = \frac{k - k^{-n}}{k - 1}$

Name

▶ **LESSON MASTER 1-1** *page 2*

Properties Objective H

10. Consider the following statement. *The sum of any nonzero real number and its reciprocal is greater than the original number.*
   a. Write this statement in the form $\forall$ *x in S, p(x)*.
   $\forall x$ in S, $x \ne 0$, $x + \frac{1}{x} > x$.
   b. Provide a counterexample to show that this statement is false.
   Sample: If $x = -1$, then $-1 + \frac{1}{-1} = -2$ and $-2 \not> -1$.

Uses Objective I

In 11–15, refer to the table below, which gives the number of Gold (G), Silver (S), and Bronze (B) Medals won by six countries in each of four different sporting events in the 1998 winter Olympics held in Nagano, Japan.

	Alpine Skiing			Figure Skating			Cross-Country Skiing			Speed Skating		
Country	G	S	B	G	S	B	G	S	B	G	S	B
Germany	3	1	2	0	0	1	0	0	0	2	3	1
Norway	1	3	0	0	0	0	4	3	2	1	0	0
Russian Fed.	0	0	0	3	2	0	5	2	1	0	0	0
Austria	3	4	4	0	0	0	0	1	1	0	0	0
Canada	0	0	0	0	1	0	0	0	0	1	2	2
United States	1	0	0	1	1	0	0	0	0	0	1	1

Let *C* be the set of the six listed countries and *E* be the set of the four listed sporting events. Use the table to determine if each statement is true or false.

11. $\exists$ a country *c* in *C* such that $\forall$ sporting events *e* in *E*, *c* won a medal in *e*. False
12. $\forall$ sporting events *e* in *E*, $\exists$ a country *c* in *C* such that *c* won a Bronze medal in *e*. True
13. $\forall$ countries *c* in *C*, $\exists$ a sporting event *e* in *E* such that *c* won a Gold medal in *e*. True
14. $\exists$ a sporting event *e* in *E* such that $\forall$ countries *c* in *C*, *c* won a medal in *e*. False
15. $\exists$ a country *c* in *C* and a sporting event *e* in *E* such that *c* won Gold, Silver, and Bronze medals in *e*. True

Name

LESSON MASTER 1-2 — **Questions on SPUR Objectives** See pages 71–75 for objectives.

Skills Objective C

In 1–4, write the negation of the statement.

1. *All true wisdom is found on T-shirts.*
Some true wisdom is not found on T-shirts.
2. $\exists$ *real numbers x such that* $x^2 + 1 = 0$.
$\forall$ real numbers x, $x^2 + 1 \ne 0$.
3. *At least one integer is irrational.* All integers are rational. or No integers are irrational.
4. $\exists$ *a real number x such that* $\forall$ *real numbers y*, $x - y \ne y - x$. $\forall$ real numbers x, $\exists$ a real number y such that $x - y = y - x$.

Skills Objective D

5. Consider the statement let *p*: *Some parabolas have no lines of symmetry.*
   a. Write $\sim p$ as a universal statement.
   All parabolas have at least one line of symmetry.
   b. Which is true, p or $\sim p$? $\sim p$

Properties Objective E

6. Suppose *p* is a false statement. Is the statement $\sim(\sim p)$ true or false? False
7. Suppose the statement $\forall$ *z in M*, $\sim r(z)$ is true. What is the truth value of $\exists$ *z in M such that* $\sim p(z)$? True
8. Suppose the statement $\exists$ *x in S such that* $\sim p(x)$ is true. What is the truth value of $\forall$ *x in S*, $\sim p(x)$? Cannot tell

Uses Objective I

In 9–11, let *m(x)* be the sentence *x is male* and *f(x)* be the sentence *x is female*. Tell which is true, the statement or its negation. (as of 1998)

9. $\forall$ *U.S. Presidents y, m(y).* the statement
10. $\exists$ a *U.S. Vice President v, such that* $\sim f(v)$. the statement
11. $\forall$ *U.S. Secretaries of State z*, $\sim f(z)$. the negation

Name

LESSON MASTER  **1-3** — **Questions on SPUR Objectives** See pages 71–75 for objectives.

Skills Objective B

In 1–4, express the inequality by writing out each implied *and* or *or*.

1. $m \le -5$
$m < -5$ or $m = -5$
2. $0 \le k < 1.2$
$(0 < k$ or $0 = k)$ and $k < 1.2$
3. $|z| > 3$
$z > 3$ or $z < -3$
4. $|t - 1| < \frac{1}{2}$
$t - 1 < \frac{1}{2}$ and $t - 1 > -\frac{1}{2}$

Skills Objective C

In 5–7, use De Morgan's Laws to write the negation of the statement.

5. *Jill is well and Mel is ill.*
Jill is ill or Mel is well.
6. $\forall$ *integers x, x is odd or x is not prime.*
$\exists$ an integer x such that x is even and prime.
7. $\exists$ *real numbers x and y such that* $x < y$ *and* $y < x$.
$\forall$ real numbers x and y, $x \ge y$ or $y \ge x$.

Skills Objective D

In 8–13, suppose the statement *p* is true and the statement *q* is false. Determine the truth value of the given statement.

8. *p and q* False
9. $\sim(p$ *and* $\sim q)$ *or* $(\sim p$ *or* $\sim q)$ False
10. $\sim p$ *or* $\sim q$ True
11. $\sim p$ *and* $\sim q$ False
12. $(\sim p$ *or* $q)$ *or* $\sim(p$ *or* $\sim q)$ False
13. $\sim(p$ *and* $q)$ True

Properties Objective E

14. Use DeMorgan's Laws to show that the statements of Questions 12 and 13 are logically equivalent.
$\sim(p$ and $\sim q) \equiv \sim p$ or $\sim\sim q \equiv \sim p$ or q and
$\sim(p$ or $\sim q) \equiv \sim p$ and $\sim\sim q \equiv \sim p$ and q. So,
$\sim(p$ and $\sim q)$ or $(\sim p$ and $q) \equiv \sim(p$ or $q)$ or
$\sim(p$ or $\sim q)$.

Name

Properties Objective H

15. Show that the following statement is false. $\forall$ *real numbers x, $x \geq 0$ or $\sin x \leq 0$.*

$x = -\frac{3\pi}{2}$ is a real number and the statements $-\frac{3\pi}{2} > 0$ and $\sin -\frac{3\pi}{2} \leq 0$ are both false

Uses Objective I

In 16–18, refer to the table below, which lists the amenities available at five hotels with rooms reserved for an upcoming convention. H = Handicapped Access; FC = Fitness Center; IP = Indoor Pool; L = Lounge; R = Restaurant; D = Distance to Convention Center; S = Single Price

Hotel	H	FC	IP	L	R	D	S
1	*	*	*	*	*	15 blocks	$180
2	*				*	6 blocks	$100
3	*					4 miles	$146
4	*	*		*	*	12 blocks	$175
5		*		*	*	15 blocks	$109

Use the table to determine whether the given statement is true or false.

16. $\exists$ *a hotel h such that h has an indoor pool and S < $180.* False

17. $\forall$ *hotels h, h has a restaurant or D > 3 miles.* True

18. $\forall$ *hotels h, h has a restaurant and lounge or h has handicapped access.* True

Representations Objective L

19. Use a truth table to show that *p and (q or r)* ≡ *(p and q) or (p and r)*.

p	q	r	q or r	p and (q or r)	p and q	p and r	(p and q) or (p and r)
F	F	F	F	F	F	F	F
F	F	T	T	F	F	F	F
F	T	F	T	F	F	F	F
F	T	T	T	F	F	F	F
T	F	F	F	F	F	F	F
T	F	T	T	T	F	T	T
T	T	F	T	T	T	F	T
T	T	T	T	T	T	T	T

Name

LESSON MASTER 1-4

Questions on SPUR Objectives
See pages 71–75 for objectives.

Representations Objective K

1. Consider the following network.

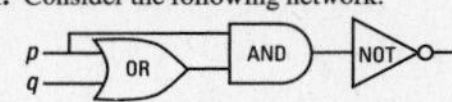

a. Write an input-output table for the network.

p	q	p OR q	p OR q AND p	NOT ((p OR q) AND p)
0	0	0	0	1
0	1	1	0	1
1	0	1	1	0
1	1	1	1	0

b. Draw a functionally equivalent network that has only one logic gate.

2. Consider the following network.

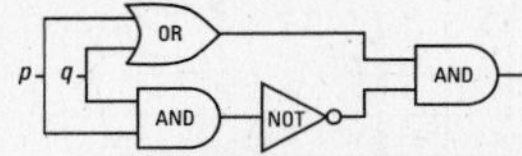

a. Write the logical expression that corresponds to the network. (p or q and ~(p and q)

b. Write an input-output table for the network.

p	q	p OR q	p AND q	NOT (p AND q)	(p OR q) and NOT (p AND q)
0	0	0	0	1	0
0	1	1	0	1	1
1	0	1	0	1	1
1	1	1	1	0	0

Name

3. Are the two networks shown below, each with four inputs *p, q, r,* and *s*, functionally equivalent? Justify your answer.

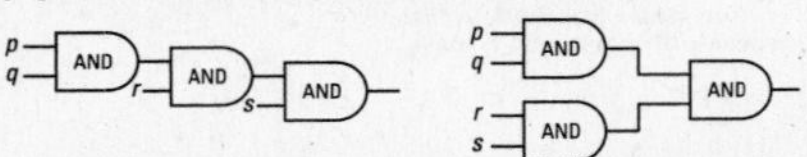

Yes; the output of each network is high only when all four inputs are high.

4. Consider the following network.

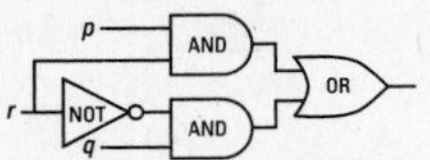

a. Fill in the input-output table below for this network.

p	q	r	NOT r	p AND r	q AND NOT r	(p AND r) OR (q AND NOT r)
0	0	0	1	0	0	0
0	1	0	1	0	1	1
1	0	0	1	0	0	0
1	1	0	1	0	1	1
0	0	1	0	0	0	0
0	1	1	0	0	0	0
1	0	1	0	1	0	1
1	1	1	0	1	0	1

b. What effect does input *r* have on the output?

When *r* is 0, the final output is equal to the input for *q*. When *r* is 1, the final output is equal to the input for *p*.

Name

LESSON MASTER 1-5

Questions on SPUR Objectives
See pages 71–75 for objectives.

Skills Objective A

In 1–3, let *p* be the following statement: *If you do not know arithmetic, then you cannot get a job.* Determine whether the given statement is the inverse, converse, or contrapositive of *p*.

1. *If you know arithmetic, then you can get a job.* inverse

2. *If you cannot get a job, then you do not know arithmetic.* converse

3. *If you can get a job, then you know arithmetic.* contrapositive

Skills Objective B

4. Write the following statement as an *if-then* conditional. *Getting a B+ on her final exam is a necessary condition for Michelle to get an A for the quarter.*

If Michelle gets an A for the quarter, then she got at least an B+ on her final exam.

5. Write two *if-then* conditionals contained in the following statement: *For any polynomial f(x), a number c is a solution to f(x) = 0 if and only if (x − c) is a factor of f(x).*

If *c* is a solution to $f(x) = 0$, then $(x - c)$ is a factor of $f(x)$. If $(x - c)$ is a factor of $f(x)$, then *c* is a solution to $f(x) = 0$.

Skills Objective C

6. Consider the statement p: $\forall x, x^2 - 5x + 6 = 0 \Rightarrow x = 3$. Write $\sim p$.

$\exists$ x such that $x^2 - 5x + 6 = 0$ and $x \neq 3$.

7. Write the negation of the following statement as a conditional statement: *There is a substance which is metal and not a good conductor.* If any substance is a metal, then it is a good conductor.

Skills Objective D

In 8–11, let $r(x)$: $\frac{1}{x} = \frac{2}{x^2}$ and let $s(x)$: $x^2 = 2x$. Determine whether the given statement is true or false.

8. $\forall$ *real numbers x*, $r(x) \Rightarrow s(x)$. True

9. $\forall$ *real numbers x*, $\sim r(x) \Rightarrow \sim s(x)$. False

10. $\forall$ *real numbers x*, $s(x) \Rightarrow r(x)$. False

11. $\forall$ real numbers *x*, $\sim s(x) \Rightarrow \sim r(x)$. True

Name

▶ **LESSON MASTER 1-5** *page 2*

Properties Objective E

12. Suppose p and $p \Rightarrow q$ are both true statements. What is the truth value of q? **True**

13. Suppose q and $p \Rightarrow q$ are both true statements. What is the truth value of p? **Cannot tell**

14. *Multiple choice.* Which statement is logically equivalent to $\forall$ *x, if p(x) then q(x)*? **c**

    (a) $\exists$ *x such that p(x) and ~ q(x).* (b) $\forall$ *x, p(x) or ~q(x).*

    (c) $\forall$ *x, ~p(x) or q(x).* (d) $\forall$ *x, p(x) and q(x).*

Uses Objective I

In 15–17, refer to the table below, which shows the types of paints that can be used on different exterior surfaces. Determine whether the given statement is true or false.

	Wood				Masonry			Metal			
	Clapboard	Shutters/trim	Window frames	Natural siding/trim	Brick	Cement/cinder block	Stucco	Metal siding	Copper surfaces	Galvanized surfaces	Iron surfaces
Latex house	✓	✓	✓		✓	✓	✓	✓		✓	✓
Alkyd house	✓	✓	✓		✓	✓	✓	✓		✓	✓
Cement powder					✓	✓	✓				
Trim		✓		✓				✓		✓	✓
Aluminum			✓		✓	✓	✓	✓		✓	✓

15. $\forall$ *paints p, if p can be used on brick then p can be used on metal siding.* **False**

16. $\forall$ *surfaces s, a latex paint can be used on s if and only if an alkyd paint can be used on s.* **True**

Representations Objective L

17. Complete the truth table for $p \Rightarrow (s \text{ or } r)$.

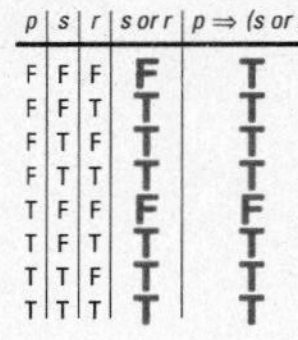

p	s	r	s or r	$p \Rightarrow (s \text{ or } r)$
F	F	F	**F**	**T**
F	F	T	**T**	**T**
F	T	F	**T**	**T**
F	T	T	**T**	**T**
T	F	F	**F**	**F**
T	F	T	**T**	**T**
T	T	F	**T**	**T**
T	T	T	**T**	**T**

Name

LESSON MASTER 1-6

Questions on SPUR Objectives
See pages 71–75 for objectives.

Properties Objective G

In 1–3, supply the missing premise so that the argument is valid.

1. $s \Rightarrow t$
   ~t
   $\therefore \sim s$

2. **$n \Rightarrow q$**
   $q \Rightarrow r$
   $\therefore n \Rightarrow r$

3. $a \Rightarrow b$
   a
   $\therefore b$

Properties Objective H

In 4–6, draw a valid conclusion from the given premises and state whether the conclusion is true or false. If the conclusion is false, circle the false premise or premises.

4. $\forall$ *integers* $n \geq 1$, *if n is not prime then n has a factor less than or equal to* $\sqrt{n}$. *101 has no factor less than or equal to* $\sqrt{101}$.
   101 is prime; true

5. *If a quadrilateral's diagonals are not perpendicular, then it is not a kite. If a quadrilateral is not a kite, then it is not a rhombus.* **If a quadrilateral's diagonals are not perpendicular, then it is not a rhombus. True**

6. $\forall$ *x and y, if x and y are irrational numbers then their product is an irrational number.* π *and* $\frac{1}{\pi}$ *are irrational numbers.*
   $\pi \cdot \frac{1}{\pi} = 1$ is irrational; false.

Uses Objective J

In 7 and 8, tell whether the argument uses the Law of Detachment (modus ponens), the Law of Indirect Reasoning (modus tollens), or the Law of Transitivity.

7. *The movie that wins the Academy Award for "Best Picture" is the most critically acclaimed movie of the year.* Titanic *won the Academy Award for "Best Picture" of 1997. So* Titanic *was the most critically acclaimed movie for that year.*
   Law of Detachment

8. *If we do not increase federal funding for education, our nation's students will not be prepared for the jobs of the 21st century. And if they are not prepared for the jobs of the 21st century, America will not be able to compete in the global marketplace. America will not be able to compete in the global marketplace, if we do not increase federal funding for education.*
   Law of Transitivity

Name

LESSON MASTER 1-7

Questions on SPUR Objectives
See pages 71–75 for objectives.

In 1–6, tell whether the argument is valid or invalid. Support your answer with a reference to one or more of the following.

I. Law of Detachment
II. Law of Indirect Reasoning
III. Law of Transitivity
IV. Converse Error
V. Inverse Error
VI. Improper Induction

Properties Objective G

1. $\forall$ *x, if* $x^2 \leq 64$ *then* $x \leq 8$.
   $9 > 8$
   $\therefore 9^2 > 64$
   valid; Law of Indirect Reasoning

2. $\forall$ *x, if* $x^2 \leq 64$ *then* $x \leq 8$.
   $(-9)^2 > 64$
   $\therefore -9 > 8$
   invalid; Inverse Error

3. $\forall$ *x, if* $x^2 \leq 64$ *then* $x \leq 8$.
   $-9 \leq 8$
   $\therefore (-9)^2 \leq 64$
   invalid; Converse Error

4. $2^{2^0} + 1 = 3$ (prime), $2^{2^1} + 1 = 5$ (prime), $2^{2^2} + 1 = 17$ (prime), $2^{2^3} + 1 = 257$ (prime), $2^{2^4} + 1 = 65{,}337$ (prime)
   $\therefore \forall$ *integers* $n \geq 0$, $2^{2^n} + 1$ *is a prime number.*
   invalid; Improper Induction

Uses Objective J

5. *If Carolyn does not finish her homework, then she will not be allowed to watch television. Carolyn was not allowed to watch television. Therefore, she did not finish her homework.*
   invalid; Converse Error

6. *Mr. Thompson did not commit the crime, if the lab results do not show a match between his DNA and the DNA found at the crime scene. The test results did show a match between Mr. Thompson's DNA and the DNA found at the crime scene, so he must have committed the crime.*
   invalid; Inverse Error

Name

LESSON MASTER

Questions on SPUR Objectives
See pages 71–75 for objectives.

Properties Objective H

In 1 and 2, steps in the solution of an equation are given. Provide the justifications that allow you to conclude the given conditionals.

1. p: $4x - 7 = 2x - 9$
   q: $4x = 2x - 2$
   r: $4x - 2x = -2$
   s: $x(4 - 2) = -2$
   t: $2x = -2$
   u: $x = -1$

   a. $p \Rightarrow q$ **Addition Property of Equality**
   b. $r \Rightarrow s$ **Distributive Property**
   c. $t \Rightarrow u$ **Multiplication Property of Equality**
   d. $p \Rightarrow u$ **Law of Transitivity**

2. p: $x^2 + 3x = 10$
   q: $x^2 + 3x - 10 = 0$
   r: $(x + 5)(x - 2) = 0$
   s: $x = -5$ or $x = 2$

   a. $p \Rightarrow q$ **Addition Property of Equality**
   b. $q \Rightarrow r$ **Distributive Property**
   c. $r \Rightarrow s$ **Zero Product Property**
   d. $p \Rightarrow s$ **Law of Transitivity**

Uses Objective J

3. If it rains today, Andrew will have to drive Amy to work. If Andrew drives Amy to work, he will be late for work. If he is late for work, he will have to reschedule a meeting. If he reschedules his meeting, he won't make it home until late. If he doesn't come home until late, he won't be able to make Amy dinner. If Andrew doesn't make dinner for Amy, Amy must make dinner for Andrew.

   a. Who will make dinner if it rains today? **Amy**
   b. What is the weather like if Amy doesn't make dinner for Andrew? **not rainy**

Name

LESSON MASTER 2-1

Questions on SPUR Objectives
See pages 142–145 for objectives.

Properties Objective C

1. The table below shows how tornadoes/wind storms are classified using the Fujita Scale. Let r = rank, w = wind speed, d = damage, s = strength, and let f, g, and h be the relations: f: rank $\to$ wind speed, g: wind speed $\to$ strength, and h: strength $\to$ damage.

Rank	Wind Speed	Damage	Strength
0	up to 72 mph	Light	weak
1	73–112 mph	Moderate	weak
2	113–157 mph	Considerable	strong
3	158–206 mph	Severe	strong
4	207–260 mph	Devastating	violent
5	> 261 mph	Incredible	violent

a. Evaluate $f(3)$. $\{w: 158 \le w \le 206\}$

b. Evaluate $g(200)$. strong

c. Among f, g, and h, which one is *not* a function? Explain.
f is not a function, because it does not determine a unique wind speed for a given rank.

In 2 and 3, a function is given. a. Give a reasonable domain for the function. b. Is the function discrete?

2. $p(x)$ = the number of people in the family of student x in Class A
a. students in class A b. Yes

3. $q(x)$ = the average temperature in a city in month x
a. months of the year b. Yes

In 4 and 5, use interval notation to describe the domain of the real function.

4. $f(x) = \sqrt{x^2 - 3x + 2}$
$(-\infty, 1]$ or $[2, \infty)$

5. $g(z) = \frac{1}{z^3 - 8} + \frac{1}{\sqrt{z - 1}}$
b. $(1, 2)$ or $(2, \infty)$

6. Suppose the price of regular gasoline is \$1.25 per gallon. You want to find the cost if you pump g gallons of gasoline into a tank with a full capacity of 16.5 gallons.
a. Identify a formula for the function mapping g onto the cost. $c = 1.25g$
b. Identify the independent variable of this function, and its domain. g, $0 \le g \le 16.5$ gal
c. Identify the dependent variable of this function, and its range. c, \$0 $\le c \le$ \$20.63

13

Name

LESSON MASTER 2-2

Questions on SPUR Objectives
See pages 142–145 for objectives.

Skills Objective A

1. Let $g(t) = \frac{1 + 8t}{1 + t^2}$. Estimate its range and its maximum and minimum values.
$\approx -3.53 \le g(t) \le \approx 4.53$
max.: ≈ 4.53; min.: ≈ -3.53

Properties Objective C

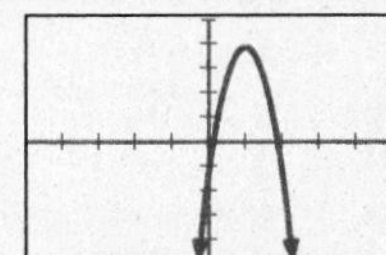

2. Let $f(x) = -4x^2 + 8x - 1$.
a. Find the exact range. $\{y: y \le 3\}$
b. Check your answer to part a by using an automatic grapher. Sketch the graph in the screen at the right.

$-5 \le x \le 5$, x-scale = 1
$-5 \le y \le 5$, y-scale = 1

Uses Objective F

3. Fred wants to use a wire to make an isosceles triangle for a decoration. Assume the wire has a length of 6 meters.
a. Express A, the area of the triangle, as a function of x.
$A(x) = (3 - x)(\sqrt{6x - 9})$
b. What is the domain of $A(x)$?
$\{x: \frac{3}{2} < x < 3\}$
c. Use an automatic grapher to graph $A(x)$. Sketch the graph in the screen at the right.
d. What is the maximum area of the triangle Fred can make?
$\sqrt{3} \approx 1.73$ m²

$-1 \le x \le 5$, x-scale = 1
$-1 \le y \le 5$, y-scale = 1

Representations Objective G

4. Sketch a graph of the function f with the following characteristics.
(a) Domain: $(-3, 4]$
(b) Range: $[-2, 5]$
(c) Maximum value: $f(0)$; minimum values: $f(-2)$ and $f(4)$

Sample:

14

Name

LESSON MASTER 2-3

Questions on SPUR Objectives
See pages 142–145 for objectives.

Skills Objective G

1. The table at the right shows the number of persons below the poverty level in the U.S. between 1975 and 1995. Let $P(x)$ be the number of persons below the poverty level in year x.

Year	Persons Below the Poverty Level (thousands)
1975	25,877
1976	24,975
1977	24,720
1978	24,497
1979	26,072
1980	29,272
1981	31,822
1982	34,398
1983	35,303
1984	33,700
1985	33,064
1986	32,370
1987	32,221
1988	31,745
1989	31,528
1990	33,585
1991	35,708
1992	38,014
1993	39,625
1994	38,059
1995	36,425

a. Find the longest interval over which P is increasing. 1978–1983
b. Find the longest interval over which P is decreasing. 1983–1989
c. What are the relative minima of P? 24,497 and 31,528
d. What are the relative maxima of P? 35,303 and 39,625
e. Solve $P(x) = 35{,}708$. $x = 1991$

2. Let $f(x) = 2x^2 - x + 15$. Give the interval(s) on which f is
a. decreasing $\left(-\infty, \frac{1}{4}\right)$
b. increasing $\left(\frac{1}{4}, \infty\right)$

Representations Objective G

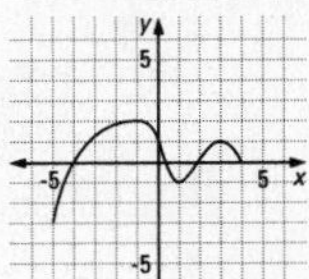

3. The graph of a function $g(x)$ is given at the right.
a. Over which intervals is g increasing? $(-\infty, 1)$ and $(1, 3)$
b. Find any relative maxima and relative minima of g.
rel. max.: $g(-1) = 2$, $g(3) = 1$
rel. min.: $g(1) = -1$

15 ▶

Name

▶ LESSON MASTER 2-3 *page 2*

4. Use an automatic grapher to estimate the relative maximum and relative minimum of the function h with $h(t) = t^3 - 4t^2 + 3t - 4$ on the interval $-1 \le t \le 4$. Sketch the graph in the screen at the right.
rel. max.: ≈ -3.4
rel. min.: ≈ -6.1

$-1 \le x \le 4$, x-scale = 1
$-8 \le y \le 8$, y-scale = 1

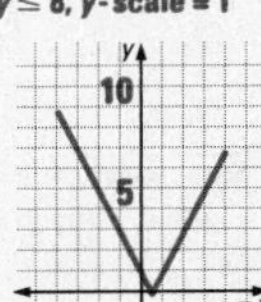

5. Graph $y = |2x - 1|$ over $-4 \le x \le 4$. Describe all intervals on which the function $x \to y$ is increasing.
$\left(\frac{1}{2}, \infty\right)$

16

Name

LESSON MASTER 2-4 Questions on SPUR Objectives
See pages 142–145 for objectives.

Properties Objective D

1. Consider the function f with $f(x) = \frac{x-1}{x+1}$.

a. Complete the table below to give decimal approximations to values of $f(x)$ as x increases.

x	10	100	1,000	10,000	100,000
$f(x)$	0.82	0.98	0.998	0.9998	0.99998

b. What is $\lim_{x\to\infty} f(x)$? 1

c. Write an equation of the horizontal asymptote of f. $y = 1$

2. Let $g(x) = 5 + \frac{1}{x^3}$.

a. Find $\lim_{x\to\infty} g(x)$ and $\lim_{x\to-\infty} g(x)$.

$\lim_{x\to\infty} g(x) = \lim_{x\to-\infty} g(x) = 5$

b. Is g *odd, even,* or *neither*? neither

c. For what values of x is $g(x)$ within 0.001 of the limit? $\{x: x < -10 \text{ or } x > 10\}$

3. If $\varphi(x)$ is an even function and $\lim_{x\to\infty} \varphi(x) = -1$, find $\lim_{x\to-\infty} \varphi(x)$. -1

4. Describe the end behavior of $y = -2x^3$.

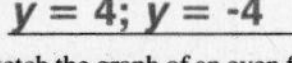

$\lim_{x\to\infty} y = -\infty$; $\lim_{x\to-\infty} y = \infty$

Representations Objective G

5. The function f is graphed at the right.

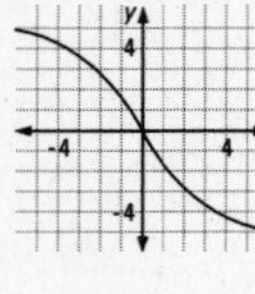

a. Is f *odd, even* or *neither*? odd

b. Describe its end behavior.

$\lim_{x\to\infty} f(x) = -4$; $\lim_{x\to-\infty} f(x) = 4$

c. Write the equations of the horizontal asymptotes.

$y = 4$; $y = -4$

6. Sketch the graph of an even function f that has a relative maximum at $x = 2$ and a relative minimum at $x = 1$, with $\lim_{x\to\infty} f(x) = 3$.

Sample:

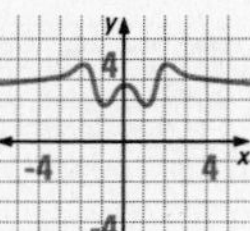

Name

LESSON MASTER 2-5 Questions on SPUR Objectives
See pages 142–145 for objectives.

Representations Objective H

In 1–3, graph the parametric equations.

1. $\begin{cases} x(t) = 2t - 1 \\ y(t) = 2t^2 + 1 \end{cases}$

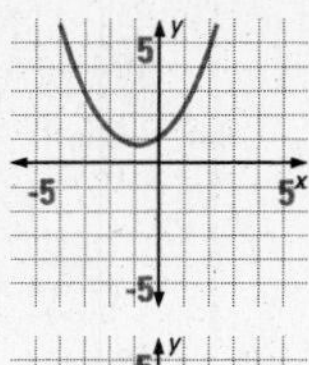

2. $\begin{cases} x(\theta) = \theta + \frac{\pi}{2} \\ y(\theta) = \cos\theta - 1 \end{cases}$

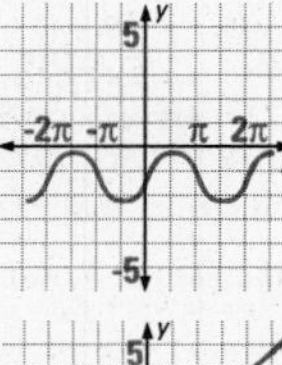

3. $\begin{cases} x(t) = e^t - e^{-t} \\ y(t) = e^t + e^{-t} \end{cases}$ $0 \le t \le 5$

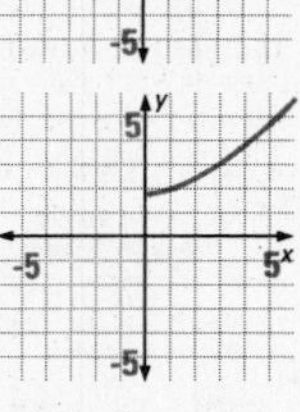

4. Suppose that a ball is thrown with an initial horizontal velocity of 25 ft/sec and an initial vertical velocity of $25\sqrt{3}$ ft/sec, and assume that the only force acting on the object is due to gravity. Let t = time in seconds since ball was thrown.

a. Find the parametric equations for the path of the ball. Assume that the starting point is the origin.

$\begin{cases} x = 25t \\ y = -16t^2 + 25\sqrt{3}t \end{cases}$

b. Graph the equations in the x-y plane.

c. Use the graph to find the maximum height attained by the ball.

≈ 29.3 ft

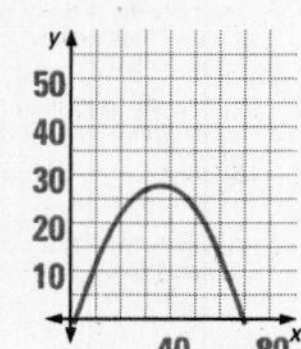

Name

LESSON MASTER 2-6 Questions on SPUR Objectives
See pages 142–145 for objectives.

Properties Objective D

1. Consider the function with equation $y = 2\sin(3x) - 3$.

a. Give its domain and range. domain: $(-\infty, \infty)$; range: $[-5, -1]$

b. What is the fundamental period of the function? $\frac{2\pi}{3}$

c. Find its maximum and minimum values. max.: -1; min.: -5

d. For how many values of x does the function reach its maximum and minimum values? infinitely many

e. Describe the end behavior of the function.

$\lim_{x\to\infty} y$ and $\lim_{x\to-\infty} y$ do not exist.

Representations Objective G

In 2–4, a function is given. Tell whether the function is *odd, even,* or *neither.*

2. $f(x) = \cos x$ even

3. $g(x) = \sin x$ odd

4. $h(x) = \sin x + \cos x$ neither

5. Consider the function f with $f(x) = -\sin(2x)$ on the interval $0 \le x \le 2\pi$.

a. Over what intervals is f increasing? $\left[\frac{\pi}{4}, \frac{3\pi}{4}\right]$; $\left[\frac{5\pi}{4}, \frac{7\pi}{4}\right]$

b. For what values of x does f reach its minimum value? $x = \frac{\pi}{4}$; $x = \frac{5\pi}{4}$

c. What is the fundamental period of f? π

6. a. On the x-y plane, graph the curve defined by the parametric equation

$\begin{cases} x(t) = \cos t + 1 \\ y(t) = 2\sin t - 1 \end{cases}$

b. Prove that every point on this curve is on the ellipse with equation $(x-1)^2 + \frac{(y+1)^2}{4} = 1$.

$x = \cos t + 1$, so $(x-1)^2 =$

$((\cos t + 1) - 1)^2 = \cos^2 t$. $y = 2\sin t + 1$, so

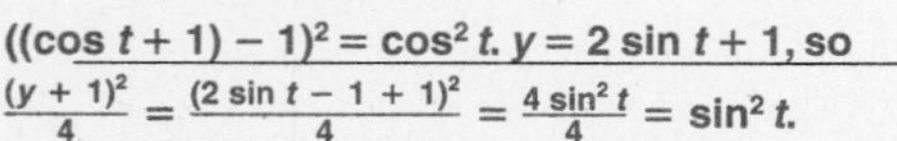

$\frac{(y+1)^2}{4} = \frac{(2\sin t - 1 + 1)^2}{4} = \frac{4\sin^2 t}{4} = \sin^2 t$.

$\cos^2 t + \sin^2 t = 1$

Name

LESSON MASTER 2-7 Questions on SPUR Objectives
See pages 142–145 for objectives.

Skills Objective B

In 1 and 2, rewrite the expression without using "+" or "–".

1. 5^{1-x} $\frac{5}{5^x}$

2. e^{x+y} $e^x \cdot e^y$

Properties Objective D

3. Contrast the end behavior of $f: x \to 2^x$ with that of $g: x \to 2^{-x}$.

$\lim_{x\to\infty} f(x) = \infty$ but $\lim_{x\to\infty} g(x) = 0$; $\lim_{x\to-\infty} f(x) = 0$ but $\lim_{x\to\infty} g(x) = \infty$

Uses Objective E

In 4–6, use the following table, which shows the GDP (gross domestic product) of the U.S. from 1992 to 1996 in billions of dollars.

Year	1992	1993	1994	1995	1996
GDP	6,038.5	6,343.3	6,736.1	7,265.4	7,636.0

4. Find the formula predicting the GDP of the United States x years after 1992, assuming a discrete model and an annual growth rate of 5.1%.

$y = 6038.5(1 + 0.051)^x$

5. Calculate the GDP predicted by the formula in Question 4 for

a. 1993. 6346.5

b. 1994. 6670.1

c. 1995. 7010.3

d. 1996. 7367.8

e. Compare the predicted GDP and the actual GDP between 1993 and 1996. How accurate is the formula for the prediction?

The predicted GDP for each year is several hundred billions less than the actual GDP

6. Use the formula in Question 4 to predict the GDP of the United States in the year 2000. $8989.8 billions

Name

► **LESSON MASTER 2-7** *page 2*

7. A lake has been polluted by a certain chemical. To have the water safe for use, the concentration of that chemical must be equal to or less than 15% of its present level. If the chemical naturally dissipates so that 3% of it is lost each year, use the Continuous Change Model to find about how many years it will take for the lake water to become usable. **about 63.24 years**

Representations Objective G

8. Let f be defined by $f(x) = ab^x$. For what values of a and b is f a decreasing function?

$a < 0$, $b > 1$; $a > 0$, $b < 1$

9. Use an automatic grapher to graph $y = e^{\sqrt{x}}$. Sketch the graph at the right. Then analyze the function from its graph.

$-1 \le x \le 5$, x-scale = 1
$-2 \le y \le 5$, y-scale = 1

domain: $[0, \infty)$; range $[1, \infty)$; maxima: none; minimum: 1 when $x = 0$; relative maxima: none; relative minima: none; increasing over entire domain $\lim_{x\to\infty} y = \infty$

Name

LESSON MASTER 2-8

Questions on SPUR Objectives
See pages 142–145 for objectives.

Properties Objective D

1. Find $\lim_{n\to\infty} a_n$ if $\begin{cases} a_1 = -5 \\ a_{k+1} = \frac{a_k}{4}\ \forall k \ge 1 \end{cases}$. **0**

2. Let $\begin{cases} c_1 = 3 \\ c_{k+1} = \frac{1}{3}c_k\ \forall k \ge 1 \end{cases}$.

   a. What is the limit of c_n as $n \to \infty$? **0**

   b. For what values of n is c_n within 0.001 of the limit? **$n \ge 9$**

3. Use limit notation to describe and then find the limit of $S_n = \left(-\frac{4}{5}\right)^{2n+1}$ as n increases without bound.

$\lim_{n\to\infty} S_n = \lim_{n\to\infty}\left(-\frac{4}{5}\right)^{2n+1} = 0$

Uses Objective E

4. Square $ABCD$ has sides of length a, A_1, B_1, C_1, and D_1 are the midpoints of $\overline{AB}$, $\overline{BC}$, $\overline{CD}$, and $\overline{DA}$, respectively. Also, from $n \ge 2$, A_n, B_n, C_n, and D_n, are the midpoints of $\overline{A_{n-1}B_{n-1}}$, $\overline{B_{n-1}C_{n-1}}$, $\overline{C_{n-1}D_{n-1}}$, and $\overline{D_{n-1}A_{n-1}}$, respectively. Let S_n be the area of square $A_nB_nC_nD_n$.

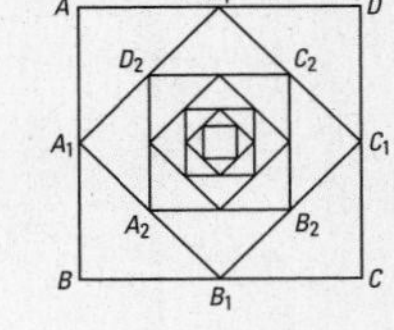

   a. Find S_1.

   $S_1 = \frac{1}{2}a^2$

   b. Give an equation relating S_n and S_{n-1}. **$S_n = \frac{1}{2}S_{n-1}$**

   c. Find $\lim_{x\to\infty} S_n$ and explain what it means.

   $\lim_{n\to\infty} S_n = 0$; this means that the squares approach the point at the center of $ABCD$.

Name

► **LESSON MASTER 2-8** *page 2*

5. A traveler brought 10 rabbits initially into an unpopulated island. Left undisturbed, the rabbit population will triple each year.

   a. Write a difference equation for the sequence P of the rabbit population at the end of the nth year (assuming an unlimited growth model.)

   $P_n = P_{n-1} + 2P_{n-1}$ or $P_n = 3P_{n-1}$

   b. Instead of assuming an unlimited growth model, suppose that the island has a support limit of 10,000 rabbits. Modify the difference equation of part **a** to account for this limitation.

   $P_n = P_{n-1} + 2P_{n-1}\left(\frac{10{,}000 - P_{n-1}}{10{,}000}\right)$

Representations Objective G

In 6 and 7, graph the first five terms of the sequence, and find its limit as $n \to \infty$.

6. $a_n = \frac{2n^2 - 1}{n^2}\ \forall n \ge 1$

$\lim_{n\to\infty} a_n = 2$

7. $\begin{cases} b_1 = 3 \\ b_{n+1} = 2b_n + 1\ \forall n \ge 1 \end{cases}$

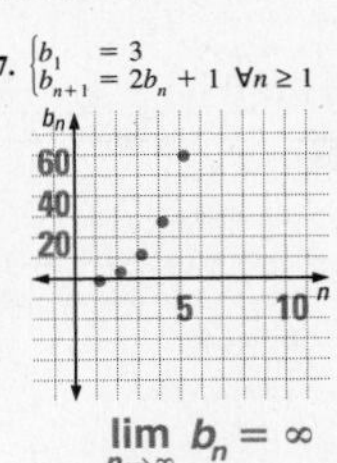

$\lim_{n\to\infty} b_n = \infty$

Name

LESSON MASTER 

Questions on SPUR Objectives
See pages 142–145 for objectives.

Skills Objective B

1. Evaluate each expression.

   a. $\log_2\left(\frac{1}{2}\right)^5$ **-5**

   b. $\log_{10}\sqrt{1{,}000}$ **$\frac{3}{2} = 1.5$**

   c. $\ln\frac{1}{e^3}$ **-3**

2. Express $\log_a\left(\frac{n^3}{m^2}\right)^{\frac{1}{5}}$ in terms of $\log_a n$ and $\log_a m$.

$\frac{3}{5}\log_a n - \frac{2}{5}\log_a m$

3. Given log 7 = 0.8451 and log 8 = 0.9030. Find

   a. log 2. **0.3010**

   b. log 14. **1.1461**

   c. log 28. **1.4471**

4. Solve for x: $\log_x 169 = 2$ **$x = 13$**

Properties Objective D

5. *True or false.* $\lim_{x\to\infty} \log_b x = 0$ for any $b > 1$. Justify your answer.

False; $\log_b n$ is undefined for $x \le 0$.

Uses Objective E

In 6 and 7, refer to the table below, which gives population data for Tokyo and Mexico City, the world's two most populous urban areas in 1995.

	Population (1995, in thousands)	Annual Growth rate 1990–1995 (percent)
Tokyo, Japan	26,959	1.4%
Mexico City, Mexico	16,562	1.81%

6. Assuming a discrete model, what was the population of each urban area in 1990?

   Tokyo **25,086.7 thousand**

   Mexico City **15,141.2 thousand**

7. Assume that the annual growth rates in both areas remain constant. In what year will Mexico City's population exceed Tokyo's? **in 2133**

Name

Representations Objective G

8. a. Graph the function f with $f(x) = \log_{\frac{1}{2}} x$.

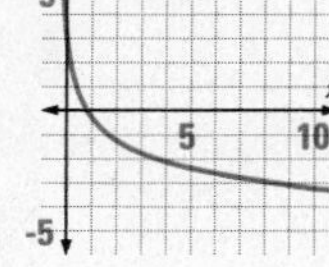

b. Give the domain and range of f.
domain: $(0, \infty)$;
range: $(-\infty, \infty)$

c. Use the Change of Base Theorem to express $f(x)$ in terms of $\log_{10} x$.
$f(x) = -\frac{\log_{10} x}{\log_{10} 2}$

d. Describe the interval of x over which f is increasing or decreasing.
$f(x)$ is decreasing over its entire domain.

e. Compare the graph of f to the graph of g where $g(x) = \log_2 x$
Each graph is the reflection image of the other over the x-axis.

Name

LESSON MASTER 3-1

Questions on SPUR Objectives
See pages 218–221 for objectives.

Skills Objective B

In 1–3, find a formula for $h(x)$ and state the domain for the indicated function h.

1. $f(x) = x$, $g(x) = x + 3$; $h = \frac{f}{g}$
$h(x) = \frac{x}{x+3}$
$\{x: x \neq 3\}$

2. $f(x) = 3^x$, $g(x) = 3^{-x}$; $h = f \cdot g$
$h(x) = 1$
all real numbers

3. $f(x) = \frac{1}{1-x}$, $g(x) = \frac{1}{1+x}$; $h = f - g$
$h(x) = \frac{2x}{(1+x)(1-x)}$
$\{x: x \neq 1 \text{ and } x \neq -1\}$

4. $f(x) = \sin x$, $g(x) = \cos x$; $h = \frac{f-g}{f+g}$
$h(x) = \frac{\sin x - \cos x}{\sin x + \cos x}$
$\left\{x: x \neq \frac{3\pi}{4} + n\pi, \text{ for integers } n\right\}$

Uses Objective I

5. Suppose for a trip to Egypt, a tour organizer charges $2,200 per person for groups of a minimum of 15 people. For each additional person in the group, however, the organizer reduces the entire group's per-person rate by $25. The organizer's expenses for the trip included a fixed cost of $3,000 and a per-person cost of $1,575.

a. Write a formula for $P(x)$, the per-person rate for a group of x people.
$P(x) = 2575 - 25x$

b. Write a formula for $R(x)$, the revenues generated from a group of x people.
$R(x) = x(P(x)) = 2575x - 25x^2$

c. Write a formula for $E(x)$, the expenses incurred from a group of x people.
$E(x) = 3000 + 1575x$

d. How is $I(x)$, the net income generated by the organizer, related to $R(x)$ and $E(x)$?
$I(x) + R(x) - E(x)$

e. Write a formula for $I(x)$ in terms of x.
$I(x) = -25x^2 + 1000x - 3000$

f. Use an automatic grapher to graph $I(x)$ from part e on a relevant domain and use the graph to determine the group size x for which the organizer receives its maximum net income.
20 people

Name

Representations Objective K

6. Let $f(x) = e^{-\frac{x}{3}}$ and $g(x) = \sin(4x)$. On the grid at the right, sketch graphs of the functions f and $f \cdot g$ over the interval $[-2\pi, 2\pi]$.

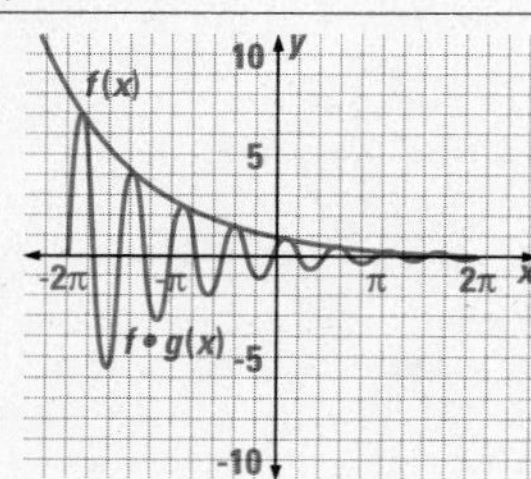

7. The functions f and g are graphed at the right.
a. Sketch the graph of $f + g$.
b. Sketch the graph of $f \cdot g$.

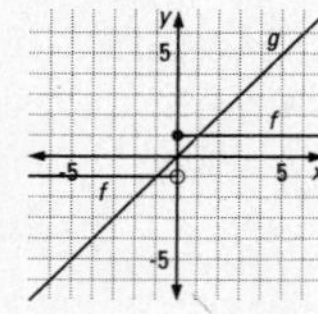

a.

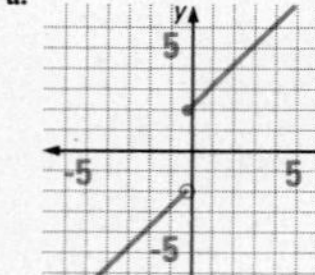

b.

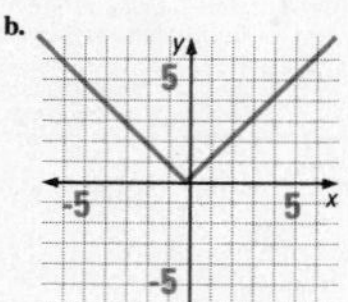

Name

LESSON MASTER 3-2

Questions on SPUR Objectives
See pages 218–221 for objectives.

Skills Objective B

In 1–3, find a formula for $h(x)$ and state the domain for the indicated function h.

1. $f(x) = 3x + 2$, $g(x) = 5x$; $h = g \circ f$
$h(x) = 15x + 10$
all real numbers

2. $f(x) = \log_3 x$, $g(x) = x^3$; $h = f \circ g$
$h(x) = 3 \log_3 x$
$\{x: x > 0\}$

3. $t(x) = \tan x$, $g(x) = \frac{x-2}{3}$; $h = t \circ g$
$h(x) = \tan\left(\frac{x-2}{3}\right)$
$\left\{x: x \neq (2n+1)\frac{3\pi}{2} + 2, n \text{ any integer}\right\}$

Properties Objective F

4. Are $g: x \to |x| + 1$ and $h: x \to |x - 1|$ inverse functions? Justify your answer.
No; $g(h(-1)) = 3 \neq -1$, so $g(h(x)) \neq x$ for all x.

Uses Objective I

5. The power output of a 1 k Ω resistor, as a function of the voltage across the resistor, is given by $P(V) = \frac{V^2}{1000}$. Suppose the voltage across the resistor as a function of time is given by $V(t) = 25 \sin\left(\frac{\pi t}{30}\right)$.

a. Find a formula for $P(V(t))$.
$P(V(t)) = 0.625 \sin^2\left(\frac{\pi t}{30}\right)$

b. What does $P(V(t))$ represent?
The power output of a 1 k Ω resistor at time t

Representations Objective K

6. At the right is a graph of the function $f: x \to \ln x + 2$. On the same grid, sketch a graph of f^{-1}.

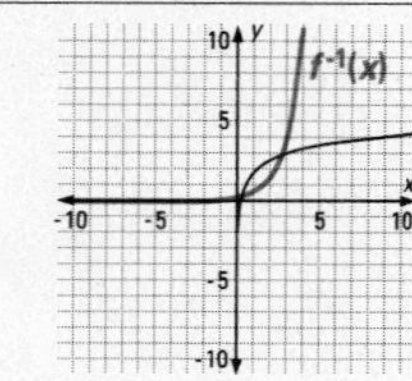

Name

LESSON MASTER 3-3

Questions on SPUR Objectives
See pages 218–221 for objectives.

Skills Objective A

In 1–8, find all real solutions.

1. $(2 + y)^2 = (3 + y)^2$ — $y = -\frac{5}{2} = -2.5$
2. $(z - 26)^2 = z^2$ — $z = 13$
3. $\sqrt{5r + 6} = -r$ — $r = -1$
4. $\sqrt{2t + 1} + \sqrt{2t - 1} = 10$ — $t = 12.505$
5. $e^{2k+2} = e^{4k-3}$ — $k = \frac{5}{2} = 2.5$
6. $3^{(2x^2+3x)} = \frac{1}{3}$ — $x = \frac{1}{2} = 0.5, x = 1$
7. $\frac{1}{a^2 + 2a - 15} = \frac{1}{3 - a}$ — $a = -6$
8. $\ln(3d + 2) = \ln(2d + 7)$ — $d = 5$

Properties Objective E

9. Consider the following solution of $\log(x^2 - 18) = \log(-3x + 10)$.
   0. $\log(x^2 - 18) = \log(-3x + 10)$
   1. $x^2 - 18 = -3x + 10$
   2. $x^2 + 3x - 28 = 0$
   3. $(x + 7)(x - 4) = 0$
   4. $x = -7$ or $x = 4$

   a. Are there any nonreversible steps in the solution? If so, where?
   Yes; step 0 does not follow from step 1.

   b. Are both $x = -7$ and $x = 4$ solutions to the original equation? Why or why not?
   No; -7 is a solution, since $(-7)^2 - 18 = -3(-7) + 10 = 31$; 4 is not a solution, since $4^2 - 18 = -2$ is not in the domain of the log function.

Uses Objective H

10. On January 1, 1998, Penny deposited $5,000 in an account with an annual interest rate of 5%, compounded continuously. One year later, on January 1, 1999, Penny's sister Rupee deposited $5,000 in an account with an annual interest rate of 7%, also compounded continuously. Give the date on which the balances in Penny's and Rupee's accounts will be equal. — July 1, 2001

Name

LESSON MASTER 3-4

Questions on SPUR Objectives
See pages 218–221 for objectives.

Properties Objective G

1. a. Tell whether the function $f: x \rightarrow \frac{1}{\cos x}$ is continuous on the given interval.

   i. $\left[0, \frac{\pi}{4}\right]$ — Yes
   ii. $\left[\frac{\pi}{4}, \frac{3\pi}{4}\right]$ — No
   iii. $\left[-\frac{\pi}{4}, 0\right]$ — Yes

   b. For the function of part a, $f\left(\frac{\pi}{4}\right) > 0$ and $f\left(\frac{3\pi}{4}\right) < 0$, yet there is no x in the interval $\left[\frac{\pi}{4}, \frac{3\pi}{4}\right]$ such that $f(x) = 0$. Does this contradict the Intermediate Value Theorem? Why or why not?
   No; $f(x)$ is not continuous on the interval $\left[\frac{\pi}{4}, \frac{3\pi}{4}\right]$.

2. *True or false.* If a function g is continuous on the interval [3, 6], $g(3) = 12$, and $g(6) = 19$, then, according to the Intermediate Value Theorem, $12 \le g(4) \le 19$. — False

Uses Objective H

3. On January 1, 1998, Frank deposited $5,000 in an account with an annual interest rate of 5%, compounded continuously. One year later, on January 1, 1999, Frank's brother Mark deposited $5,000 in an account with an annual interest rate of 7%, also compounded continuously. Give the date on which Mark's account will have $10 more than Frank's account. — Aug. 1, 2001

Representations Objective M

4. Consider the equation $e^{-x} \sin x = 1$.

   a. *Multiple choice.* In which one of the following intervals must there be a solution to the equation? — a
   (a) $\left[\frac{3\pi}{2}, -\pi\right]$ (b) $\left[-\pi, \frac{\pi}{2}\right]$ (c) $\left[\frac{\pi}{2}, 0\right]$ (d) $\left[0, \frac{\pi}{2}\right]$

   b. Use an automatic grapher to find an interval of length 0.05 that contains a solution to the equation. — Sample: [-3.20, -3.15]

Name

LESSON MASTER 3-5

Questions on SPUR Objectives
See pages 218–221 for objectives.

Skills Objective D

In 1–8, solve the inequality for all real-number solutions.

1. $-7n + 3 > 38$ — $n < -5$
2. $\ln z \le -2$ — $0 < z \le e^{-2} \approx 0.135$
3. $3^r > 3^{2-r}$ — $r < 1$
4. $\log_7(2t + 3) \ge \log_7(5t - 4)$ — $\frac{4}{5} < t \le \frac{7}{3}$
5. $k^{1.5} \ge 20$ — $k \ge 20^{\frac{2}{3}} \approx 7.37$
6. $\sqrt[3]{x} - 5 < -2$ — $x < -3$
7. $(7x - 3.2)^5 \ge (-x + 4.8)^5$ — $x \ge 1$
8. $x^3 + 3x^2 + 3x + 1 < 125$ — $x < 4$

Properties Objective E

9. Consider the following solution of $\frac{1}{x} > \frac{1}{x+1}$.

Conclusion	Justification
0. $\frac{1}{x} > \frac{1}{x+1}$	Given
1. $x < x + 1$	Apply $h(x) = \frac{1}{x}$ to both sides.
2. $0 < 1$	Add $-x$ to both sides.
3. All real values of x are solutions.	

   a. The solution is not correct. Give the values of x which are not solutions to the original inequality.
   No; $-1 \le x \le 0$

   b. The function h in the solution is 1 - 1 and is decreasing on the intervals $(-\infty, 0)$ and $(0, \infty)$, so where is the mistake in the solution?
   h is not always decreasing, so step 1 is invalid.

Name

▶ **LESSON MASTER 3-5** *page 2*

Properties Objective F

In 10 and 11, *true or false*.

10. If a real function f is either increasing or decreasing throughout its entire domain, then the inverse of f is also a function. — True
11. If the inverse of a real function f is also a function, then f is either increasing or decreasing throughout its entire domain. — False

Uses Objective J

12. The atmospheric pressure p (in lb/in²) as a function of altitude above sea level h (in feet) can be approximated by the formula $p = 14.7e^{-\frac{h}{28,300}}$. For what altitudes is the atmospheric pressure at least 12 lb/in²? — $h \le \approx 5743$ ft

Representations Objective K

13. *Multiple choice.* If f is a real function which is decreasing throughout its entire domain, which of the following could be the graph of f^{-1}? — d

(a)

(b)

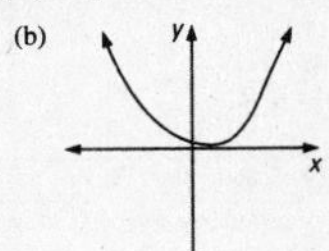

(c)

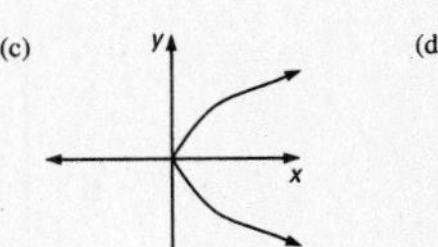

(d)

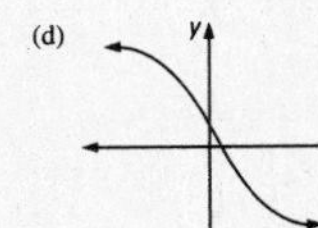

Name

LESSON MASTER 3-6

Questions on SPUR Objectives
See pages 218–221 for objectives.

Skills Objective C

In 1–4, find all exact zeros of the given function.

1. $f(m) = 3(2^m) - 384$ — $m = 7$
2. $g(t) = 5^{2t} - 26(5^t) + 25$ — $t = 0; t = 2$
3. $k(r) = (\log r)^2 + 0.5 \log r - 0.5$ — $r = \frac{1}{10}; r = \sqrt{10}$
4. $h(\theta) = \sin^2\theta - \sqrt{3} \sin \theta + \frac{3}{4}$ — $\theta = \frac{\pi}{3} + 2n\pi; \theta = \frac{2\pi}{3} + 2n\pi$ for integers n

In 5–8, find all solutions to the given equation.

5. $x^6 + 9x^3 = 2x^3 + 8$ — $x = -2; x = 1$
6. $\frac{1}{x^2} + 8 = \frac{6}{x}$ — $x = \frac{1}{4}; x = \frac{1}{2}$
7. $\cos^4 x + \frac{1}{4} = \cos^2 x$ — $x = \frac{\pi}{4} + n\pi; x = \frac{3\pi}{4} + n\pi$
8. $(5^x - 4)^3 + 7 = 5^x + 3$ — $x = 1, \frac{\ln 3}{\ln 5}, \frac{\ln 4}{\ln 5}$

Uses Objective H

9. Ms. Yuan wishes to invest $2,000 by placing half the money in an insured no-risk certificate of deposit with an annual interest rate of 3.5%, compounded continuously, and the other half in a higher-risk bond fund with an annual interest rate of 7%, also compounded continuously.
   a. Write a formula for $V(t)$, the total value of Ms. Yuan's investment as function of time.
   $V(t) = 1{,}000e^{0.07t} + 1{,}000e^{0.035t}$
   b. Determine the time it will take Ms. Yuan's initial investment of $2,000 to reach $6,000.
   $1{,}000e^{0.07t} + 1{,}000e^{0.035t} = 6{,}000 \Rightarrow 1{,}000e^{0.07t} + 1{,}000e^{0.035t} - 6{,}000 = 0 \Rightarrow e^{0.07t} + e^{0.035t} - 6 = 0.$
   Let $u = e^{0.035t}$. Then $u^2 = e^{0.07t}$. $u^2 + u - 6 = 0$
   $\Rightarrow (u + 3)(u - 2) = 0$. So, $e^{0.035t} = 2$.
   $0.035t = \ln 2$, and $t = \frac{\ln 2}{0.035} \approx 19.8$ years.

Name

LESSON MASTER 3-7

Questions on SPUR Objectives
See pages 218–221 for objectives.

Skills Objective D

In 1–8, find the exact solution set to each inequality.

1. $\frac{x^2 - 4}{x + 3} < 0$ — $\{x: -2 < x < 2 \text{ or } x < -3\}$
2. $e^{x^2} > e^{7x+8}$ — $\{x: x < -1 \text{ or } x > 8\}$
3. $(7v - 2)(4v - 3) \le 0$ — $\{x: \frac{2}{7} \le x \le \frac{3}{4}\}$
4. $\frac{x^2 - 9}{x} < 0$ — $\{x: x < -3 \text{ or } 0 < x < 3\}$
5. $t^8 - 4t^6 \ge 0$ — $\{x: x < -2, x = 0, x \ge 2\}$
6. $\log(c^2 - 9c) \le \log(c - 24)$ — no solution
7. $(b + 5)(b - 2)(b - 3) > 0$ — $\{x: -5 < x < 2 \text{ or } x > 3\}$
8. $10^{x^2-3x} < 10^{x-1}$ — no solution

9. Fill in the blanks to determine when $\frac{x^2 + 5x}{x^2 - 5x + 6} < 0$.

	$(-\infty, -5)$	$(-5, 0)$	$(0, 2)$	$(2, 3)$	$(3, \infty)$
$x + 5$	−	+	+	+	+
$x - 3$	−	−	−	−	+
$x - 2$	−	−	−	+	+
x	−	−	+	+	+

$\{x: -5 < x < 0 \text{ or } 2 < x < 3\}$

Name

LESSON MASTER 

Questions on SPUR Objectives
See pages 218–221 for objectives.

Skills Objective D

In 1–3, solve the inequality.

1. a. $x^2 < 25x$ — $0 < x < 25$
   b. $(y + 2)^2 < 25(y + 2)$ — $-2 < y < 23$
2. a. $c^2 > 3c - 2$ — $c < 1; c > 2$
   b. $(a - 1)^2 > 3(a - 1) - 2$ — $a < 2; a > 3$
3. a. $v^2 < 16v$ — $0 < v < 16$
   b. $(4u)^2 < 16(4u)$ — $0 \le u < 4$

Representations Objective L

4. The circle $x^2 + y^2 = 1$ is transformed by $S_{5,4}$ and then $T_{2,6}$.
   a. Find the equation of the image under $S_{5,4}$. — $\frac{x^2}{25} + \frac{y^2}{16} = 1$
   b. Find the equation of the image under the transformation $T \circ S$. — $\frac{(x - 2)^2}{25} + \frac{(y - 6)^2}{16} = 1$
5. From the parametric equations, give an equation relating x and y.
   $\begin{cases} x = 4 \cos t - 1 \\ y = \frac{1}{2} \sin t + 2 \end{cases}$ — $\left(\frac{x + 1}{4}\right)^2 + \left(\frac{y - 2}{\frac{1}{2}}\right)^2 = 1$

Representations Objective M

In 6–8, use an automatic grapher to estimate the zeros of the function.

6. $f(x) = e^{x-3436} - 3$ — ≈ 3437.0986
7. $g(x) = 3^{\frac{x}{4}-7}$ — ≈ 3.5425
8. $h(x) = \ln(x - 525) + 2$ — ≈ 525.1353

Name

LESSON MASTER 

Questions on SPUR Objectives
See pages 218–221 for objectives.

Skills Objective A

In 1–4, solve the equation.

1. $|a + 5| = 3a$ — $a = \frac{5}{2} = 2.5$
2. $1 = |3x - 2|$ — $x = 1; x = \frac{1}{3}$
3. $|c^2 - 9| = 7$ — $c = \pm\sqrt{2}; c = \pm 4$
4. $|d^3 - 13| = 14$ — $d = -1; d = 3$

Skills Objective D

In 5–8, solve the inequality.

5. $|x + 5| \le 3$ — $8 \le x \le -2$
6. $|4t - 5| > t + 1$ — $t < \frac{4}{5}; t > 2$
7. $4 > |s^2 + 3|$ — $-1 < s < 1$
8. $6 < |x^2 - 5x|$ — $x < -1; 2 < x < 3; x > 6$

Uses Objective J

9. A poll is conducted to calculate the approval rating of a politician. The poll results vary from the true amount by at most 5% with a confidence of 90%. The poll finds the approval rating to be 60%.
   a. Write the possible values t for the 90% confidence interval using a double inequality. — $55\% \le t \le 65\%$
   b. Describe the possible values t for the 90% confidence interval using an absolute value. — $|t - 60\%| \le 5\%$

Name ______

LESSON MASTER 4-1

Questions on SPUR Objectives
See pages 278–281 for objectives.

Skills Objective D

1. Express $(x - 5)(x^2 - 3x + 2) + (x - 5)(x^2 - 1)$ as a product of three polynomials.
   $(x - 5)(x - 1)(2x - 1)$

2. Express $y^8 + 4y^4 - 5$ as a product of four polynomials.
   $(y^4 + 5)(y^2 + 1)(y - 1)(y + 1)$

Properties Objective F

3. For what values of k is x^k a factor of $a_nx^n + a_{n-1}x^{n-1} + \ldots + a_mx^m$, where $0 < m < n$? $\{k: 0 \le k \le m\}$

In 4 and 5, determine whether the statement is true or false and explain your answer.

4. -4 is a factor of $64 \cdot 77$.
   True; $64 \cdot 77 = (-4 \cdot -16) \cdot 77 = -4(-16 \cdot 77)$

5. $y + 2$ is a factor of $17y^2 + 37y + 6$.
   True; $17y^2 + 37y + 6 = (y + 2)(17y + 3)$

In 6–8, prove the conjecture or give a counterexample to disprove it.

6. 3 is a factor of the sum of any three consecutive integers.
   Let m, $m + 1$, and $m + 2$ be three consecutive integers. Then $m + (m + 1) + (m + 2) = 3m + 3 = 3(m + 1)$. So, 3 is a factor of the sum.

7. 4 is a factor of the sum of any four consecutive integers.
   Counterexample: 4 is not a factor of $1 + 2 + 3 + 4 = 10$.

Name ______

LESSON MASTER 4-2

Questions on SPUR Objectives
See pages 278–281 for objectives.

Skills Objective A

In 1 and 2, values for n and d are given. Find the values of q and r as defined in the Quotient-Remainder Theorem for Integers.

1. $n = 61{,}302$, $d = 179$ — $q = 342$, $r = 84$
2. $n = -173$, $d = 11$ — $q = -16$, $r = 3$

3. When the polynomial $p(x) = x^5 + 2x^4 + 3x^2 + 3x + 1$ is divided by $x^3 + 1$, the quotient is $x^2 + 2x$.
   a. Find the remainder. $2x^2 + x + 1$
   b. Write $p(x)$ in the form of the Quotient-Remainder Theorem for Polynomials.
   $(x^2 + 2x)(x^3 + 1) + 2x^2 + x + 1$

Properties Objective H

In 4 and 5, $d > 0$ and $n = q \cdot d + r$ in accordance with the Quotient-Remainder Theorem for Integers.

4. Suppose that q is negative.
   a. What can be said about n? n is negative
   b. What can be said about r? $0 \le r < d$

5. Suppose that q is a factor of n.
   a. What can be said about d? d is a factor of n
   b. What can be said about r? $r = 0$

6. Suppose that $d = 11$ and $r = 9$.
   a. Give a possible positive value of n. Sample: $n = 20$
   b. Give a possible negative value of n. Sample: $n = -2$

Name ______

► **LESSON MASTER 4-2** *page 2*

In 7 and 8, $p(x) = q(x) \cdot d(x) + r(x)$ in accordance with the Quotient-Remainder Theorem for Polynomials.

7. If the degree of $r(x)$ is 10 and the degree of $q(x)$ is 4, what is the minimum possible degree of $p(x)$? 15

8. If $p(x)$ has lower degree than $d(x)$, what can be said about $q(x)$ and $r(x)$? $q(x) = 0$; $r(x) = p(x)$

Uses Objective K

9. John decides on a Wednesday to leave on a trip exactly 115 days later. On what day of the week will he begin his trip? Saturday

10. A market sells a certain bottled soft drink packaged three ways: individually for 70¢ a bottle, in 6-packs for $3.50 per pack, and in cases (four 6-packs per case) for $11 per case. Suppose n bottles are bought using c cases, s 6-packs, and b individual bottles, in such a way that the total cost is minimized.
    a. What are the values of c, s, and b if $n = 64$? $c = 2$, $s = 2$, $b = 4$
    b. What are the values of c, s, and b if $n = 100$? $c = 4$, $s = 0$, $b = 4$
    c. Are your answers to parts a and b unique? Explain.
    Yes; if a case is replaced by 6-packs or a 6-pack is replaced by individual bottles, the cost will be greater.

Name ______

LESSON MASTER 

Questions on SPUR Objectives
See pages 278–281 for objectives.

Skills Objective B

In 1 and 2, use long division to find the quotient $q(x)$ and remainder $r(x)$ when $p(x)$ is divided by $d(x)$.

1. $p(x) = x^5 + x^4 - x^3 - 3x^2 - 2x$, $d(x) = x^2 + x + 1$
   $q(x) = x^3 - 2x - 1$
   $r(x) = x + 1$

2. $p(x) = 3x^3 + 7x^2 + 11x + 6$, $d(x) = x + \frac{1}{3}$
   $q(x) = 3x^3 - 6x + 9$
   $r(x) = 3$

3. What is the height of a rectangular box, if the bottom of the box measures $(m + 6)$ inches by $(m + 4)$ inches and the volume of the box in cubic inches is $m^3 + 7m^2 - 6m - 72$? $(x - 3)$ in.

Properties Objective H

4. Consider the polynomials $p(x) = x^6 - 9x^4 - x^2 + 9$ and $d(x) = x^2 + 1$.
   a. Use long division to find the quotient $q(x)$ and remainder $r(x)$ when $p(x)$ is divided by $d(x)$.
   $q(x) = x^4 - 10x^2 + 9$
   $r(x) = 0$
   b. Divide the quotient found in part b by $x^2 - 9$.
   $x^2 - 1$
   c. Using the results of parts a and b, express $p(x)$ as a product of five polynomials.
   $(x^2 + 1)(x + 1)(x - 1)(x + 3)(x - 3)$
   d. Find the values of $p(1)$, $p(-1)$, $p(3)$, $p(-3)$.
   $p(1)$ 0 $p(-1)$ 0 $p(3)$ 0 $p(-3)$ 0

5. If $f(x)$ is a polynomial, $f(-3) = 5$, and the quotient is $x^2 + x + 1$ when $f(x)$ is divided by $x + 3$, what is $p(x)$?
   $x^3 + 4x^2 + 4x + 8$

6. *Multiple choice.* If $p(x)$ is divided by $x + \frac{7}{2}$, the remainder is given by which of the following? c
   (a) $p(7)$ (b) $p(\frac{7}{2})$ (c) $p(-\frac{7}{2})$ (d) $p(2)$

Name

LESSON MASTER 4-4

Questions on SPUR Objectives
See pages 278–281 for objectives.

Skills Objective D

1. Factor the polynomial $3x^6 - 39x^4 + 108x^2$ completely over the reals.
$3x^2(x - 2)(x + 2)(x - 3)(x + 3)$

Skills Objective E

2. a. Show that -1 is a zero of the polynomial $g(x) = 6x^3 - 5x^2 - 46x - 35$.
$g(-1) = 6(-1)^3 - 5(-1)^2 - 46(-1) - 35 =$
$-6 - 5 + 46 - 35 = 0$

b. Find the remaining real zeros of $g(x)$. $-\frac{5}{3}, \frac{7}{2}$

3. Given that $x - 4$ is a factor of $p(x) = x^4 - 23x^2 + 18x + 40$ and that -1 is a zero of $p(x)$, find all real zeros of $p(x)$. -5, -1, 2, 4

4. Given that $t^2 + 1$ is a factor of $f(t) = t^5 - 3t^4 - 39t^3 - 3t^2 - 40t$, find all real zeros of $f(t)$. -5, 0, 8

Properties Objective H

5. *Multiple choice.* If the graph of the equation $y = p(x)$, where $p(x)$ is a polynomial function, crosses the line $y = b$ five times, which of the following statements is not necessarily correct? b

(a) $p(x)$ has degree at least 5.
(b) $p(x)$ has 5 real zeros.
(c) $f(x) = p(x) - b$ has 5 real zeros.
(d) $f(x) = p(x) - b$ has degree at least 5.

6. Suppose that $g(x)$, $h(x)$, and $k(x)$ are all factors of the polynomial $f(x)$. If 5 is a zero of $g(x)$, -5 and 2 are zeros of $h(x)$, and -2 is a zero of $k(x)$, find a polynomial of degree 4 that is a factor of $f(x)$.
Sample: $(x - 5)(x + 5)(x - 2)(x + 2) =$
$x^4 - 29x^2 + 100$

7. Fill in the blanks in the following sentence. If $ax + b$ is a factor of $p(x)$, then $-\frac{b}{a}$ is a zero of $p(x)$, provided that $a \neq 0$.

Name

LESSON MASTER 4-5

Questions on SPUR Objectives
See pages 278–281 for objectives.

Skills Objective C

1. Name two elements in each of the congruence classes modulo 5.
Sample: $R_0 = \{0, 5\}$, $R_1 = \{1, 6\}$, $R_2 = \{2, 7\}$,
$R_3 = \{3, 8\}$, $R_4 = \{4, 9\}$

In 2 and 3, give the smallest positive integer that makes the congruence true.

2. $m \equiv 11 \text{ mod } 5$ 1

3. $x \equiv -9 \pmod{21}$ 12

4. Consider the congruence classes $R_0, R_1, R_2, \ldots R_{10}$ for integers modulo 11.

a. If you add an element of R_1 to an element of R_{10}, which class contains the sum? R_0

b. If you multiply an element of R_4 and an element of R_7, which class contains the product? R_6

Properties Objective G

5. If a "special leap year" is defined as a year divisible by 4 but not divisible by 100, express any special leap year y as a solution to congruence sentences.
$y \equiv 0 \pmod 4$ and $y \not\equiv 0 \pmod{100}$

6. If $m \equiv 3 \pmod{14}$ and $n \equiv 7 \pmod{14}$, write a congruence statement for

a. $m - n$. $m - n \equiv 10 \pmod{14}$

b. mn. $mn \equiv 7 \pmod{14}$

Uses Objective L

7. Find the last three digits of 11^{12}. 721

8. The first 11 digits of the Universal Product Code (UPC) for a product give information; the last digit is the *Modulo 10 Check Character.* To calculate this check digit, add the values in the even-numbered positions of the first 11 digits starting from right to left. Then multiply this sum by 3, and add the product and the sum of the values in the odd-numbered positions. The check digit is the least number that when added to the above result gives a number that is a multiple of 10. Find the check digit for each number.

a. 0-212000-15577-? 8

b. 0-87547-36720-? 5

Name

LESSON MASTER 4-6

Questions on SPUR Objectives
See pages 278–281 for objectives.

Representations Objective M

In 1 and 2, find the base-2 representation of the number.

1. 38 100110_2

2. 111 1101111_2

In 3–6, find the base-10 representation of the number.

3. 1100011_2 99

4. 100001_2 33

5. 327_8 215

6. BF21_{16} 48,929

7. Express 100 in base n where

a. $n = 2$. 1100100_2

b. $n = 5$. 400_5

c. $n = 8$. 144_8

d. $n = 6$. 244_6

In 8 and 9, perform the indicated addition and then verify your answer by finding the base 10 representations of the numbers.

8. $101_2 + 1110_2$
10011_2

$101_2 = 5$
$+ 1110_2 = + 14$
$10011_2 = 19$

9. $1110110_2 + 100111_2$
10011101_2

$1110110_2 = 118$
$+ 100111_2 = + 39$
$10011101_2 = 159$

Name

LESSON MASTER 4-7

Questions on SPUR Objectives
See pages 278–281 for objectives.

Skills Objective D

In 1–4, factor completely into prime polynomials over the reals.

1. $6x^2 + 11x - 10$
$(2x + 5)(3x - 2)$

2. $20t^4 - 31t^2 + 12$
$(\sqrt{5}t + 2)(\sqrt{5}t - 2) \cdot (2t + \sqrt{3})(2t - \sqrt{3})$

3. $g(x) = 8x^3 + 22x^2 - x - 15$, given that $x + 1$ is a factor of $g(x)$
$(x + 1)(2x + 5)(4x - 3)$

4. $(x^2 - xy)(x + y - 4) - (x^2 - xy)(x^2 + y - 7)$
$-x(x - y)\left(x - \frac{1 + \sqrt{13}}{2}\right)\left(x - \frac{1 - \sqrt{13}}{2}\right)$

Properties Objective I

In 5, write the assumption that you would make to begin the proof of the given statement by contradiction.

5. For any integer n, $\log n^2 > 0$.
There exists an integer n, such that $\log n^2 \leq 0$.

6. Consider the statement: *If a and b are real numbers, then* $a^2 + b^2 < 2ab$.

a. To write a proof by contradiction, with what assumption would you start?
Suppose $a^2 + b^2 < 2ab$.

b. Complete the proof.
Then $a^2 + b^2 - 2ab < 0$ and $(a - b)^2 < 0$. But a and b are real numbers, so $(a - b)^2 \geq 0$. Thus, the assumption is false and $a^2 + b^2 \geq 2ab$.

Properties Objective J

In 7 and 8, list the numbers that must be tested as factors to determine whether n is prime, then tell whether n is prime.

7. $n = 151$
2, 3, 5, 7, 11; n is prime.

8. $n = 1147$
2, 3, 5, 7, 11, 13, 17, 19, 23, 29, 31; n is not prime.

In 9 and 10, give the standard prime factorization of the number.

9. 160 $2^5 \cdot 5$

10. 221,850 $2 \cdot 3^2 \cdot 5^2 \cdot 17 \cdot 29$

Name

LESSON MASTER 5-1

Questions on SPUR Objectives
See pages 344–347 for objectives.

Skills Objective B

In 1–4, show that each result is rational by expressing it as the ratio of two integers.

1. $4.3 - 6.2$ $\dfrac{-19}{10}$
2. $\sqrt{\frac{1}{64}}$ $\dfrac{1}{8}$
3. $\frac{12}{7} + \frac{2}{13}$ $\dfrac{170}{91}$
4. $\log_9 27$ $\dfrac{3}{2}$

Properties Objective F

5. What is wrong with the following argument that π is a rational number? All rational numbers can be written as the ratio of two numbers. $\pi = \frac{\pi}{1}$, π can be written as the ratio of two numbers. Therefore π is rational.

   Sample: Since π is not an integer, $\frac{\pi}{1}$ is not the ratio of two integers.

6. Prove or find a counterexample: The square of any rational number is rational.

   Sample: Let r be a rational number $\frac{x}{y}$, where x and y are integers. Then $r^2 = \frac{x^2}{y^2}$. Since x^2 and y^2 are integers, $\frac{x^2}{y^2}$ is the ratio of two integers and r^2 is rational.

Uses Objective I

7. A company hires N people to work on a construction project. All but 4 of the people work on Phase I of the project, and all but 6 of the people work on Phase II of the project. The company has a total of $12,000 budgeted for labor expenses, $7,000 allocated for Phase I and $5,000 allocated for Phase II. All workers on a given phase of the project are paid equally. Find an expression in terms of N for the wage of a person who works

   a. only on Phase I. $\dfrac{7{,}000}{N-4}$

   b. only on Phase II. $\dfrac{5{,}000}{N-6}$

   c. on both phases. $\dfrac{12{,}000N - 62{,}000}{N^2 - 10N + 24}$

Name

LESSON MASTER 5-2

Questions on SPUR Objectives
See pages 344–347 for objectives.

Skills Objective A

In 1 and 2, rewrite the expression in lowest terms.

1. $\dfrac{3x^2 + 9x - 84}{2x^2 + 13x - 7}$ $\dfrac{3(x - y)}{2x - 1}$
2. $\dfrac{2y^3 + 4y^2 - 30y}{8y^2 + 64y + 120}$ $\dfrac{y(y - 3)}{4(y + 3)}$

In 3 and 4, rewrite the expression as a simple fraction and state any restrictions on the variable.

3. $\dfrac{\frac{1}{7} - \frac{7}{a^2}}{\frac{1}{a} + \frac{1}{3a^2}}$ $\dfrac{3(a - 7)(a + 7)}{7(3a + 1)}$ $a \neq -\frac{1}{3}$ and $a \neq 0$
4. $\dfrac{\frac{1}{t} + \frac{t}{4}}{\frac{t^3 - 15}{5t^2}}$ $\dfrac{5t(t^2 + 4)}{4(t^3 - 15)}$ $t \neq \sqrt[3]{15}$ and $t \neq 0$

In 5–7, write the result as a simple rational expression in lowest terms and state any restrictions on the variable.

5. $\dfrac{2m - 4}{m + 6} \div \dfrac{3m + 8}{m^2 + 4m - 12}$ $\dfrac{2(m - 2)^2}{3m + 8}$

   $m \neq -6$, $m \neq -\frac{8}{3}$, $m \neq 2$

6. $\dfrac{r^2 + 1}{r^2 - 4r + 4} + \dfrac{r^2 - 7}{r^2 + r - 6}$ $\dfrac{2r^3 + r^3 - 6r + 17}{(r - 2)^2(r + 3)}$

   $r \neq 2$ and $r \neq -3$

7. $\dfrac{s^2 + 10s + 9}{s^2 + 5s + 6} \cdot \dfrac{s^2 - 5s - 14}{s^2 - 5s - 6}$ $\dfrac{(s + 9)(s - 7)}{(s + 3)(s - 6)}$

   $s \neq -3$, $s \neq -2$, $s \neq -1$, $s \neq 6$

Uses Objective I

8. At a constant temperature, the pressure P of a real gas varies as a function of its volume V according to the formula $P(V) = \frac{RT}{(V - b)} - \frac{a}{V^2}$, where R, a, and b are constants and T is the temperature in kelvins.

   Rewrite $P(V)$ as a rational expression. $\dfrac{RTV^2 - aV + ab}{V^2(V - b)}$

Name

LESSON MASTER 5-3

Questions on SPUR Objectives
See pages 344–347 for objectives.

Skills Objective J

1. Consider the functions $f: x \to \frac{-2}{x^2}$ and $g: x \to \frac{-2}{(x + 3)^2} + 6$.

   a. State the domain and range of f.

   domain: $\{x: x \neq 0\}$; range: $\{y: y < 0\}$

   b. Give equations for all asymptotes to the graph of f.

   $x = 0$; $y = 0$

   c. State the domain and range of g.

   domain: $\{x: x \neq -3\}$; range: $\{y: y < 6\}$

   d. What transformation maps the graph of f onto the graph of g?

   $T_{-3, 6}: (x, y) \to (x - 3, y + 6)$

   e. Give equations for all asymptotes to the graph of g.

   $x = -3$; $y = 6$

   f. On the grid at the right sketch the graphs of f and g, showing their asymptotes.

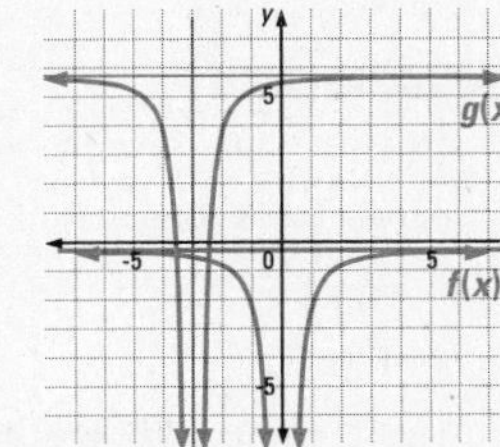

Representations Objective K

In 2 and 3, graph the function defined by the equation. Then use the limit notation to describe all vertical asymptotes.

2. $h(x) = \frac{7}{x - 2}$

   $\lim_{x \to -\infty} h(x) = \lim_{x \to \infty} h(x) = 0$; $\lim_{x \to 2^-} h(x) = -\infty$, $\lim_{x \to 2^+} h(x) = \infty$

3. $k(x) = \frac{1}{3x^4} - 5$

   $\lim_{x \to -\infty} k(x) = \lim_{x \to \infty} k(x) = -5$; $\lim_{x \to 0^+} k(x) = \lim_{x \to 0^-} k(x) = \infty$

Name

LESSON MASTER 5-4

Questions on SPUR Objectives
See pages 344–347 for objectives.

Skills Objective D

In 1–4, state whether the function defined by the given rule is a rational function. If it is a rational function, determine the values of the independent variable which are excluded from the domain.

1. $f(t) = \dfrac{t + 1}{t^2 + 3t + 2}$ rational; $t = -1$, $t = -2$
2. $g(x) = \dfrac{\frac{1}{x^2} - x}{x^2 - 7}$ rational; $x = 0$, $x = \pm\sqrt{7}$
3. $h(v) = \dfrac{v^3 + 5v + 13}{v^2 + 5}$ rational
4. $k(n) = \dfrac{n^2 - 7}{e^n}$ not rational

Properties Objective G

5. Consider the function f defined by $f(x) = \frac{x^2 + 5x + 6}{x^2 + x - 6}$. Find each limit.

   a. $\lim_{x \to -3^+} f(x)$ $\frac{1}{5}$

   b. $\lim_{x \to -3^-} f(x)$ $\frac{1}{5}$

   c. $\lim_{x \to 2^+} f(x)$ ∞

   d. $\lim_{x \to 2^-} f(x)$ $-\infty$

Properties Objective H

6. Consider the function h with $h(x) = \frac{x^2 - 1}{x^3 - x}$.

   a. For what values of x is the function undefined? $x = 0$, $x = 1$, $x = -1$

   b. At which of the values in part a is there an essential discontinuity? $x = 0$

   c. At which of the values in part a is there a removable discontinuity? $x = 1$, $x = -1$

   d. Redefine the function at the value(s) in part c so that the discontinuity is removed. $h(1) = 1$, $h(-1) = -1$

7. Define a function which has a removable discontinuity at $x = 7$ and an essential discontinuity at $x = -2$. Sample: $\dfrac{x - 7}{x^2 + 5x - 14}$

Name

► **LESSON MASTER 5-4** *page 2*

8. *True or false.* Suppose f is a rational function having no essential discontinuities with $f(x) = \frac{p(x)}{q(x)}$, where $p(x)$ and $q(x)$ are polynomials over the reals. Then $\forall$ real numbers x, $q(x) = 0 \Rightarrow p(x) = 0$. Justify your answer.
True; if $q(x) = 0$ and $p(x) \neq 0$, then $f(x)$ has an essential discontinuity, and this violates the assumption.

Representations Objective J

9. a. Graph the rational function $h: x \rightarrow \frac{5x^2 - 8}{x^2 + 1}$.
b. Does h have any essential discontinuities? If so, list them.
No
c. Does h have any removable discontinuities? If so, list them.
No

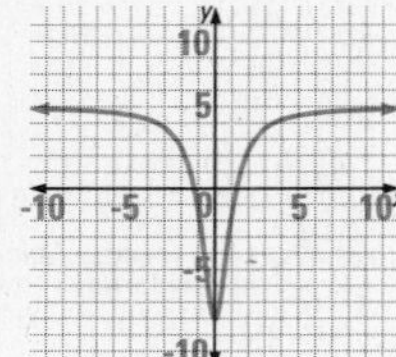

Representations Objective K

10. Suppose a rational function g has the following properties: The domain of g is $\{x: x \neq 0 \text{ and } x \neq 5\}$, $\lim_{x\to 0^-} g(x) = 1$, $\lim_{x\to 0^+} g(x) = 1$, $\lim_{x\to 5^+} g(x) = \infty$, and $\lim_{x\to 5^-} g(x) = -\infty$.
a. Write an equation for a vertical asymptote of g.
$x = 5$
b. Construct a possible rule for the function of g.
$g(x) = \frac{5x}{x^2 - 5x}$
c. Graph the function of part b.

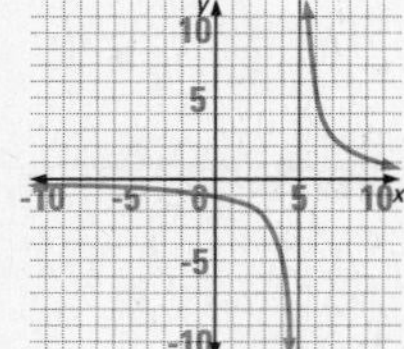

Name

LESSON MASTER 5-5

Questions on SPUR Objectives
See pages 344–347 for objectives.

Properties Objective G

In 1–3, use limit notation to describe the end behavior of the given function.

1. $f(x) = \frac{7x^2 - 17}{6x^2 - 5x + 2}$ $\lim_{x\to\infty} f(x) = \frac{7}{6}$; $\lim_{x\to-\infty} f(x) = \frac{7}{6}$

2. $g(z) = \frac{7z + 1}{9z^3 - 6z + 3}$ $\lim_{z\to\infty} g(z) = 0$; $\lim_{z\to-\infty} g(z) = 0$

3. $h(t) = \frac{4t^3 + 3t^2 + 2t + 1}{t^2 + 2t + 3}$ $\lim_{t\to\infty} h(t) = \infty$; $\lim_{t\to-\infty} h(t) = -\infty$

Representations Objective J

4. a. Graph the function. $h: x \rightarrow \frac{2x^2 - 7x - 1}{7x - 63}$.
b. Give equations for all vertical asymptotes of h.

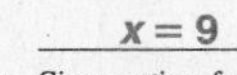

c. Give equations for all horizontal asymptotes of h.

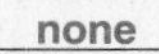

d. Give equations for all oblique asymptotes of h.
$y = \frac{2}{7}x + \frac{11}{7}$

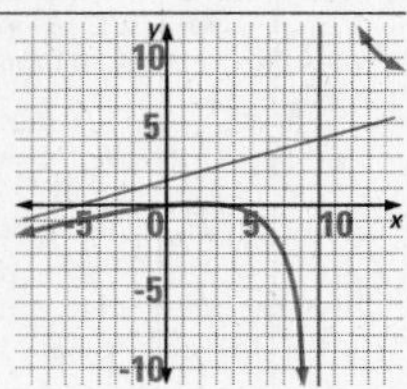

Representations Objective K

5. The function k is graphed at the right, showing its end behavior, a removable discontinuity at $x = 5$, and an essential discontinuity at $x = 8$.
a. Use limit notation to describe the behavior of the function near $x = 5$.
$\lim_{x\to 5^+} k(x) = 2$; $\lim_{x\to 5^-} k(x) = 2$
b. Use limit notation to describe the behavior of the function near $x = 8$.
$\lim_{x\to 8^+} k(x) = \infty$; $\lim_{x\to 8^-} k(x) = -\infty$
c. Use limit notation to describe the end behavior of the function.
$\lim_{x\to\infty} k(x) = 6$; $\lim_{x\to-\infty} k(x) = 6$

Name

LESSON MASTER 5-6

Questions on SPUR Objectives
See pages 344–347 for objectives.

Skills Objective B

In 1–5, identify each number as rational or irrational. Justify your reasoning.

1. $6 + \sqrt{2}$ irrational; rational + irrational = irrational

2. $\sqrt{72}$ irrational; $\sqrt{72} = 6\sqrt{2}$; rational × irrational = irrational

3. $0.134\overline{134}$ rational; repeating decimals are rational

4. $\frac{3\pi}{6}$ irrational; $\frac{3\pi}{6} = \frac{\pi}{2}$; irrational ÷ rational = irrational

5. $\frac{43e^2}{4e^3}$ rational; $\frac{43e^3}{34e^3} = \frac{43}{4}$; $\frac{43}{4}$ is rational

Skills Objective C

In 6–9, rationalize the denominator.

6. $\frac{7}{3 - \sqrt{2}}$ $\sqrt{2} + 3$

7. $\frac{\sqrt{5}}{7 - \sqrt{10}}$ $\frac{7\sqrt{5} + 5\sqrt{2}}{39}$

8. $\frac{\sqrt{3} + 2}{\sqrt{5} - 1}$ $\frac{\sqrt{15} + 2\sqrt{5} + \sqrt{3} + 2}{4}$

9. $\frac{13}{1 - \sqrt{3}}$ $\frac{-13 - 13\sqrt{3}}{2}$

Properties Objective F

10. Prove or find a counterexample: The square root of any irrational number is irrational.
Sample: Assume the square root is rational. Then $\sqrt{x} = \frac{a}{b}$, where a and b are integers, then $x = \frac{a^2}{b^2}$. Since the square of an integer is an integer, a^2 and b^2 are both integers. Thus x is rational, which is a contradiction. So, the square root of any irrational number is irrational.

Name

LESSON MASTER 5-7

Questions on SPUR Objectives
See pages 344–347 for objectives.

Skills Objective D

In 1 and 2, determine if the function defined by the given rule is a rational function.

1. $f(x) = \frac{1}{\cos x}$ not rational

2. $g(x) = \frac{1}{\cot x}$ not rational

Properties Objective H

In 3 and 4, a function and its rules are given.
a. List all values of θ at which the function is discontinuous.
b. Tell which discontinuities are removable.

3. $h(\theta) = \frac{1 - 2\cos\theta}{\sin\theta}$
a. $n\pi$, n an integer
c. none

4. $g(\theta) = \frac{1 - \sin^2\theta}{\cos\theta}$
b. $\frac{(2n + 1)\pi}{2}$, n an integer
d. All are removable

Representations Objective K

5. Consider the function $k: x \rightarrow \frac{x}{\sin x}$. Use an automatic grapher to graph k.
a. At what values of x is k undefined? $n\pi$, n an integer
b. Find $\lim_{x\to 0^-} \frac{x}{\sin x}$. 1
c. Find $\lim_{x\to 0^+} \frac{x}{\sin x}$. 1
d. Is 0 a removable or essential discontinuity of the function k? removable

Representations Objective L

In 6–8, use the triangle below to rewrite the trigonometric expression in terms of x.

6. tan α $\frac{7 - x}{x}$

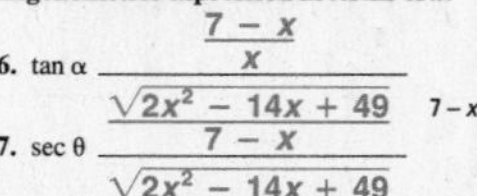

7. sec θ $\frac{\sqrt{2x^2 - 14x + 49}}{7 - x}$

8. csc α $\frac{\sqrt{2x^2 - 14x + 49}}{7 - x}$

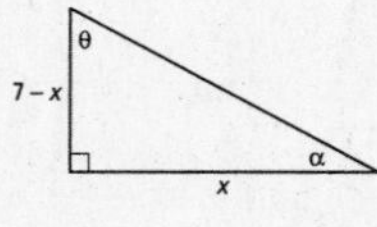

Name

LESSON MASTER 5-8

Questions on SPUR Objectives
See pages 344–347 for objectives.

Skills Objective E

In 1–4, solve the equation.

1. $\frac{5}{x-2} + \frac{3}{x-1} = 0$ $x = \frac{11}{8}$

2. $\frac{7}{y+2} + \frac{4}{y-3} = 3$ $y = 5, y = \frac{-1}{3}$

3. $\frac{z}{z+1} - \frac{z}{z+11} = \frac{-1}{(z+1)(z+11)}$ $z = -\frac{1}{10}$

4. $\frac{t}{t+2} + t = \frac{2-t}{t+2}$ $t = \sqrt{6} - 2, t = -\sqrt{6} - 2$

Uses Objective I

5. A ship's hull was punctured and filled with water before being sealed off. A pump removed water at a steady rate of 5 gallons per minute, but after 75% of the water was removed, the pump slowed. If the water was removed at an average rate of 4 gallons per minute, at what rate was the remaining 25% of the water removed? 25 gal/min

6. In an electrical circuit, if two capacitors with capacitances C_1 and C_2 are connected in series, then the equivalent capacitance, C, is found using the equation $\frac{1}{C} = \frac{1}{C_1} + \frac{1}{C_2}$. If C is 8 microfarads less than C_1 and C is two fifths the capacitance of C_2, what are the values of C_1, C_2 and C?
$C = 12$, $C_1 = 20$, $C_2 = 30$ microfarads

Name

LESSON MASTER 6-1

Questions on SPUR Objectives
See pages 401–403 for objectives.

Representations Objective H

In 1–6, use an automatic grapher to conjecture whether or not the equation appears to be an identity. If so, identify the domain of the identity. If not, give a counterexample. Sample counter-examples are given.

1. $\tan^2\theta - \cot^2\theta = \sec^2\theta - \csc^2\theta$
Yes; $\{\theta: \theta \neq \frac{n\pi}{2}$, n an integer$\}$

2. $\csc 2x + \frac{1}{2}\csc x \sec x$
Yes; $\{x: x \neq \frac{n\pi}{2}$, n an integer$\}$

3. $\sec 2x = \sec^2 x - \csc^2 x$
No; for $\frac{\pi}{6}$, $\sec 2x = \sec\frac{\pi}{3} = 2$ and $\sec^2 x - \csc^2 x = \frac{-8}{3}$

4. $\tan 2x = 2\tan x$
No; for $x = \frac{\pi}{6}$, $\tan 2x = \tan\frac{\pi}{3} = \sqrt{3}$ and $2\tan x = 2\tan\frac{\pi}{6} = \frac{2\sqrt{3}}{4}$

5. $\cot(y - \pi) = \tan\left(\frac{\pi}{2} - y\right)$
Yes; $\{y: y \neq n\pi$, n an integer$\}$

6. $\cos^3 x + \sin^3 x = \cos x + \sin x$
No; for $\frac{\pi}{4}$, $\cos^3 x + \sin^3 x = \frac{\sqrt{2}}{2}$ and $\cos x + \sin x = \sqrt{2}$

7. Use an automatic grapher to determine over what domain $f: x \to \sin x$, with x in radians, can be approximated by $g: x \to x - \frac{x^3}{3!} + \frac{x^5}{5!}$ to within 0.01. $\approx [-1.76, 1.76]$

8. Explain why it is difficult to use an automatic grapher to determine the domain of the identity $\sin\theta\cot\theta = \cos\theta$.
The graph of $\sin\theta\cot\theta$ is not defined at $\theta = k\pi$, $k = 0,1,2\ldots$, but only a very careful choice of window range reveals the "holes" on the grapher screen.

Precalculus and Discrete Mathematics © Scott Foresman Addison Wesley

Name

LESSON MASTER 6-2

Questions on SPUR Objectives
See pages 401–403 for objectives.

Properties Objective D

In 1–4, prove the identity and specify its domain. Sample proofs are given.

1. $\sec^2 x + \csc^2 x = \sec^2 x \csc^2 x$

$\sec^2 x + \csc^2 x = \frac{1}{\cos^2 x} + \frac{1}{\sin^2 x} = \frac{\sin^2 x + \cos^2 x}{\cos^2 x \sin^2 x} =$
$\frac{1}{\cos^2 x \sin^2 x} = \frac{1}{\cos^2 x} \cdot \frac{1}{\sin^2 x} = \sec^2 x \csc^2 x$
domain: $\{x: x \neq \frac{n\pi}{2}$, n an integer$\}$

2. $\sin^4 x - \cos^4 x = \frac{\tan x - \cot x}{\sec x \csc x}$ domain: $\{x: x \neq \frac{n\pi}{2}$, n an integer$\}$

$\sin^4 x - \cos^4 x = \frac{\frac{\sin x}{\cos x} - \frac{\cos x}{\sin x}}{\frac{1}{\cos x} \cdot \frac{1}{\sin x}}$
$= \frac{\sin^2 x - \cos^2 x}{\cos x \sin x} \cdot \frac{\cos x \cdot \sin x}{1} = \sin^2 x - \cos^2 x \cdot 1$
$= (\sin^2 x - \cos^2 x)(\sin^2 x + \cos^2 x)$
$= \sin^4 x - \cos^4 x$

3. $\tan\theta + \cot\theta = \sec\theta\csc\theta$

$\tan\theta + \cot\theta = \frac{\sin\theta}{\cos\theta} + \frac{\cos\theta}{\sin\theta} = \frac{\sin^2\theta + \cos^2\theta}{\cos\theta\sin\theta} =$
$\frac{1}{\cos\theta\sin\theta} = \sec\theta\csc\theta$
domain: $\{x: x \neq \frac{n\pi}{2}$, n an integer$\}$

4. $\cot 2x \tan 2x = \sin 2x \csc 2x$

$\cot 2x \tan 2x = \frac{1}{\tan 2x} \cdot \tan 2x = 1 =$
$\sin 2x \cdot \frac{1}{\sin 2x} = \sin 2x \csc 2x$
domain: $\{x: x \neq \frac{n\pi}{4}$, n an integer $\}$

5. Fill in the blank to make an identity: $\cos x + \sin x \tan x =$ $\sec x$

Precalculus and Discrete Mathematics © Scott Foresman Addison Wesley

Name

Representations Objective H

In 6 and 7, use an automatic grapher to determine whether the equation appears to be an identity. If so, prove it and identify its domain. If not, give a counterexample. Samples are given.

6. $\sin 4x = 4\sin x$ Not an identity; counterexample
Let $x = \frac{\pi}{4}$, then $\sin 4\left(\frac{\pi}{4}\right) = \sin\pi = 0$ but
$4\sin\frac{\pi}{4} = 4 \cdot \frac{\sqrt{2}}{2} = 2\sqrt{2}$; $2\sqrt{2} \neq 0$

7. $\cos^4 x + \sin^4 x = 1 - 2\cos^2 x \sin^2 x$

Yes; $\cos^4 x + \sin^4 x = \cos^4 x + 2\cos^2 x \sin^2 x +$
$\sin^4 x - 2\cos^2 x \sin^2 x = (\cos^2 x + \sin^2 x) -$
$2\cos^2 x \sin^2 x = 1 - 2\cos^2 x \sin^2 x$
domain: all real numbers

Precalculus and Discrete Mathematics © Scott Foresman Addison Wesley

Name

LESSON MASTER 6-3

Questions on SPUR Objectives
See pages 401–403 for objectives.

Representations Objective G

1. How is the graph of $y = 1 + \cos 3x$ related to the graph of $y = \cos x$?
It is the image under $T: (x, y) \to \left(\frac{1}{3}x, y + 1\right)$

2. Consider the sine wave with the following graph.

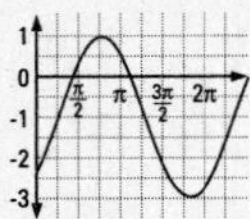

Determine the following.

a. Amplitude 2 b. Period 2π

c. Phase shift $\frac{\pi}{4}$ d. Vertical Shift -1

e. An equation for the graph $y = 2\sin\left(x - \frac{\pi}{4}\right) - 1$

3. a. Write an equation for the image of $y = \sin x$ under the transformation $T(x, y) = \left(\frac{1}{2}x - \frac{\pi}{3}, 3y - 1\right)$.
$y = 3\sin\left(2x + \frac{2\pi}{3}\right) - 1$

b. Give the amplitude, vertical shift, period, and phase shift of the image.
amplitude: 3 period: π
vertical shift: -1 phase shift: $-\frac{\pi}{3}$

Name

▶ **LESSON MASTER 6-3** *page 2*

4. a. Write an equation for the image of $y = \sec x$ under the rubberband transformation $(x, y) \to \left(x + \frac{\pi}{2}, y + 3\right)$.
$y = \sec\left(x - \frac{\pi}{2}\right) + 3$

b. Give the asymptotes and vertical shift of the image.
asymptote: $x = n\pi$, n an integer;
vertical shift: 3

5. Under what transformation is the graph of $y = 7\cos\left(5x + \frac{5\pi}{4}\right) - 2$ the image of the graph of $y = \cos x$?
$T: (x, y) \to \left(\frac{x}{5} - \frac{\pi}{4}, 7y - 2\right)$

6. a. Write parametric equations for the image of the graph $\begin{cases} x = \cos t \\ y = \sin t \end{cases}$ under the transformation $(x, y) \to (5x - 2, 3y + 2)$.
$\begin{cases} x = 5\cos t - 2 \\ y = 3\sin t + 2 \end{cases}$

b. Write a single equation in x and y for the image graph.
$\frac{(x + 2)^2}{25} + \frac{(y - 2)^2}{9} = 1$

c. What type of figure is the parent graph? What type of figure is the image?
a circle an ellipse

Name

LESSON MASTER 6-4

Questions on SPUR Objectives
See pages 401–403 for objectives.

Skills Objective A

1. Suppose $-\pi < \beta < -\frac{\pi}{2} < \alpha < 0$, $\sin\alpha = -\frac{1}{2}$, and $\cos\beta = -\frac{3}{5}$.
Find exact values of the following.

a. $\cos\alpha$ $\frac{\sqrt{3}}{2}$ b. $\cos(\alpha + \beta)$ $-\frac{1}{10}(3\sqrt{3} + 4)$

c. $\sin\beta$ $-\frac{4}{5}$ d. $\cos(\alpha - \beta)$ $-\frac{1}{10}(3\sqrt{3} + 4)$

In 2–5, express the following in terms of rational numbers and radicals.

2. $\cos\left(\frac{\pi}{3} + \frac{\pi}{4}\right)$ $\frac{\sqrt{2} - \pm\sqrt{6}}{4}$ 3. $\cos\frac{13\pi}{12}$ $-\frac{\sqrt{2} + \sqrt{6}}{4}$

4. $\cos\frac{7\pi}{16}\cos\frac{3\pi}{16} + \sin\frac{7\pi}{16}\sin\frac{3\pi}{16}$ $\frac{\sqrt{2}}{2}$ 5. $\cos\frac{\pi}{12}$ $\frac{\sqrt{2} + \sqrt{6}}{4}$

Properties Objective D

In 6–8, prove the identity and state its domain. Sample proofs are given.

6. $\cos(x + 210°) = \frac{-\sqrt{3}\cos x + \sin x}{2}$
$\cos(x + 210°) = \cos x\cos 210° - \sin x\sin 210°$
$= \cos x\left(-\frac{\sqrt{3}}{2}\right) - \sin x\left(-\frac{1}{2}\right) = \frac{-\sqrt{3}\cos x + \sin x}{2}$
domain: all real numbers

7. $\cos(\pi + x + y) = \sin x\sin y - \cos x\cos y$
$\cos(\pi + x + y) = \cos\pi\cos(x + y) - \sin\pi \cdot \sin(x + y) = -\cos(x + y) = -(\cos x\cos y - \sin x\sin y) = \sin x\sin y - \cos x\cos y$
domain: all real numbers

8. $\cos(A - B)\cos(A + B) = \cos^2 A - \sin^2 B$
$(\cos A\cos B + \sin A\sin B)(\cos A\cos B - \sin A\sin B) = (\cos A\cos B)^2 - (\sin A\sin B)^2 = \cos^2 A(1 - \sin^2 B) - (1 - \cos^2 A)\sin^2 B = \cos^2 A - \cos^2 A\sin^2 B - \sin^2 B + \cos^2 A\sin^2 B = \cos^2 A - \sin^2 B$ domain: all real numbers

Name

LESSON MASTER  **6-5**

Questions on SPUR Objectives
See pages 401–403 for objectives.

Skills Objective A

In 1–4, express in terms of rational numbers and radicals.

1. $\sin\frac{5\pi}{12}$ $\frac{\sqrt{6} + \sqrt{2}}{4}$ 2. $\tan\frac{\pi}{12}$ $2 - \sqrt{3}$

3. $\sin\frac{15\pi}{11}\cos\frac{4\pi}{11} - \cos\frac{15\pi}{11}\sin\frac{4\pi}{11}$ 0 4. $\frac{\tan\frac{7\pi}{8} - \tan\frac{\pi}{8}}{1 + \tan\frac{7\pi}{8}\tan\frac{\pi}{8}}$ -1

5. Given that $\tan\theta = b$, find an expression for $\tan\left(\theta + \frac{\pi}{4}\right)$ and indicate the values of b for which it is defined.
$\tan\left(\theta + \frac{\pi}{4}\right) = \frac{1 + b}{1 - b}$; $b \neq 1$

6. Suppose that $\frac{\pi}{2} < x < \pi < y < \frac{3\pi}{2}$, $\sin x = \frac{\sqrt{3}}{2}$, and $\cos y = -\frac{4}{5}$.
Find exact values of the following.

a. $\cos x$ $-\frac{1}{2}$ b. $\sin y$ $-\frac{3}{5}$

c. $\sin(x + y)$ $\frac{-4\sqrt{3} + 3}{10}$ d. $\tan(x + y)$ $\frac{48 + 25\sqrt{3}}{11}$

Properties Objective D

In 7–8, prove the identity and specify its domain. Sample proofs are given

7. $\sin(A - B)\sin(A + B) = \sin^2 A - \sin^2 B$
$\sin(A - B)\sin(A + B) = (\sin A\cos B - \cos A\sin B) \cdot (\sin A\cos B + \cos A\sin B) = \sin^2 A\cos^2 B - \cos^2 A\sin^2 B = \sin^2 A(1 - \sin^2 B) - (1 - \sin^2 A)\sin^2 B = \sin^2 A - \sin^2 A\sin^2 B - \sin^2 B + \sin^2 A\sin^2 B = \sin^2 A - \sin^2 B$ domain: set of real numbers

8. $\tan(45° - x)\tan(135° - x) = -1$ $\tan(45° - x)\tan(135° - x)$
$= \frac{\tan 45° - \tan x}{1 + \tan 45°\tan x} \cdot \frac{\tan 135° - \tan x}{1 + \tan 135°\tan x} = \frac{1 - \tan x}{1 + \tan x} \cdot \frac{-1 - \tan x}{1 - \tan x} = 1(1 - 1) = -1$
domain: $\{x: x \neq (2n + 1)\frac{\pi}{4}$, n an integer

Name

LESSON MASTER 6-6 **Questions on SPUR Objectives** See pages 401–403 for objectives.

Skills Objective A

1. Given that $\cos\theta = \frac{12}{13}$ and $\sin\theta = -\frac{5}{13}$, find exact values of $\cos 2\theta$, $\cos\frac{\theta}{2}$, $\sin 2\theta$, and $\sin\frac{\theta}{2}$.

$\cos 2\theta = \frac{119}{169}$ $\sin 2\theta = \frac{-120}{169}$

$\cos\frac{\theta}{2} = \frac{-5\sqrt{26}}{26}$ $\sin\frac{\theta}{2} = \frac{\sqrt{26}}{26}$

In 2 and 3, express the following in terms of rational numbers and radicals.

2. $\sin\frac{\pi}{8}$ $\frac{1}{2}\sqrt{2-\sqrt{2}}$ 3. $\cos 15°$ $\frac{1}{2}\sqrt{2+\sqrt{3}}$

4. a. Use the identity for $\sin(\alpha+\beta)$ to find $\sin\frac{5\pi}{12}$. $\frac{1}{4}(\sqrt{6}+\sqrt{2})$

b. Use the identity $\cos 2\alpha = 1 - 2\sin^2\alpha$ to find $\sin\frac{5\pi}{12}$. $\frac{1}{2}(\sqrt{2+\sqrt{3}})$

c. Show that your answers to parts a and b are equal.

$\left(\frac{\sqrt{6}+\sqrt{2}}{4}\right)^2 = \frac{6+2+4\sqrt{3}}{16} = \frac{2+\sqrt{3}}{4}$; $\left(\frac{\sqrt{2+\sqrt{3}}}{2}\right)^2 = \frac{2+\sqrt{3}}{4}$; Thus, $\frac{\sqrt{6}+\sqrt{2}}{4} = \frac{\sqrt{2+\sqrt{3}}}{4}$.

Properties Objective D

5. Prove that $\sin 3x = 3\sin x - 4\sin^3 x$. (Hint: Express $\sin 3x$ in the form $\sin(2x + x)$ and expand.)

$\sin 3x$
$= \sin(2x + x) = \sin 2x\cos x + \cos 2x \sin x$
$= 2\sin x\cos x \cdot \cos x + (\cos^2 x - \sin^2 x)\sin x$
$= 2\sin x\cos^2 x + \cos^2 x\sin x - \sin^3 x$
$= 3\sin x\cos^2 x - \sin^3 x$
$= 3\sin x(1 - \sin^2 x) - \sin^3 x$
$= 3\sin x - 3\sin^3 x - \sin^3 x$
$= 3\sin x - 4\sin^3 x$

Name

In 6–9, prove the identity and specify its domain. Sample proofs are given.

6. $\frac{\sin 2\theta}{\sin\theta} - \frac{\cos 2\theta}{\cos\theta} = \sec\theta$

$\frac{\sin 2\theta}{\sin\theta} - \frac{\cos 2\theta}{\cos\theta} = \frac{2\sin\theta\cos\theta}{\sin\theta} - \frac{\cos^2\theta - \sin^2\theta}{\cos\theta} =$
$2\cos\theta - \cos\theta + \frac{\sin^2\theta}{\cos\theta} = \cos\theta + \frac{\sin^2\theta}{\cos\theta} =$
$\frac{\cos^2\theta + \sin^2\theta}{\cos\theta} = \frac{1}{\cos\theta} = \sec\theta$
domain: $\{x: x = \frac{n\pi}{2}$, n an integer$\}$

7. $\left(\sin\frac{\theta}{2} - \cos\frac{\theta}{2}\right)^2 = 1 - \sin\theta$

$\left(\sin\frac{\theta}{2} - \cos\frac{\theta}{2}\right)^2 = \sin^2\frac{\theta}{2} - 2\sin\frac{\theta}{2}\cos\frac{\theta}{2} +$
$\cos^2\frac{\theta}{2} = \left(\sin^2\frac{\theta}{2} + \cos^2\frac{\theta}{2}\right) - 2\sin\frac{\theta}{2}\cos\frac{\theta}{2} =$
$1 - \sin\left(2\cdot\frac{\theta}{2}\right) = 1 - \sin\theta$
domain: $\{\theta: \theta \neq \frac{n\pi}{2}$, n an integer$\}$

8. $\tan\frac{1}{2}\theta = \frac{1-\cos\theta}{\sin\theta}$

$\tan\frac{\theta}{2} = \sqrt{\frac{1-\cos\theta}{1+\cos\theta}}\cdot\sqrt{\frac{1-\cos\theta}{1-\cos\theta}} = \sqrt{\frac{(1-\cos\theta)^2}{1-\cos^2\theta}}$
$= \sqrt{\frac{(1-\cos\theta)^2}{\sin^2\theta}} = \frac{1-\cos\theta}{\sin\theta}$
domain $\{\theta: \theta \neq 0 + n\pi$, n an integer$]$

9. $\cos(A+B) + \cos(A-B) = 2\cos A\cos B$

$\cos(A+B) + \cos(A-B) = \cos A\cos B -$
$\sin A\sin B + \cos A\cos B + \sin A\sin B =$
$2\cos A\cos B$
domain: $\{A, B$: A and B are real numbers.$\}$

Name

LESSON MASTER 6-7 **Questions on SPUR Objectives** See pages 401–403 for objectives.

Skills Objective B

In 1 and 2, *true or false*.

1. $\forall x$ in the interval $-1 \le x \le 1$, $\cos(\sin^{-1}x) \ge 0$. True

2. $\forall x$, $\sin(\tan^{-1}x) \ge 0$. False

In 3–6, give exact values.

3. $\cos^{-1}\left(-\frac{\sqrt{2}}{2}\right)$ $\frac{3\pi}{4}$ 4. $\sec\left(\sin^{-1}\left(-\frac{\sqrt{3}}{2}\right)\right)$ 2

5. $\sin^{-1}\left(\sin\frac{5\pi}{4}\right)$ $-\frac{\pi}{4}$ 6. $\tan\left(\cos^{-1}\left(\sin\left(-\frac{\pi}{6}\right)\right)\right)$ $-\sqrt{3}$

7. Use $\triangle PQR$ to evaluate each expression.

a. $\tan^{-1}\left(\frac{r}{p}\right)$ α

b. $\csc\left(\cos^{-1}\left(\frac{r}{q}\right)\right)$ $\frac{q}{p}$

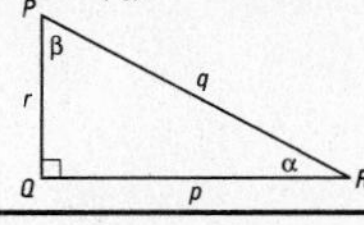

Uses Objective E

8. A 24-foot ladder is used to reach the top of an 18-foot wall. If the ladder extends 2 feet beyond the top of the wall, what angle does it make with the horizontal? $\approx 55°$

9. An aircraft is flying eastward at an altitude of 2 miles and a speed of 240 miles per hour. An observer standing directly under the flight path of the aircraft initially spots it overhead and watches it until it is 12 miles east of his position.

a. Express the angle of elevation of the line of sight from the observer to the aircraft as a function of the time in minutes after he initially spots the aircraft. (Assume the observer is at the origin and that east is the positive direction along the horizontal axis.) $\theta = \tan^{-1}\left(\frac{1}{2t}\right)$

b. What is the angle of elevation at time $t = 0.5$ minute? $\frac{\pi}{4} = 45°$

Name

LESSON MASTER  **6-8** **Questions on SPUR Objectives** See pages 401–403 for objectives.

Skills Objective C

In 1–4, solve over the interval $0 \le x \le 2\pi$ without using a calculator.

1. $\cot x \ge 1$ $0 \le x \le \frac{\pi}{4}$ or $\pi < x \le \frac{5\pi}{4}$

2. $\sec 3x = 2$ $x = \frac{\pi}{9}, \frac{5\pi}{9}$

3. $2\sin^2 x = 1 + \cos x$ $x = \frac{\pi}{3}, \pi$, or $\frac{5\pi}{3}$

4. $2\cos^2 x - \sqrt{3}\cos x > 0$ $0 < x < \frac{\pi}{6}, \frac{\pi}{2} < x < \frac{3\pi}{2}, \frac{11\pi}{6} < x < 2\pi$

In 5–6, solve over the reals without using a calculator.

5. $2\sin^2\theta + (\sqrt{2} - 1)\sin\theta - \frac{\sqrt{2}}{2} = 0$
$\theta = \frac{\pi}{6} \pmod{2\pi}$ or $\theta = \frac{5\pi}{6} \pmod{2\pi}$ or
$\theta = \frac{5\pi}{4} \pmod{2\pi}$ or $\theta = \frac{7\pi}{4} \pmod{2\pi}$

6. $\tan 2x = -\sqrt{3}$
$x = \frac{\pi}{3} \pmod{\pi}$ or $x = \frac{5\pi}{6} \pmod{\pi}$

Uses Objective F

7. If an object is thrown upward with an initial velocity of v ft/sec and at an angle of θ to the horizontal, the maximum height in feet that it reaches above the starting point is given by $h_{max} = \frac{v^2}{512}(16\sin\theta - \sin^2\theta)$. If a projectile hurled with an initial velocity of 60 feet per second reaches a maximum height of 56.25 feet above the starting point, at what angle was it thrown? $\approx 31°$

Representations Objective I

8. a. Use an automatic grapher to approximate to the nearest hundredth all solutions to the equation $\sin x + \cos x = 1.2$ over the inverval $0 \le x \le 2\pi$.
$x \approx 0.23$, $x \approx 1.34$

b. Use the results of part a to solve $\sin x + \cos x \ge 1.2$ over the interval $0 \le x \le 2\pi$.
$0.23 \le x \le 1.34$

Name

LESSON MASTER 7-1 **Questions on SPUR Objectives** See pages 467–469 for objectives.

Skills Objective A

In 1–6, find the first five terms of the sequence defined by the given formula.

1. $a_n = 1 - \left(-\frac{1}{2}\right)^n$ $\quad \frac{3}{2}, \frac{3}{4}, \frac{9}{8}, \frac{15}{16}, \frac{33}{32}$

2. $b_n = (1 + n)^{\lceil \frac{n}{3} \rceil}$ $\quad$ 2, 3, 4, 25, 36

3. $\begin{cases} c_1 = 2 \\ c_k = 1 + c_{k-1}^2 \ \forall k \geq 2. \end{cases}$ $\quad$ 2; 5; 26; 677; 458,330

4. $\begin{cases} s_1 = 2, s_2 = -1 \\ s_k = s_{k-2} + ks_{k-1} \ \forall k \geq 3. \end{cases}$ $\quad$ 2, -1, -1, -5, -26

5. $f_n = \lfloor \frac{n}{2} \rfloor \lceil \frac{n}{4} \rceil$ $\quad$ 0, 1, 1, 2, 4

6. $d_n = \tan\left(\frac{(2n+1)\pi}{4}\right)$ $\quad$ -1, 1, -1, 1, -1

7. In which of the Questions 1–6 are the sequences defined explicitly? $\quad$ 1, 2, 5, and 6

Skills Objective B

In 8–11, a sequence is defined recursively.
a. Write the first five terms of the sequence.
b. Conjecture an explicit formula for the sequence that works for the first five terms.

8. $\begin{cases} a_1 = 0 \\ a_k = a_{k-1} + \frac{1}{2} \text{ for } k \geq 2. \end{cases}$
 a. $0, \frac{1}{2}, 1, \frac{3}{2}, 2$
 b. $a_n = \frac{1}{2}(n - 1)$

9. $\begin{cases} a_1 = 1 \\ a_k = \frac{1 - a_{k-1}}{1 + a_{k-1}} \text{ for } k \geq 2. \end{cases}$
 a. 1, 0, 1, 0, 1
 b. $a_n = \frac{1 - (-1)^n}{2}$

10. $\begin{cases} a_1 = 49 \\ a_k = \frac{1}{7}a_{k-1} \text{ for } k \geq 2. \end{cases}$
 a. $49, 7, 1, \frac{1}{7}, \frac{1}{49}$
 b. $a_n = 49 \cdot \left(\frac{1}{7}\right)^{n-1} = 7^{3-n}$

11. $\begin{cases} a_1 = 1, a_2 = 3 \\ a_{k+2} = \frac{a_{k+1} + a_k}{2} + 3 \text{ for } k \geq 3. \end{cases}$
 a. 1, 3, 5, 7, 9
 b. $a_n = 2n - 1$

Name

Uses Objective H

12. During a period of rapid growth in Haywire County, telegraph lines were run from each town directly to every other town in the county. Let n and l_n be the number of towns and the number of telegraph lines in Haywire County, respectively.
 a. Find the first six terms of the sequence $l_1, l_2, l_3, \ldots$. $\quad$ 0, 1, 2, 4, 6, 9
 b. Find a recursive formula for l_n. $\quad l_1 = 0, l_{n+1} = l_n + n$
 c. Conjecture an explicit formula for l_n and check to see whether it gives you the correct recursive formula.
 Let $l_n = \frac{n(n-1)}{2}$. Then $l_{n+1} = \frac{(n+1)n}{2} = \frac{n^2 + n}{2} = \frac{n^2 - n}{2} + n = l_n + n$

Representations Objective J

13. a. List the terms generated by the program at the right. $\quad$ 2; 4; 16; 256; 65,536

```
10 TERM = 2
20 FOR J = 1 TO 5
30 PRINT TERM
40 TERM = TERM * TERM
50 NEXT J
60 END
```

 b. Write a recursive formula for the sequence generated by the program. $\quad t_1 = 2, t_n = (t_{n-1})^2$
 c. Write an explicit formula for the sequence. $\quad t_n = 2^{2^{n-1}}$

Name

LESSON MASTER 7-2 **Questions on SPUR Objectives** See pages 467–469 for objectives.

Skills Objective C

1. If $n = 2$, find $\sum_{k=-n}^{n+1} k^3 - 2k$. $\quad$ 21

In 2–3, use summation notation to express the sum

2. $(-2)^{-2} + (-1)^{-1} + 0^0 + 1^1 + 2^2 + \ldots + n^n$ $\quad \sum_{k=-2}^{n} k^k$

3. $\frac{m^2}{n^2} + \frac{m}{n} + 1 + \frac{n}{m} + \frac{n^2}{m^2} + \frac{n^3}{m^3}$ $\quad \sum_{k=-2}^{3} \left(\frac{n}{m}\right)^k$

4. a. Rewrite the equation $(1 + 1) + (2 + 4) + (3 + 9) + \ldots + (n + n^2) = (1 + 2 + 3 + \ldots + n) + (1 + 4 + 9 + \ldots + n^2)$ using summation notation.
 $\sum_{i=1}^{n} (i + i^2) = \sum_{i=1}^{n} i + \sum_{i=1}^{n} i^2$
 b. Show that the equation is true for $n = 6$.
 $\sum_{k=1}^{6} (k + k^2) = 112; \sum_{k=1}^{6} k + \sum_{k=1}^{6} k^2 = 21 + 91 = 112$

Skills Objective D

5. a. Express $\sum_{i=0}^{101} (i + i^3)$ in terms of $\sum_{i=0}^{100} (i + i^3)$. $\quad \sum_{i=0}^{100} (i + i^3) + (101 + 101^3)$
 b. Given that $\sum_{i=0}^{100} (i + i^3) = 25{,}507{,}550$, find $\sum_{i=0}^{101} (i + i^3)$. $\quad$ 26,537,952

6. Let $S(n)$ be the statement $\sum_{k=1}^{n} (k^2 + 2k) = \frac{n(n+1)(2n+7)}{6}$.
 a. Find $\sum_{k=1}^{4} (k^2 + 2k)$ and show that $S(4)$ is true.
 $\sum_{k=1}^{4} (k^2 + 2k) = 50; \frac{4 \cdot 5 \cdot 15}{6} = 50$
 b. Rewrite $\sum_{k=1}^{n+1} (k^2 + 2k)$ in terms of $\sum_{k=1}^{n} (k^2 + 2k)$.
 $\sum_{k=1}^{n} (k^2 + 2k) + (n + 1)^2 + 2(n + 1)$
 c. Use your answers to parts a and b to find $\sum_{k=1}^{5} (k^2 + 2k)$? $\quad$ 85
 d. Use the answer to part c to determine if $S(5)$ is true. $\quad$ True; $\frac{5 \cdot 6 \cdot 17}{6} = 85$

Name

LESSON MASTER 7-3 **Questions on SPUR Objectives** See pages 467–469 for objectives.

Properties Objective F

1. Prove that the sequence defined by $\begin{cases} s_1 = 1 \\ s_{k+1} = s_k + (k + 1)^3 \ \forall k \geq 1. \end{cases}$ satisfies the explicity formula $s_n = \frac{1}{4}n^2(n + 1)^2$.

Basis step: $s_1 = \frac{1}{4} \cdot 1^2 \cdot 2^2 = 1$, so the formula is valid for $n = 1$.
Inductive step: Suppose $s_k = \frac{1}{4}k^2(k + 1)^2$ is true. Then, $s_{k+1} = s_k + (k + 1)^3 = \frac{1}{4}k^2(k + 1)^2 + (k + 1)^3 = \frac{1}{4}(k + 1)^2 \cdot [k^2 + 4(k + 1)] = \frac{1}{4}(k + 1)^2(k + 2)^2$. So, the assumption that the formula is valid for s_k implies the formula is valid for s_{k+1}.

2. a. Find an explicit formula for the sequence defined by $\begin{cases} a_1 = 1 \\ a_{k+1} = a_k + (-1)^{k+1} \ \forall k \geq 1. \end{cases}$ $\quad a_n = \frac{(-1)^n + 3}{2}$
 b. Use mathematical induction to prove that the formula found in part a is correct.

Basis step: $a_1 = \frac{3 + (-1)^1}{2} = 1$, so the formula is valid for $n = 1$.
Inductive step: Suppose $a_k = \frac{(-1)^k + 3}{2}$. Then $a_{k+1} = a_k + (-1)^{k+1} = \frac{(-1)^k + 3}{2} + (-1)^{k+1} = \frac{2(-1)^{k+1} + (-1)^k + 3}{2} = \frac{2(-1)^k(-1) + (-1)^k + 3}{2} = \frac{(-1)(-1)^k + 3}{2} = \frac{(-1)^{k+1} + 3}{2}$. So, the assumption that the formula is valid for a_k implies the formula is valid for a_{k+1}.

Name

Properties Objective G

3. Let $S(n)$ be the statement: $\sum_{i=0}^{n} 3^i = \frac{1}{2}(3^{n+1} - 1)$. Use mathematical induction to prove that $S(n)$ is true for all positive integers n.

Basis step: $\sum_{i=0}^{1} 3^i = 3^0 + 3^i = 1 + 3 = 4 = \frac{1}{2}(3^2 - 1) = 4$, so the formula is valid for $i = 1$.

Inductive step: Suppose that $\sum_{i=0}^{k} 3^i = \frac{1}{2}(3^{k+1} - 1)$.

Then $\sum_{i=0}^{k+1} 3^i = \sum_{i=0}^{k} 3^i + 3^{k+1} = \frac{1}{2}(3^{k+1} - 1) + 3^{k+1} = \frac{1}{2}(3^{k+1}) - \frac{1}{2} + 3^{k+1} = \frac{3}{2}(3^{k+1}) - \frac{1}{2} = \frac{1}{2}(3^{k+2} - 1)$. So, the assumption that the statement is true for $S(n)$ implies that the statement is true for $S(n + 1)$.

Representations Objective J

4. Consider the program at the right.

```
10 INPUT N
20 SUM = 0
30 FOR I = 1 TO N
40 SUM = SUM + 3
50 PRINT SUM
60 NEXT I
70 END
```

a. Write a recursive definition for the sequence generated by the program.

$a_1 = 3$, $a_k = a_{k-1}, + 3$

b. Find an explicit formula for the sequence. $a_k = 3 + (k - 1)3k$

c. What modification to the program would you make so that the computer uses the explicit formula, rather than the recursive definition, to generate the sequence?

40 SUM = 3I

Name

LESSON MASTER 7-4

Questions on SPUR Objectives
See pages 467–469 for objectives.

Properties Objective G

In 1–3, use mathematical induction to prove that the statement is true. Samples are given.

1. For all integers a, a is a factor of $(a + 1)^n - 1$ ∀ positive integers n.

$(a + 1)^1 - 1 = a + 1 - 1 = a$, and a is a factor of a. Assume that a is a factor of $(a + 1)^k - 1$. Then $(a + 1)^{k+1} - 1 = (a + 1)(a + 1)^k - 1 = a(a + 1)^k + (a + 1)^k - 1$. By the inductive assumption, a is a factor of $(a + 1)^k$. a is clearly a factor of $a(a + 1)^k$. So, a is a factor of $(a + 1)^{k+1} - 1$. Thus, the assumption that a is a factor of $(a + 1)^k - 1$ implies that a is a factor of $(a + 1)^{k+1} - 1$.

2. 2 is a factor of $n^2 + n$ for all positive integers n.

$1^2 + 1 = 1 + 1 = 2$, and 2 is a factor of 2. Assume that 2 is a factor of $k^2 + k$. Then $(k + 1)^2 + (k + 1) = k^2 + 2k + 1 + k + 1 = (k^2 + k) + 2(k + 1)$. By the inductive assumption, 2 is a factor of $k^2 + k$. 2 is clearly a factor of $2(k + 1)$. So, 2 is a factor of $(k + 1)^2 + (k + 1)$. Thus, the assumption that 2 is a factor of $k^2 + k$ implies that 2 is a factor of $(k + 1)^2 + (k + 1)$.

3. 4 is a factor of $n^4 + n^2$ for all positive integers n.

$1^4 + 1^2 + 2 \cdot 1 = 1 + 1 + 2 = 4$, and 4 is a factor of 4. Assume that 4 is a factor of $k^4 + k^2 + 2k$. Then $(k + 1)^4 + (k + 1)^2 + 2(k + 1) = k^4 + 4k^3 + 6k^2 + 4k + 1 + k^2 + 2k + 1 + 2k + 2 = (k^4 + k^2 + 2k) + 4(k^3 + k^2 + k + 1) + 2k^2 + 2k$. By the inductive assumption, 4 is a factor of $k^4 + k^2 + 2k$. 4 is clearly a factor of $4(k^3 + k^2 + k + 1)$. Since $2k^2 + 2k = 2k\,(k + 1)$ and either k or $k + 1$ is even, 4 is a factor of $2k^2 + 2k$, and thus a factor of the entire expression. Thus, the assumption that the statement is true for k implies that the statement is true for $k + 1$.

Name

4. Suppose that the functions f and g are such that $f(x)$ and $g(x)$ are both integers whenever x is an integer. Suppose further that the integer is a factor of $f(n)$ when $n \geq 5$ and is a factor of $g(n)$ when $n \geq 9$. For what values of n can you be sure that n is a factor of the given expression?

a. $f(n) + g(n)$ $n \geq 9$

b. $f(n) \cdot g(n)$ $n \geq 5$

5. Prove that $x + y$ is a factor of $x^{2n} - y^{2n}$ ∀ positive integers n. (Hint: In the inductive step, add and subtract x^2y^{2k}).

True when $n = 1$; $S(1)$: $x^2 - y^2 = (x - y)(x + y)$
Assume true for $n = k$; $S(k)$: $(x + y)$ is a factor of $x^{2k} - y^{2k}$

$S(k + 1)$: $x^{2(k+1)} - y^{2(k+1)}$
$= x^{2k+2} - y^{2k+2}$
$= x^{2k+2} + x^2y^{2k} - x^2y^{2k} - y^{2k+2}$
$= (x^{2k}x^2 - x^2y^{2k}) + (x^2y^{2k} - y^{2k}y^2)$
$= x^2(x^{2k} - y^{2k}) + y^{2k}(x^2 - y^2)$

$x + y$ is a factor of $x^{2k} - y^{2k}$ by the inductive assumption and is therefore a factor of $x^2(x^{2k} - y^{2k})$. It is also a factor of $x^2 + y^2$, as proved in the base case, and is therefore a factor of $y^{2k}(x^2 - y^2)$. By the Factor of an Integer Sum Theorem, $x + y$ is a factor of $x^{2(k+1)} - y^{2(k+1)}$. Thus, the assumption $S(k)$ implies $S(k + 1)$ is true.

Name

LESSON MASTER 

Questions on SPUR Objectives
See pages 467–469 for objectives.

Properties Objective G

In 1–3, prove the statement using the Principle of Mathematical Induction.

1. For all integers $n \geq 1$, if $0 < a < 1$, then $0 < a^n < 1$.

Basis step: If $0 < a < 1$, then $0 < a^1 < 1$, since $a^1 = a$.
Inductive step: Assume that $0 < a^k < 1$. Then $0 = a \cdot 0 < a \cdot a^k = a^{k+1} < a \cdot 1$, or $0 < a^{k+1} < a$, since $a > 0$. $0 < a^{k+1} < a$ and $a < 1 \Rightarrow 0 < a^{k+1} < 1$. So, the assumption that the inequalities are true for a^k implies that these inequalities are true for a^{k+1}.

2. For all integers $p \geq 2$, $4^p > p^2 + 2p + 1$.

Basis step: $4^2 = 16 > 2^2 + 2 \cdot 2 + 1 = 9$
Inductive step: Assume that $4^k > k^2 + 2k + 1$ for $k \geq 1$. Then $4^{k+1} = 4 \cdot 4^k > 4(k^2 + 2k + 1) = 4k^2 + 8k + 4 = (k^2 + 2k + 1) + 2(k + 1) + 1 + (3k^2 + 4k) = (k + 1)^2 + 2(k + 1) + 1 + (3k^2 + 4k) > (k + 1)^2 + 2(k + 1) + 1$. So, the assumption that the inequality is true for k implies that the inequality is true for $k + 1$.

3. For all integers $n \geq 1$ and all real θ such that $\cos\theta \neq 0$, $|\sec^n\theta| \geq |\cos^n\theta|$.

Basis step: $\cos\theta \neq 0 \Rightarrow 0 < |\cos\theta| \leq 1 \Rightarrow |\sec\theta| = \left|\frac{1}{\cos\theta}\right| = \frac{1}{|\cos\theta|} \geq 1 \geq |\cos\theta|$

Inductive step: Assume that $|\sec^k\theta| \geq |\cos^k\theta|$. Then $|\sec^{k+1}\theta| = |\sec\theta||\sec^k\theta| \geq |\sec\theta| \cdot |\cos^k\theta| \geq |\cos\theta||\cos^k\theta| = |\cos^{k+1}\theta|$. So, the assumption that the inequality is true for k implies that the inequality is true for $k + 1$.

4. a. *True or false.* For all integers $n \geq 1$, if $x > y$, then $x^n > y^n$. False

b. If your answer to part a is "true," give a proof. If your answer is "false," give a counterexample.

Sample: $-2 > -3$, but $(-2)^2 < (-3)^2$.

Name

LESSON MASTER 7-6

Questions on SPUR Objectives
See pages 467–469 for objectives.

Skills Objective E

In 1–3, a series is given. a. Find its value when $n = 5$. b. Find its limit as $n \to \infty$.

1. $\sum_{k=0}^{n} \frac{8}{(-2)^k}$
   a. $\frac{21}{4}$
   b. $\frac{16}{3}$

2. $\sum_{j=1}^{n} 3(0.7)^j$
   a. ≈ 5.8
   b. 7

3. $\sum_{i=1}^{n} (1.5)^i$
   a. ≈ 19.8
   b. ∞

4. Let s be the sequence defined by $\begin{cases} s_1 = 4 \\ s_{k+1} = s_k \cdot \sin\frac{\pi}{4} \text{ for } k \geq 1. \end{cases}$
   Let S_n be the nth partial sum of the sequence.
   a. Find a formula for S_n. $S_n = \dfrac{4 - 4\left(\frac{\sqrt{2}}{2}\right)^n}{1 - \frac{\sqrt{2}}{2}}$
   b. Find S_5. $3\sqrt{2} + 7$
   c. Find $\lim_{n\to\infty} S_n$. $\dfrac{4}{1 - \frac{\sqrt{2}}{2}}$ or $\dfrac{8}{2 - \sqrt{2}}$

5. Give an example of a sequence for which the partial sums, S_n, satisfy $\lim_{n\to\infty} S_n = 3$.
   Sample: $2, \frac{2}{3}, \frac{2}{9}, \ldots$

6. Consider the finite geometric series $c + \frac{3}{2}c + \frac{9}{4}c + \ldots + \frac{243}{32}c$.
   a. Use sigma notation to express the series. $\sum_{k=0}^{5}\left[\left(\frac{3}{2}\right)^k \cdot c\right]$
   b. If the value of the series is 332.5, find c. $c = 16$

Representations Objective J

7. Consider the computer program at the right.

```
10 TERM = 7
20 SUM = TERM
30 FOR J = 2 TO 10
40 TERM = 3 * (TERM/4)
50 SUM = SUM + TERM
60 NEXT J
70 PRINT SUM
80 END
```

   a. Use summation notation to express the sum that is calculated by the program. $\sum_{j=1}^{10} 7\left(-\frac{3}{4}\right)^{j-1}$
   b. Use the formula for a finite geometric series to find the sum in part a. ≈ 3.78
   c. What would be the approximate value of the sum if the 10 in line 30 were changed to 1 trillion? ≈ 4

Name

LESSON MASTER 7-7

Questions on SPUR Objectives
See pages 467–469 for objectives.

Properties Objective G

1. Let $S(n)$ be a sentence in n. Suppose that $S(1)$ is false. Also suppose that for all integers $k \geq 1$, the assumption that $S(1), S(2), \ldots S(k-1), S(k)$ are all false implies that $S(k+1)$ is also false. What can you conclude? Explain your answer.
   Sample: It is true that $S(n)$ is false for all integers n. The Strong Form of Mathematical Induction requires a statement of truth.

In 2–4, use the Strong Form of Mathematical Induction.

2. Let a be the sequence defined by
$$\begin{cases} a_1 = bq \\ a_2 = cq \\ a_{k+1} = da_k + ea_{k-1}\ \forall\ k \geq 2, \end{cases}$$
   where $b, c, d, e,$ and q are all integers. Prove that q is a factor of every term of the sequence.
   Sample: By definition q is a factor of a_n for $n = 1$ and $n = 2$. Assume that q is a factor of $a_1, a_2, \ldots$, and a_k for $k \geq 2$. Then $a_k = rq$ for some integer r, and $a_{k-1} = sq$, for some integer s. So, $a_{k+1} = da_k + ea_{k-1} = drq + esq = (dr + es)q$; and thus q is a factor of a_{k+1}. So, the assumption that q is a factor of $a_1, a_2, \ldots$, and a_k implies that q is a factor of a_{k+1}.

Name

► **LESSON MASTER 7-7** *page 2*

Sample proofs are given.

3. Let a be the sequence defined by
$$\begin{cases} a_1 = 7q \\ a_2 = 13q^2 \\ a_{k+1} = 4qa_k + 10q^2a_{k-1}\ \forall\ k \geq 2, \end{cases}$$
   where q is an integer.
   Prove that q^n is a factor of $a_n\ \forall\ n \geq 1$.
   For $S(n)$ use $S(n)$: q^n is a factor of a_n. $S(1)$: $a_1 = 7q$ is true. $S(2) = a_2 = 13q^2$ is true. $S(k)$: $a_k = 4qa_{k-1} + 10q^2a_{k-2}$ is true for $k = 2, 3, \ldots k$. $S(k+1) = 4qa_k + 10q^2a_{k-1} = 4q \cdot q^k p(q) + 10q^2q^{k-1}r(q)$, where $p(q)$ and $r(q)$ are the other factors, $= q^{k+1}(4p(q) + 10r(q))$. So by the Strong Form of the Principle of Mathematical Induction, $S(n)$ is true for all n.

4. Let b be the sequence defined by
$$\begin{cases} b_1 = 1 \\ b_2 = 2 \\ b_{k+1} = k(b_k + b_{k-1})\ \forall\ k \geq 2. \end{cases}$$
   Prove that $b_n = n!$ for all positive integers n.
   $b_1 = 1 = 1!$, $b_2 = 2 = 2 \cdot 1 = 2!$, so $b_n = n!$ for $n = 1$ and $n = 2$.
   Assume that $b_i = i!$ for $i = 1, 2, \ldots, k$. Then, $b_{k+1} = k(b_k + b_{k-1}) = k(k! + (k-1)!) = k(k(k-1)! + (k-1)!) = k(k-1)!(k+1) = k!(k+1) = (k+1)!$. Thus, the assumption that the statement is true for all positive integers less than $k+1$ implies that the statement is true for $k+1$.

Name

LESSON MASTER 7-8

Questions on SPUR Objectives
See pages 467–469 for objectives.

Uses Objective I

In 1–3, use the specified algorithm to arrange the given list in increasing order. Show all intermediate steps.

1. 5, 0, -1, 3 (Bubblesort)

3	5	5
-1	3	3
0	-1	0
5	0	-1

   -1, 0, 3, 5

2. $\frac{3}{2}$, -2, 1, 3, 2, $\frac{5}{2}$, 0 (Bubblesort)

0	after 1st Pass	final
$\frac{5}{2}$	0	$\frac{5}{2}$
2	$\frac{5}{2}$	2
3	2	$\frac{3}{2}$
1	$\frac{3}{2}$	1
-2	1	0
$\frac{3}{2}$	-2	-2

   -2, 0, 1, $\frac{3}{2}$, 2, $\frac{5}{2}$, 3

3. 10, -2, 9, 11, 4, -3, 7 (Quicksort)

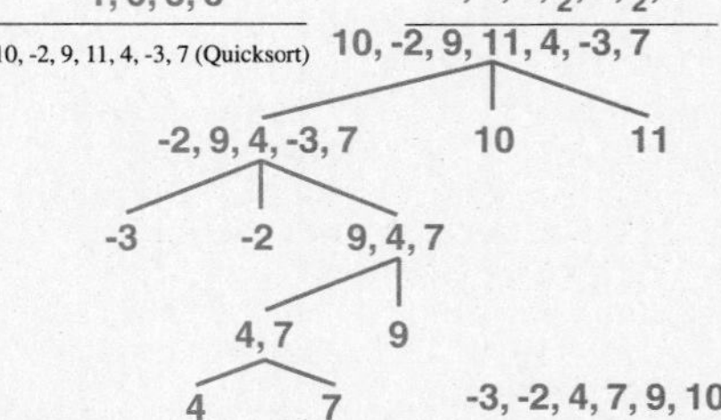

   -3, -2, 4, 7, 9, 10, 11

4. What is the maximum number of passes needed for the Bubblesort algorithm to arrange a list of n numbers in increasing order? $n - 1$

5. Refer to the description of the Quicksort algorithm on page 452. Suppose that you want to modify the algorithm so that it will arrange a list L of numbers in decreasing order. What change(s) would you make in the algorithm?
   In step 2, place numbers that are greater than or equal to f in L_ℓ and those that are less than f in L_r. Then place f between L_ℓ and L_r.

Name

LESSON MASTER 8-1

Questions on SPUR Objectives
See pages 547–549 for objectives.

Skills Objective A

In 1–3, give the real part and the imaginary part of the complex number.

1. $18 - 13i$ real 18 imaginary -13
2. $-i$ real 0 imaginary -1
3. $\sqrt{7}$ real $\sqrt{7}$ imaginary 0

In 4 and 5, write the complex number as an ordered pair.

4. $7 + 9i$ (7, 9)
5. $-i + \sqrt{5}$ $(\sqrt{5}, -1)$

In 6 and 7, write the complex number in $a + bi$ form.

6. (0, -8) $-8i$
7. $\left(-\frac{2}{3}, 1\right)$ $-\frac{2}{3} + i$

Skills Objective B

In 8–13, perform the indicated operation and write the answer in $a + bi$ form.

8. $(6 - i) - (10 + 7i)$ $-4 - 8i$
9. $(1 + 6i)(3 - 4i)$ $27 + 14i$
10. $\frac{\sqrt{-72}}{3}$ $2\sqrt{2}i$
11. $\frac{9 - 2i}{2 + 5i}$ $\frac{8}{29} - \frac{49}{29}i$
12. $\frac{7i}{2 + 2i} + 1 - 12i$ $\frac{11}{4} - \frac{41}{4}i$
13. $(-5 + 8i)^2$ $-39 - 80i$

In 14 and 15, solve the equation and express the solution in $a + bi$ form.

14. $-5 + 6i = v + 8 - i$ $v = -13 + 7i$
15. $w^2 = -19$ $w = \pm\sqrt{19}i$

Properties Objective F

16. Verify that $2 - i$ is a solution of $z^2 - 4z + 5 = 0$.
$(2 - i)^2 - 4(2 - i) + 5 = 4 - 4i + i^2 - 8 + 4i + 5 = 4 - 4i - 1 - 8 + 4i + 5 = 0$

17. Let $z = a + bi$ and $w = c + di$. Prove that $\overline{z + w} = \bar{z} + \bar{w}$.
$z + w = (a + c) + (b + d)i$, so $\overline{z + w} = (a + c) - (b + d)i$. But $\bar{z} = a - bi$ and $w = c - di$, so $\bar{z} + \bar{w} = (a - bi) + (c - di) = (a + c) + (b + d)i = \overline{z + w}$.

Name

▶ **LESSON MASTER 8-1** *page 2*

18. Prove that the fifth power of any imaginary number is imaginary.
For any imaginary number bi, $(bi)^5 = b^5(i^5) = b^5(i^2)(i^2)(i) = b^5(-1)(-1)(i) = b^5i$. Since b is real, b^5 is real and b^5i is imaginary. Thus, $(bi)^5$ is imaginary.

Uses Objective H

19. If the voltage in an AC circuit is $6 - 12i$ volts and the impedance is $2 + 4i$ ohms, find the current. $-\frac{9}{5} - \frac{12}{5}i$ amps

20. Two AC circuits with impedances of $-5 + 8i$ and $4 - 3i$ ohms are connected in series.
   a. Find the total impedance. $-1 + 5i$ ohms
   b. If the total current is $-\frac{1}{2} - \frac{5}{2}i$ amps, find the voltage. 13 volts

Representations Objective I

21. a. On the grid at the right, graph *EFGH*, where $E = 3 + i$, $F = -1 - i$, $G = -2 - 3i$, and $H = 2 - i$.
   b. Show that *EFGH* is a parallelogram.

Slope of $\overline{EF} = \frac{-1 - 1}{-1 - 3} = \frac{-2}{-4} = \frac{1}{2}$;

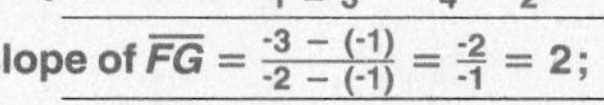
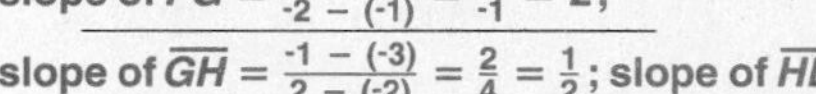

slope of $\overline{FG} = \frac{-3 - (-1)}{-2 - (-1)} = \frac{-2}{-1} = 2$; slope of $\overline{GH} = \frac{-1 - (-3)}{2 - (-2)} = \frac{2}{4} = \frac{1}{2}$; slope of $\overline{HE} = \frac{-1 - 1}{2 - 3} = \frac{-2}{-1} = 2$; since opposite sides are parallel, *EFGH* is a parallelogram.

22. Let $A = 1 + 2i$, $B = 5i$, and $C = -4$, and let $f(z) = (1 - i)z$. On the grid at the right, graph $\triangle ABC$ and $\triangle A'B'C'$, where $A' = f(A)$, $B' = f(B)$, and $C' = f(C)$. Label the vertices.

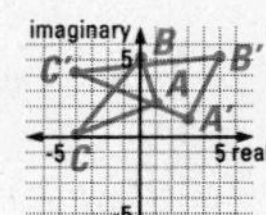

Name

LESSON MASTER 8-2

Questions on SPUR Objectives
See pages 547–549 for objectives.

Skills Objective C

In 1 and 2, find the rectangular coordinates for the point *P* whose polar coordinates are given.

1. [4, 300°] $(2, -2\sqrt{3})$
2. $\left[3\sqrt{2}, -\frac{3\pi}{4}\right]$ (-3, -3)

In 3 and 4, give one pair of polar coordinates for the (x, y) pair.

3. (-4, 5) [6.40, 128.66]
4. $(-\sqrt{3}, 1)$ $\left[2, \frac{7\pi}{6}\right]$

5. If $P = \left[r, \frac{5\pi}{3}\right] = (4, y)$, $r =$ 8 and $y =$ $-4\sqrt{3}$

6. Suppose $P = \left[6, \frac{7\pi}{4}\right]$. Give a different polar representation $[r, \theta]$ for *P* satisfying the given conditions.
   a. $r = 6$ 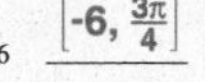 $\left[6, \frac{15\pi}{4}\right]$
   b. $r = -6$ 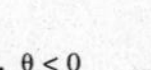 $\left[-6, \frac{3\pi}{4}\right]$
   c. $\theta < 0$ $\left[6, -\frac{\pi}{4}\right]$

Representations Objective I

7. Plot and label the following points on the polar grid at the right.
   a. $A = \left[3, \frac{\pi}{2}\right]$
   b. $B = [-2, -120°]$
   c. $C = \left[-4, -\frac{\pi}{6}\right]$
   d. $D = [0, \pi]$

8. Give two polar representations of the point *P* graphed below.

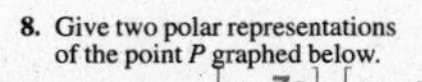

Samples: $\left[3, \frac{7\pi}{6}\right]$, $\left[-3, \frac{\pi}{6}\right]$

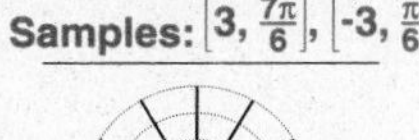
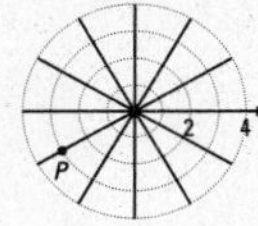

9. On the polar grid below, sketch all solutions to these equations.
   a. $r = 2.5$
   b. $\theta = -\frac{5\pi}{4}$

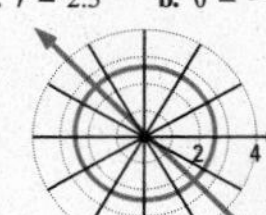

Name

LESSON MASTER 8-3

Questions on SPUR Objectives
See pages 547–549 for objectives.

Skills Objective A

In 1–4, the complex number is written in binomial, rectangular, polar, or trigonometric form. Write it in the other three forms.

1. $-4 + 2i$
   (-4, 2)
   $[2\sqrt{5}, 153.43°]$
   $2\sqrt{5}(\cos 153.43° + i \sin 153.43°)$

2. [1.4, 80°]
   $1.4(\cos 80° + i \sin 80°)$
   (0.24, 1.38)
   $0.24 + 1.38i$

3. $\frac{\sqrt{2}}{2}$
   $\left(\frac{\sqrt{2}}{2}, 0\right)$
   $\left[\frac{\sqrt{2}}{2}, 0\right]$
   $\frac{\sqrt{2}}{2}(\cos 0 + \sin 0)$

4. $3\left(\cos -\frac{\pi}{3} + i \sin -\frac{\pi}{3}\right)$
   $\left[3, -\frac{\pi}{3}\right]$
   $\left(1.5, \frac{-3\sqrt{3}}{2}\right)$
   $1.5 - \frac{3\sqrt{3}}{2}i$

In 5 and 6, give the modulus and an argument θ for the complex number.

5. $12 - 9i$ modulus = 15; $\theta \approx -36.87°$
6. $\sqrt{3}c + ci$ where $c > 0$ modulus = 2c; $\theta = \frac{\pi}{6}$

Skills Objective B

In 7–9, find *zw*. Express the result in the form of the given numbers.

7. $z = \sqrt{5}\left(\cos \frac{3\pi}{4} + i \sin \frac{3\pi}{4}\right)$, $w = \sqrt{2}\left(\cos \frac{\pi}{12} + i \sin \frac{\pi}{12}\right)$ $\sqrt{10}\left(\cos \frac{5\pi}{6} + \sin \frac{5\pi}{6}\right)$

8. $z = [4, 125°]$, $w = [3, 35°]$ [12, 160°]

9. Find z so that $z \cdot [12, 20°] = [6, 170]$. $\left[\frac{1}{2}, 150°\right]$

Properties Objective F

10. Let $z = [r, \theta]$. If z is multiplied by $w = [s, \phi]$, describe the changes to z.
size change of magnitude s and rotation of ϕ

Name

▶ **LESSON MASTER 8-3** *page 2*

11. Use polar coordinates to show that the square of any imaginary number is a real number.

Imaginary number $0 + bi = \left[b, \frac{\pi}{2}\right]$, so $(0 + bi)^2 =$

$\left[b, \frac{\pi}{2}\right]^2 = \left[b, \frac{\pi}{2}\right] \cdot \left[b, \frac{\pi}{2}\right] = [b^2, \pi] = -b^2 + 0i =$

a real number.

Representations Objective I

12. Let $A = -1 + 4i$, $B = -3 - 2i$, and $C = 1 - 2i$.
   a. Sketch $\triangle ABC$ in the complex plane.
   b. What kind of triangle is $\triangle ABC$? isosceles
   c. Prove your answer to part b.

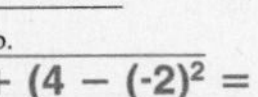

$AB = \sqrt{(-1 - (-3))^2 + (4 - (-2))^2} =$

$\sqrt{40}$; $AC = \sqrt{(-1 - 1)^2 + (4 - (-2))^2} = \sqrt{40}$;

since $AB = AC$, $\triangle ABC$ is isosceles.

13. Refer to the multiplication illustrated at the right. Give w in polar form.

$[2, 60°]$

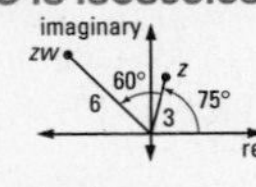

14. a. Graph $\triangle PQR$ in the complex plane where $P = 1 + i$, $Q = -2$, and $R = -1 - 2i$.
   b. Multiply each vertex by $z = 2 + i$ and graph the result as $\triangle P'Q'R'$.
   c. Find the ratio of similitude of $\triangle P'Q'R'$ to $\triangle PQR$ and relate it to the Geometric Multiplication Theorem.

Ratio of similitude $= \sqrt{5}$; Multiplication by $2 + i = [\sqrt{5}, 25.57°]$ multiplies the modulus by $\sqrt{5}$.

   d. How does the argument of R' compare to that of R? Use the Geometric Multiplication Theorem to explain your answer.

It is 25.57° greater; multiplication by $2 + i = [\sqrt{5}, 25.57°]$ increases the argument by 25.57°.

Name

LESSON MASTER 8-4

Questions on SPUR Objectives
See pages 547–549 for objectives.

Representations Objective J

In 1–4, sketch the graph of the polar equation and identify the type of curve obtained.

1. $\theta = -120°$ line

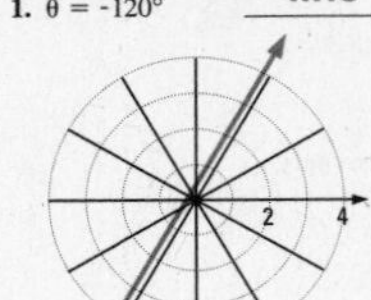

2. $r = \frac{7}{2}$ circle

3. $r = 3 + 3 \sin \theta$ cardioid

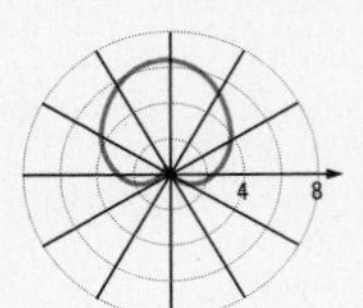

4. $r \cos \theta = -4$ line

Name

▶ **LESSON MASTER 8-4** *page 2*

5. a. Sketch the rectangular graph of the equation $r = 2 \cos \theta - 1$, $0 \le \theta \le 2\pi$.

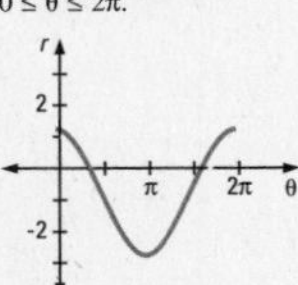

   b. Use the rectangular graph in part a to sketch its polar graph.

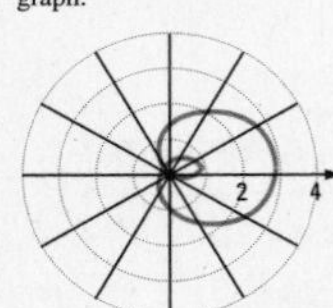

   c. Identify the type of curve in part b. limacon

6. a. Sketch the graph of $r = 3 \sin \theta$.
   b. Prove that the graph is a circle and find its center and radius.

$r = 3 \sin \theta = 3\frac{y}{r}$, so $r^2 = 3y$. Since $r^2 = x^2 + y^2$, $3y = x^2 + y^2$, or $x^2 + y^2 - 3y = 0$. Completing the square yields $x^2 + \left(y^2 - 3y + \frac{9}{4}\right) = \frac{9}{4}$, or $x^2 + \left(y - \frac{3}{2}\right)^2 = \left(\frac{3}{2}\right)^2$.

The center is $\left(0, \frac{3}{2}\right)$, and the radius is $\frac{3}{2}$.

7. Describe the polar graph of $r = k \cos \theta$.

Circle with center $\left(\frac{k}{2}, 0\right)$ and radius $\left|\frac{k}{2}\right|$

Name

LESSON MASTER 8-5

Questions on SPUR Objectives
See pages 547–549 for objectives.

Skills Objective J

In 1–4, sketch the graph of the polar equation and identify the type of curve obtained.

1. $r = 3 \sin 4\theta$ rose curve

2. $r = 2\theta + 1$, $0 \le \theta \le 2\pi$ spiral of Archimedes

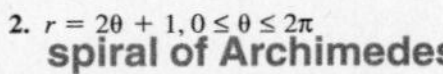

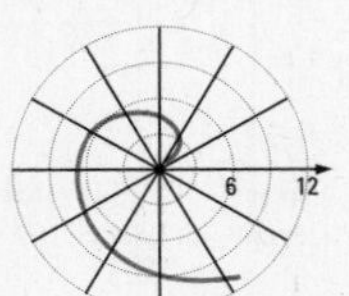

3. $r = (1.5)^\theta$, $0 \le \theta \le 2\pi$ logarithmic spiral

4. $r = 2 \cos 2\theta$ rose curve

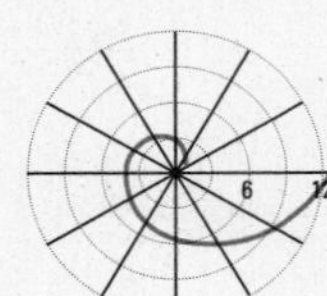

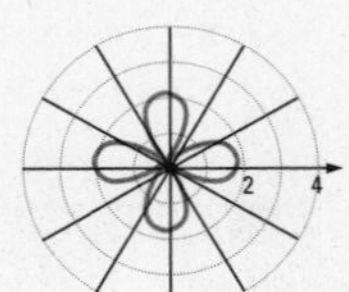

Name

▶ **LESSON MASTER 8-5** *page 2*

5. a. Graph the curve $r = 4 \cos 3\theta$.

b. Describe its reflection symmetry.
over the polar axis

c. Prove that your answer to part b is correct.
If $[r, \theta]$ is on the graph, $r = 4 \cos 3\theta$. $4 \cos 3\theta = 4 \cos (-3\theta) = 4 \cos (3 \cdot -\theta)$. So, $r = 4 \cos (3 \cdot -\theta)$, and $[r, -\theta]$ is on the graph.

6. a. Write a polar equation for a 4-leafed rose with leaves of length 3.5 that is symmetric over the line $\theta = \frac{\pi}{2}$.
$r = 3.5 \sin 2\theta$

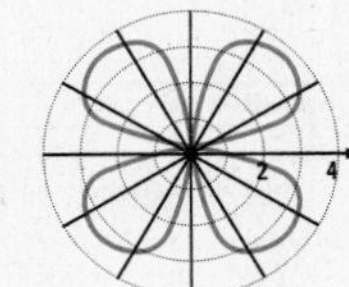

b. Graph this curve.

7. Consider the polar graph of the equation $r = a \cos n\theta$.

a. If n is a positive even integer, how many leaves does the curve have? $2n$

b. If n is a positive odd integer, how many leaves does the curve have? n

c. What is the length of each petal? a

Name

LESSON MASTER 8-6

Questions on SPUR Objectives
See pages 547–549 for objectives.

Skills Objective D

In 1–3, use DeMoivre's Theorem to compute the power. Write your answers in the same form as the base.

1. $\left[-4, \frac{\pi}{4}\right]^6$ $\left[4096, \frac{3\pi}{2}\right]$

2. $(2 - 2\sqrt{3}i)^{11}$ $2{,}097{,}152 + 2{,}097{,}152\sqrt{3}i$

3. $\left[3\left(\cos \frac{\pi}{3} + i \sin \frac{\pi}{3}\right)\right]^5$ $243\left(\cos \frac{5\pi}{3} + i \sin \frac{5\pi}{3}\right)$

In 4 and 5, write the answer in $a + bi$ form.

4. A third root of a certain complex number z is $5(\cos 150° + i \sin 150°)$. Find z. $0 + 125i$

5. An eighth root of a certain complex number w is $\left[-1, \frac{\pi}{2}\right]$. Find w. $1 + 0i$

Properties Objective F

6. Let $z = [2, 8°]$ and $w = [3, 10°]$.

a. Write a polar representation of z^3. $[8, 24°]$

b. Write a polar representation of w^3. $[27, 30°]$

c. Verify that $(z \cdot w)^3 = z^3 \cdot w^3$.
$(z \cdot w) = [2, 8°] \cdot [3, 10°] = [6, 18°]$, so $(z \cdot w)^3 = [6, 18°]^3 = [216, 54°] \cdot (z^3 \cdot w^3) = [8, 24°] \cdot [27, 30°] = [216, 54°]$. Therefore, $(z \cdot w)^3 = z^3 \cdot w^3$.

7. Let $z = [r, \theta]$. Prove that $(z^m)^n = z^{mn}$ for all positive integers m and n.
$z^m = [r, \theta]^m = [r^m, m\theta]$, so $(z^m)^n = [r^m, m\theta]^n = [r^{mn}, mn\theta]$. But, $z^{mn} = [r, \theta]^{mn} = [r^{mn}, mn\theta]$. Therefore, $(z^m)^n = z^{mn}$.

Name

▶ **LESSON MASTER 8-6** *page 2*

Representations Objective K

8. Give the polar coordinates of z^1, z^2, z^3, z^4, and z^5, where the first four are graphed at the right.

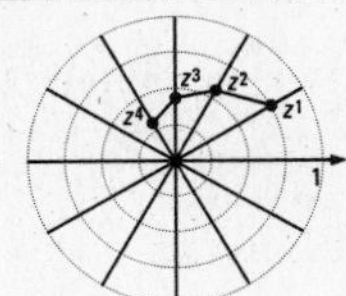

$z^1 = \left[0.75, \frac{\pi}{6}\right]$

$z^2 = \left[0.56, \frac{\pi}{3}\right]$

$z^3 = \left[0.42, \frac{\pi}{2}\right]$

$z^4 = \left[0.32, \frac{2\pi}{3}\right]$

$z^5 = \left[0.24, \frac{5\pi}{6}\right]$

9. a. Graph w^1, w^2, w^3, w^4, w^5, and w^6 when $w = 1.25\left(\cos \frac{\pi}{4} + i \sin \frac{\pi}{4}\right)$.

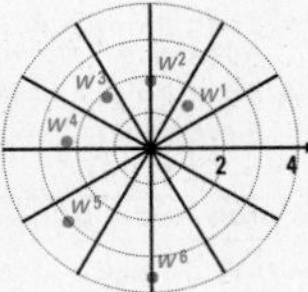

b. Are the points for this sequence of numbers getting closer to or farther from the origin?
farther from the origin

10. a. Let $v = \cos 30° + i \sin 30°$.

b. What is the value of $|v|$?
1

c. Graph the first eight points of the sequence of successive powers of v.

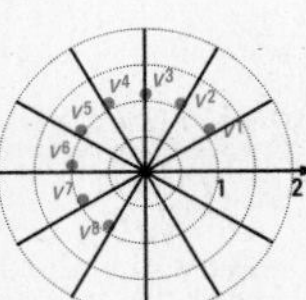

d. Is this sequence periodic? If so, how often do the terms repeat?
yes; every 12 terms

Name

LESSON MASTER 8-7

Questions on SPUR Objectives
See pages 547–549 for objectives.

Skills Objective D

In 1–3, find the roots. Write your answer in the same form as the given number.

1. cube roots of $-1000i$
$10i, 5\sqrt{3} - 5i, -5\sqrt{3} - 5i$

2. fifth roots of $243\left(\cos \frac{\pi}{2} + i \sin \frac{\pi}{2}\right)$
$3\left(\cos \frac{\pi}{10} + i \sin \frac{\pi}{10}\right), 3\left(\cos \frac{\pi}{2} + i \sin \frac{\pi}{2}\right), 3\left(\cos \frac{9\pi}{10} + i \sin \frac{9\pi}{10}\right), 3\left(\cos \frac{13\pi}{10} + i \sin \frac{13\pi}{10}\right), 3\left(\cos \frac{17\pi}{10} + i \sin \frac{17\pi}{10}\right)$

3. sixth roots of $[64, 300°]$
$[2, 50°], [2, 110°], [2, 170°], [2, 230°], [2, 290°], [2, 350°]$

4. The fourth power of a complex number z is -1. Find all possible values of z.
$\frac{\sqrt{2}}{2} + \frac{\sqrt{2}}{2}i, \frac{-\sqrt{2}}{2} + \frac{\sqrt{2}}{2}i, \frac{-\sqrt{2}}{2} - \frac{\sqrt{2}}{2}i, \frac{\sqrt{2}}{2} - \frac{\sqrt{2}}{2}i$

In 5–7, solve the equation over the set of complex numbers. Express the solution in $a + bi$ form.

5. $m^3 = -27$
$m = -3, m = \frac{3}{2} \pm \frac{3\sqrt{3}}{2}i$

6. $w^8 = 81$
$w = \pm\sqrt{3}, w = \frac{\sqrt{6}}{2} \pm \frac{i\sqrt{6}}{2}, w = \pm i\sqrt{3}, w = \frac{-\sqrt{6}}{2} \pm \frac{i\sqrt{6}}{2}$

7. $(z + 2)^8 = 81$ (Hint: Use your answer to Question 6.)
$z = -2 \pm \sqrt{3}, z = -2 \pm \sqrt{3}i, z = \left(-2 \pm \frac{\sqrt{6}}{2}\right) \pm \frac{\sqrt{6}}{2}i, z = \left(-2 - \frac{\sqrt{6}}{2}\right) \pm \frac{\sqrt{6}}{2}i$

Name

8. A sixth root of a complex number z is $\sqrt{3}(\cos 85° + \sin 85°)$.

   a. Find z. $27(\cos 150° + i \sin 150°)$

   b. Find the other sixth roots.

   $\sqrt{3}(\cos 25° + i \sin 25°)$, $\sqrt{3}(\cos 145° + i \sin 145°)$, $\sqrt{3}(\cos 205° + i \sin 205°)$, $\sqrt{3}(\cos 265° + i \sin 265°)$, $\sqrt{3}(\cos 325° + i \sin 325°)$

Representations Objective K

9. Graph the cube roots of -27 on a complex plane. (Refer to Question 5.)

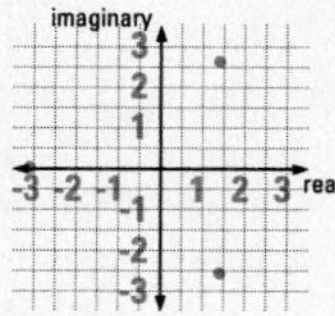

10. a. The fifth roots of $243\left(\cos \frac{\pi}{2} + i \sin \frac{\pi}{2}\right)$ form the vertices of what figure? (Refer to Question 2.) regular pentagon

    b. Graph the figure on a polar grid.

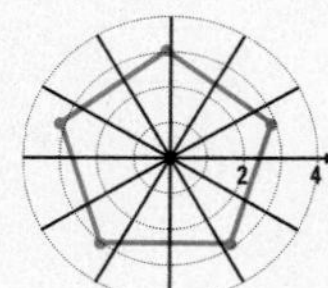

Name

LESSON MASTER 8-8 Questions on SPUR Objectives
See pages 547–549 for objectives.

Skills Objective E

In 1–3, a polynomial is given. a. Find all zeros of the polynomial. b. Give the multiplicities of the zeros.

1. $f(x) = (x + 3)^5(2x - 1)(x^2 + 1)$

   a. $-3, \frac{1}{2}, i, -i$ b. 5, 1, 1, 1

2. $g(t) = t^5 + 2t^3 - 3t$

   a. $0, 1, -1, \sqrt{3}i, -\sqrt{3}i$ b. 1, 1, 1, 1, 1

3. $h(x) = x^4 - 8x^3 + 20x^2 - 32x + 64$ given that $2i$ is a zero of $h(x)$.

   a. $2i, -2i, 4$ b. 1, 1, 2

4. Find a polynomial of degree 4 that has zeros 5, -5, i and $-i$.
   Sample: $f(x) = x^4 - 24x^2 - 25$

Properties Objective G

5. $p(x) = -2x^9 + 5x^6 + 7x^3 - 12$ has exactly __?__ complex zeros counting multiplicities. 9

6. A polynomial $f(x)$ has the following zeros: 3, 1, 0, $2i$, and $-2i$. The 3 and 0 each have multiplicity 2, and the other zeros have multiplicity 1.

   a. What is the degree of $f(x)$? 7

   b. Write a possible formula for $f(x)$ in factored form.
   Sample: $f(x) = (x - 3)^2(x - 1)(x^2)(x^2 + 4)$

7. An eighth-degree polynomial $q(x)$ has at least 2 simple zeros each with multiplicity 2.

   a. How many more zeros does $q(x)$ have, counting multiplicities? 4

   b. Write a possible formula for $f(x)$ in factored form.
   1 zero with multiplicity 4; 2 zeros with multiplicities 3 and 1; 2 zeros each with multiplicity 2; 3 zeros with multiplicities 2, 1 and 1; or 4 zeros each with multiplicity 1

Name

LESSON MASTER 8-9 Questions on SPUR Objectives
See pages 547–549 for objectives.

Skills Objective E

1. Two of the zeros of the polynomial $p(x) = x^4 - 6x^3 + 11x^2 - 6x + 10$ are $3 - i$ and i. Find the remaining zeros of $p(x)$. $3 + i, -i$

2. If i is a zero of the polynomial $f(y) = 4y^4 - 8y^3 + 9y^2 - 8y + 5$, find the remaining zeros of p(y) $i, 1 + \frac{i}{2}, 1 - \frac{i}{2}$

3. If $1 - i$ and $4i$ are zeros of a fourth degree polynomial $q(x)$ with real coefficients, give a possible formula for $q(x)$.
   Sample: $q(x) = x^4 - 2x^3 + 18x^2 - 32x + 32$

4. Find a polynomial $g(x)$ of smallest degree with real coefficients that has zeros $5 + i$ and 0.
   Sample: $g(x) = x^3 - 10x^2 + 26x$

Properties Objective G

5. If $2i$ is a zero of $h(x) = x^2 - 4xi - 4$, is $-2i$ necessarily the other zero? Explain.
   No; the Conjugates Zeros Theorem applies to polynomials with real coefficients.

6. Does there exist a polynomial $p(z)$ with real coefficients which has exactly three zeros: $5i$, $-5i$, and $3 + 2i$? Justify your answer.
   No; the Conjugates Zeros Theorem, $3 - 2i$ must also be a zero.

7. What is the smallest possible degree of a polynomial $f(x)$ with real coefficients if $-2 - 2i$, $-1 + i$, and 6 are zeros of $f(x)$? 5

8. Suppose $p(x)$ is a polynomial with real coefficients such that $p(x) = (x - 1 - 3i)q(x)$ where $q(x)$ is a polynomial. Give a factor of $q(x)$. $x - 1 + 3i$

9. Prove: If a polynomial with real coefficients has a nonreal zero z with multiplicity 2, then the degree of polynomial is at least 4.
   By the Conjugates Zeros Theorem, $\bar{z}$ is also a zero with multiplicity 2. Since there are at least 2 zeros each with multiplicity 2, the degree must be at least 4.

Name

LESSON MASTER  Questions on SPUR Objectives
See pages 596–599 for objectives.

Skills Objective A

1. Find the average rate of change in $q(x) = x^2 + 12$ from $x = -1$ to $x = 4$. 3

2. Find the average rate of change in $g(n) = 3n^3 - n^2 + 6$ over the interval $-2 \le n \le 2$. 12

3. Let $f(x) = 2x^2 + 3x$. Find the average rate of change in f over the given interval.

   a. From x to $x + \Delta x$ $4x + 3 + 2\Delta x$

   b. From 2 to 2.1 11.2

   c. From 2 to 2.01 11.02

Uses Objective D

4. A stone is thrown upward from a height of 2 meters with an initial velocity of 8 meters per second. If only the effect of gravity is considered, then the stone's height in meters after t seconds is given by the equation $h(t) = -4.9t^2 + 8t + 2$.

   a. Find a formula for the average velocity from $t = 1$ to $t = 1 + \Delta t$. $-1.8 - 4.9\Delta t$ m/sec

   b. Use your answer in part a to find the average from $t = 1$ to $t = 3\frac{1}{2}$. -14.05 m/sec

Representations Objective G

5. Refer to the graph of g at the right. Find the average rate of change in g over each interval.

   a. C to E $\frac{5}{2}$

   b. $0 \le x \le 35$ $\frac{2}{7}$

   Over what interval does the average rate of change in g have the given value?

   c. 0 B to D d. $-\frac{3}{2}$ A to C

6. Suppose $P = (3, 7)$ and $Q = (9, a)$ are points on the graph of the function h. If the average rate of change in h from $x = 3$ to $x = 9$ is $-\frac{5}{3}$, find a. $a = -3$

Name

LESSON MASTER 9-2

Questions on SPUR Objectives
See pages 596–599 for objectives.

Skills Objective B

In 1–3, find the derivative of the function at the given value of x.

1. $f(x) = 3x^2 + 4$; $x = 2$ — 12
2. $g(x) = -12x + 8$; $x = .5$ — -12
3. $h(x) = 22$; $x = 7$ — 0
4. Let $f(x) = -2x^2 + x - 3$
   a. Compute $f'(0)$. — 1
   b. Compute $f'(3)$. — -11

Uses Objective D

5. The typical number of mosquitoes $m(r)$ in hundreds of thousands in a certain county during the month of June is approximated by $m(r) = 8r - r^2$, where r is the average total rainfall for the month in inches.
   a. Find the derivative of m when $r = 2$. — 4
   b. What does your answer to part a mean?
   At a rainfall of 2 inches, the mosquito population is increasing at the rate of 400,000 mosquitoes per inch of rain.

Uses Objective E

6. The height h in feet of a small rocket t seconds after launch is approximated by $h(t) = 320t - 16t^2$.
   a. Find the instantaneous velocity at time $t = 5$. — 160 ft/sec
   b. Find the instantaneous velocity at time $t = 14$. — -128 ft/sec
   c. Find the instantaneous velocity at time $t = 10$. — 0 ft/sec
   d. At what time does the rocket reach its maximum height? — at $t = 10$ sec

Name

7. A pebble is dropped from a cliff 60 feet high. The height of the pebble in feet above the ground at time t seconds is given by $h(t) = -16t^2 + 60$.
   a. Find the instantaneous velocity of the pebble at time $t = 0.5$ second. — -16 ft/sec
   b. At what time does the pebble hit the ground? — ≈1.94 sec
   c. Find the instantaneous velocity of the ball at the moment just before it hits the ground. — ≈-61.97 ft/sec

Representations Objective H

8. Refer to the graph of f at the right. Give a value of x for which $f'(x)$ is **Samples:**
   a. positive. — -3
   b. negative. — 1
   c. zero. — -1

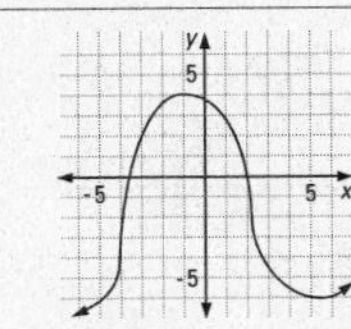

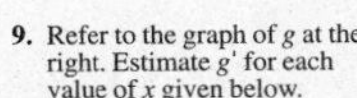

9. Refer to the graph of g at the right. Estimate g' for each value of x given below.
   a. $x = -4$ — 3
   b. $x = -1$ — 0
   c. $x = 4$ — $-\frac{3}{2}$

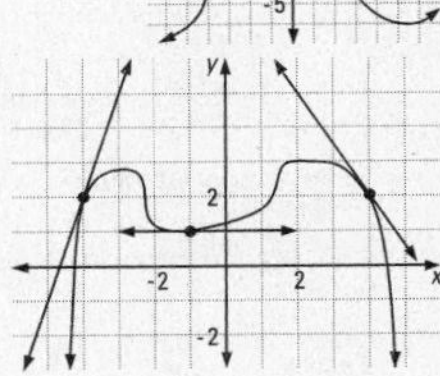

Precalculus and Discrete Mathematics © Scott Foresman Addison Wesley

Name

LESSON MASTER 9-3

Questions on SPUR Objectives
See pages 596–599 for objectives.

Skills Objective B

In 1–4, find the derivative of the function whose formula is given.

1. $f(y) = 7y^2$ — $14x$
2. $g(x) = 7x^2 - 3x$ — $14x - 3$
3. $p(v) = -4.5v$ — -4.5
4. $q(x) = 94$ — 0

Uses Objective D

5. If \$800 is invested at an interest rate of 7.5% compounded continuously, the amount in the account after t years is $A(t) = 800e^{0.075t}$ dollars. The derivative of A is $A' = 60e^{0.075t}$.
   a. Find the amount in the account after 5 years. — ≈\$1163.99
   b. Find $A'(5)$. — ≈\$87.30
   c. What does your answer to part b mean?
   At 5 years, the balance is increasing at a rate of about \$87.30 per year.

6. A certain flashlight is pointed directly at a wall. The area A in square inches of the illuminated area is $A(d) = \pi d^2 + 2\pi d + \pi$ where d is the flashlight's distance in inches from the wall.
   a. Find the illuminated area at $d = 3$ inches. — $16\pi \approx 50.27$ in²
   b. Find the derivative of $A(d)$. — $2\pi d + 2\pi$
   c. Find the instantaneous rate of change of the illuminated area when $d = 3$ inches. — $8\pi \approx 25.13$ in²/in.
   d. Find the illuminated area at $d = 6$ inches. — $49\pi \approx 153.94$ in²
   e. Calculate $A'(6)$. — $14\pi \approx 43.98$ in²/in.
   f. What does your answer to part e mean?
   The instantaneous rate of change of the illuminated area when the flashlight is 6 inches from the wall is $14\pi \frac{\text{in}^2}{\text{in.}}$

Precalculus and Discrete Mathematics © Scott Foresman Addison Wesley

Name

Uses Objective E

7. A particle moves so that the distance s traveled in meters at time t seconds is given by $s(t) = t^2 + 5t - 4$.
   a. Find the average velocity between 3 and 4 seconds. — 12 m/sec
   b. Find the instantaneous velocity of the particle at time $t = 8$. — 21 m/sec
   c. What is the initial velocity of the particle (that is, at time $t = 0$ seconds)? — 5 m/sec

Representations Objective H

8. The function j is graphed at the right.
   a. Estimate the values of $j'(x)$ when $x = -5, -3, -2, 0, 1,$ 3 and 5. **Sample:**
   $j'(-5) \approx 3$; $j'(-3) \approx \frac{1}{6}$; $j'(-2) \approx 0$; $j'(0) \approx -2$; $j'(1) \approx -2$; $j'(3) \approx -\frac{3}{2}$; $j'(5) \approx -\frac{1}{3}$
   b. Use the information from part a and the graph of j to sketch a graph of j'.

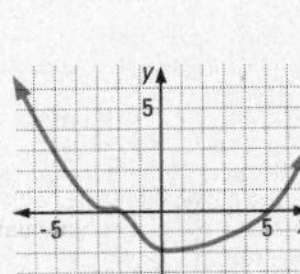

Precalculus and Discrete Mathematics © Scott Foresman Addison Wesley

Name

LESSON MASTER 9-4

Questions on SPUR Objectives
See pages 596–599 for objectives.

Skills Objective D

1. A bowl of hot soup is placed on a table to cool. The temperature in degrees Celsius of the object after t minutes is given by $C(t) = 65e^{-0.198t} + 20$. For this function, $C' = -12.87e^{-0.198t}$ and $C'' = 2.56e^{-0.198t}$.
   a. In what units is $C'(t)$? **degrees/min**
   b. In what units is $C''(t)$? **degrees/min^2**
   c. How fast is the temperature changing at time $t = 4$ minutes? **-5.83°C/min**
   d. How fast is the rate of cooling changing at time $t = 4$ minutes? **1.16°C/min^2**
   e. Is the change in the rate of cooling at $t = 7$ minutes greater or less than at $t = 4$ minutes? **less**

Uses Objective E

2. A particle moves horizontally so that its position in feet to the right of the starting point at time t seconds is given by $f(t) = -t^2 + 5t + 6$.
   a. At time $t = 8$ seconds, is the particle moving to the right, to the left, or stationary? **to the left**
   b. What is the speed of the object at time $t = 8$ seconds? **-11 ft/sec**
   c. What is the acceleration of the object at time $t = 8$ seconds? **-2 ft/sec^2**
   d. Is the acceleration increasing, decreasing, or staying the same at time $t = 8$ seconds? **staying the same**
3. A ball is thrown directly upward. Its height h in meters after t seconds is given by the equation $h(t) = -4.9t^2 + 28t + 2$.
   a. Find the instantaneous velocity at each time.
      i. 0 seconds **28 m/sec** ii. 3 seconds **-1.4 m/sec**
   b. Find the instantaneous acceleration at each time.
      i. 0 seconds **-9.8 m/sec^2** ii. 3 seconds **-9.8 m/sec^2**

Name

LESSON MASTER 9-5

Questions on SPUR Objectives
See pages 596–599 for objectives.

Skills Objective C

1. Suppose g is a function such that $g(x) = -\frac{2}{3}x^3 + 5x^2 - 12x$. Then $g'(x) = -2x^2 + 10x - 12$. Use the first derivative to find each.
   a. The interval(s) on which g is increasing. **$2 < x < 3$**
   b. The interval(s) on which g is decreasing. **$x < 1, x > 3$**
   c. The points at which g may have a relative maximum or minimum. **$\left(2, \frac{-28}{3}\right), (3, -9)$**
2. Suppose $f(x) = 3x^5 + 3x$. Then $f'(x) = 15x^4 + 3$. Is f increasing or decreasing on the set of all real numbers? Explain your answer.
   Increasing; $f'(x) > 0$ for all x, so f is everywhere increasing.

Uses Objective F

3. A rectangular pen adjacent to a shed is to be enclosed with 40 feet of fencing. What should the dimensions of the pen be in order to maximize the area? **10 ft by 20 ft**

Representations Objective I

4. Consider the function f graphed at the right.
   a. On what interval(s) is $f'(x)$ positive? **$0 < x < 1;\ 2 < x < 4$**
   b. On what interval(s) is $f'(x)$ negative? **$x < 0;\ 1 < x < 2;\ x > 4$**
   c. For what values of x is $f'(x) = 0$? **0, 1, 2, 4**
5. The derivative h' of a function h is graphed at the right. Describe the values of x where
   a. h is increasing. **$0 < x < 2,\ x > 6$**
   b. h is decreasing. **$x < 0,\ 2 < x < 6$**
   c. h has a relative maximum or minimum. **$x = 0$; $x = 2$; $x = 6$**

Name

LESSON MASTER 10-1

Questions on SPUR Objectives
See pages 653–655 for objectives.

Skills Objective A

In 1–8, describe the essential features of the problem in the question. You do not have to answer the question.

1. Mrs. Kerrigan returned from a trip to Spain with 12 different souvenirs. She wants to give one to each of her three children. In how many different ways can she do this?
   ordered symbols, repetition not allowed
2. The combination lock on a briefcase has three dial wheels with the digits from 0 through 5 on each wheel. How many different lock combinations are possible?
   ordered symbols, repetition allowed
3. A social committee of five members is to be chosen from the 44-member Student Council. In how many ways can the committee be formed?
   unordered symbols, repetition not allowed
4. The school store has construction paper in eight different colors. Angelo needs to buy five sheets for an art project. How many different selections are possible?
   unordered symbols, repetition allowed
5. How many integers from 100 to 999 have at least one digit that is a zero?
   ordered symbols, repetition allowed
6. How many different 3-letter code words, such as *SOS*, can be made from the letters *A, B, G, M, O, S, T, X*?
   ordered symbols, repetition allowed
7. Harriet wants to hang 7 skirts and 13 blouses on a rod in her closet. How many different arrangements are possible if she keeps the skirts together and the blouses together?
   ordered symbols, repetition not allowed
8. How many different ways can 5 cards be chosen from a deck of 52 cards?
   unordered symbols, repetition not allowed

Name

LESSON MASTER 10-2

Questions on SPUR Objectives
See pages 653–655 for objectives.

Uses Objective F

1. A vendor sells belts in s different sizes, c different colors, and w different widths. How many different kinds of belts are available? **scw kinds**
2. Can Doreen wear a different outfit every day of the year if she chooses from 10 pairs of slacks, 12 blouses, and 3 pairs of shoes? **No**
3. a. How many integers from 100 to 999 have at least one digit that is a zero? **171 integers**
   b. If one of the integers in part a is chosen at random, what is the probability that its first and last digits are the same? **$\frac{9}{171} \approx 0.0526$**
4. How many different 5-letter code words can be made from the letters *C, E, G, M, R, S, U*, and *W* satisfying the indicated condition?
   a. The letters can be repeated. **32,768 words**
   b. The letters cannot be repeated. **6,720 words**
   c. The first letter must be *E* and the last must be *S*, with no repetition allowed. **120 words**
5. How many c-letter codes can be created from l different letters if the letters can be repeated? **l^c words**
6. How many different license plates can be made if three letters are to be followed by four digits, but the letters *I* and *O* are not allowed? **138,240,000 plates**
7. In the computer program below, how many numbers does line 50 ask to be printed? **192 numbers**

```
10 FOR I = 0 TO 5
20 FOR J = 1 TO 4
30 FOR K = 2 TO 9
40 SUM = I + J + K
50 PRINT SUM
60 NEXT K
70 NEXT J
80 NEXT I
90 END
```

Name

Representations Objective I

8. a. Fran and Bob are planning to play a game that has four game pieces: a ship, a plane, a car, and a train engine. Each player must choose one piece. Draw a possibility tree to show the number of different ways Fran and Bob can pick their pieces.

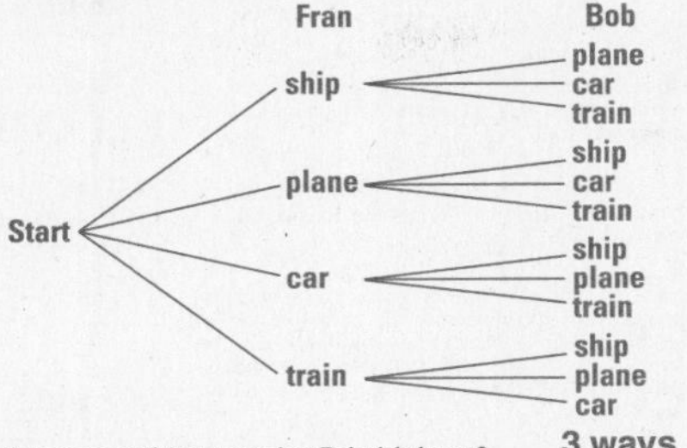

b. In how many of these ways does Bob pick the car? 3 ways

9. For the conference championship, the Darts will play the Jolts in a series of games. The first team to win either three games in all or two games in a row is the champion. Draw a possibility tree to show the possible outcomes.

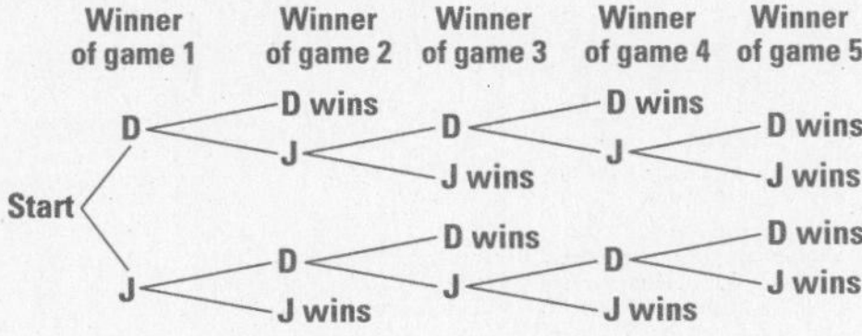

Name

LESSON MASTER 10-3

Questions on SPUR Objectives
See pages 653–655 for objectives.

Skills Objective B

In 1–4, evaluate the expression.

1. $P(11, 9)$ 19,958,400
2. $P(20, 3)$ 6,840
3. ${}_7P_4$ 840
4. $0!$ 1
5. Find a so that $P(22, a) = \frac{22!}{15!}$ $a = 7$

Skills Objective D

6. If $n! = n \cdot 18!$, what is n? 19

7. a. Verify that $P(9, 8) = P(9, 9) = 9!$.

$P(9, 8) = \frac{9!}{(9-8)!} = \frac{9!}{1!} = 9!$; $P(9, 9) = \frac{9!}{(9-9)!} = \frac{9!}{0!} = \frac{9!}{1} = 9!$

b. Generalize the results from part a.

$P(n, n-1) = P(n, n) = n!$

Skills Objective F

6. Each year Clyborn High School has a sock hop, a junior prom, and a senior prom. In how many ways can these three school dances be scheduled from a set of fourteen available Saturdays? 2,184 ways

7. A photographer is arranging three sets of triplets in a row. If each set of triplets is not to be separated, in how many ways can the nine people be arranged? 1,296 ways

8. Using the digits from 0 to 9, how many 4-digit personal identification numbers (PIN) are possible under the given conditions?

a. The digits can repeat. 10,000 numbers

b. The digits cannot repeat. 5,040 numbers

c. The first digit must be odd, the rest even, and repetition is allowed. 625 numbers

d. The first digit must be odd, the rest even, and repetition is not allowed. 300 numbers

Name

LESSON MASTER 10-4

Questions on SPUR Objectives
See pages 653–655 for objectives.

Skills Objective B

In 1–4, evaluate the expression.

1. $C(15, 6)$ 5,005
2. $C(9, 9)$ 1
3. ${}_{10}C_5$ 252
4. $\binom{7}{3}$ 35
5. Find a and b so that $C(a, 5) = \frac{11!}{b!5!}$ $a = 11, b = 6$
6. Find j and k so that $C(6, 4) \cdot 4! = P(j, k)$. $j = 6, k = 4$

Skills Objective D

7. Show that $C(n, r) \cdot r! = P(n, r)$

$C(n, r) \cdot r! = \frac{n!}{r!(n-r)!} \cdot r! = \frac{n!}{(n-r)!} = P(n, r)$

8. a. Verify that $C(10, 3) = C(10, 7)$.

$C(10, 3) = \frac{10!}{3!7!} = 120$; $C(10, 7) = \frac{10!}{7!3!} = 120$

b. Generalize the results from part a.

$C(n, r) = C(n, n-r)$

Skills Objective G

9. The high school band has been rehearsing seven pieces. The band director needs to select two of them for an audition tape. In how many ways can this choice be made? 21 ways

10. At a family party, 18 people need to be seated at two tables, a table for eight and a table for ten. In how many ways can the table assignments be made? 43,758 ways

11. Rigio's deluxe pizza offers any three toppings from a choice of nine. Armando's deluxe pizza allows any four toppings from a choice of eight. Which pizzeria offers the greater number of different possible deluxe pizzas? Rigio's

12. Lorna needs to pack 5 blouses and 4 pairs of slacks for a vacation. She has 14 blouses and 8 pairs of slacks to choose from. In how many different ways can she choose her clothes for the trip? 140,140 ways

Name

LESSON MASTER 10-5

Questions on SPUR Objectives
See pages 653–655 for objectives.

Skills Objective C

1. a. What combination yields the coefficient of x^9y^{13} in the expansion of $(x + y)^{22}$? $\binom{22}{13}$

b. What is this coefficient? 497, 420

2. What is the coefficient of xy^7 in the expansion of $(x + 4y)^8$? 131,072

3. Write the following expression as the power of a binomial: $\sum_{k=0}^{6} \binom{6}{k}(4x)^{6-k}y^k$. $(4x + y)^6$

In 4–6, expand using the Binomial Theorem.

4. $(x + y)^5$

$x^5 + 5x^4y + 10x^3y^2 + 10x^2y^3 + 5xy^4 + y^5$

5. $(2a - 5b)^4$

$16a^4 - 160a^3b + 600a^2b^2 - 1{,}000\,ab^3 + 625b^4$

6. $(x + 5)^7$

$x^7 + 35x^6 + 525x^5 + 4{,}375x^4 + 21{,}875x^3 + 65{,}625x^2 + 109{,}375x + 78{,}125$

7. Find the sixth power of $(1 + i)$. $-8i$

8. Find the tenth term of $(x + y)^{18}$. $48{,}620x^9y^9$

9. Find the first term of $(3x - y)^{10}$. $59{,}049x^{10}$

10. Find the last term of $(-2x + y)^5$. y^5

11. The coefficients of which terms of the expansion of $(x + y)^{12}$ are the same?

1st and 13th, 2nd and 12th, 3rd and 11th, 4th and 10th, 5th and 9th, 6th and 8th

Name

LESSON MASTER 10-6 — **Questions on SPUR Objectives** See pages 653–655 for objectives.

Properties Objective E

1. What combination yields the number of 5-element subsets that can be formed from a set with 9 elements? $\binom{9}{5}$

2. How is ${}_{10}C_7 + {}_{10}C_8 + {}_{10}C_9 + {}_{10}C_{10}$ related to the number of subsets that can be formed from a set? It gives the number of subsets containing at least 7 elements that can be formed from a 10-element set.

Uses Objective G

3. In how many ways is it possible to obtain at least three heads in 11 tosses of a coin? 1,981 ways

4. In how many ways is it possible to obtain at least six tails in eight tosses of a coin? 37 ways

5. A pizzeria offers ten different pizza toppings. In how many different ways can a pizza be topped if at least one topping is used? 1,023 ways

Uses Objective H

6. A long multiple-choice text is designed so that each of the choices, *A*, *B*, *C*, and *D*, is the correct answer 25% of the time. A computer randomly assigns the correct answer to *A*, *B*, *C*, and *D* in each question. What is the probability that in the first ten questions *A* is the correct answer for five questions? ≈ 0.058

7. In a board game, a player must roll a 1 or a 2 on a die to attain a bonus. In five rolls of a fair die, what is the probability that the player will roll a 1 or a 2 at least once? ≈ 0.868

8. A cereal manufacturer has packaged a small toy in 8% of its boxes of cereal. Assuming that the boxes are randomly distributed to the stores, what is the probability that a purchase of four boxes will result in
   a. exactly four toys? ≈ 0.00004
   b. no toys? ≈ 0.7164
   c. at least one toy? ≈ 0.2836
   d. at least two toys? ≈ 0.0344

Name

LESSON MASTER 10-7 — **Questions on SPUR Objectives** See pages 653–655 for objectives.

Skills Objective G

In 1–3, give the number of different terms in each expansion.

1. $(x + y + z)^8$ 45 terms
2. $(w + x + y + z)^6$ 84 terms
3. $(2a - 5b + 3c - d + 8)^{12}$ 1,820 terms

4. In how many different ways can six passengers be distributed among the cars of a four-car commuter train? 84 ways

5. Benny's Bagels offers seven different varieties. How many different half-dozen selections can be made? 924 selections

6. Suppose a die is tossed ten times. An outcome is defined as a certain number of occurrences of each number. For example, one possible outcome is two 1s, zero 2s, two 3s, four 4s, one 5, and one 6. How many different outcomes are possible in the ten tosses? 3,003 outcomes

7. How many different solutions (a, b, c) are there to the equation $a + b + c = 15$ for which a, b, and c are all nonnegative integers? 136 solutions

8. How many positive integers less than 1000 have digits whose sum is 12? 91 integers

9. a. How many positive integers less than 10,000 have digits whose sum is 18? 1330 integers
   b. How many of the numbers in part a begin with a 4? 120 numbers
   c. How many of the numbers in part a have exactly one 9? 220 numbers

10. For Homecoming, a royal court of eight students was elected from the student body at large. The court was made up of one freshman, three sophomores, one junior, and three seniors. If each possible court is defined to be the number of freshmen, sophomores, juniors, and seniors that were elected, how many *other* different courts were possible? 164 courts

Name

LESSON MASTER 

Questions on SPUR Objectives See pages 713–717 for objectives.

Uses Objective E

1. Suppose the process of producing a high school musical involves the tasks listed in the table below.

Task	Description	Time Required (days)	Prerequisite Tasks
A	Choose musical	2	none
B	Negotiate royalty agreement	5	A
C	Hold cast tryouts	3	A
D	Hold orchestra auditions	1	A
E	Design set and costumes	5	A
F	Rehearse cast (without orchestra)	20	C
G	Rehearse orchestra (without cast)	15	D
H	Construct set, sew costumes	25	E
I	Rehearse cast with orchestra	10	F, G
J	Perform technical rehearsal	2	H, I
K	Perform dress rehearsal	1	J
L	Perform musical	4	B, K

   a. Sketch a digraph to represent the process.

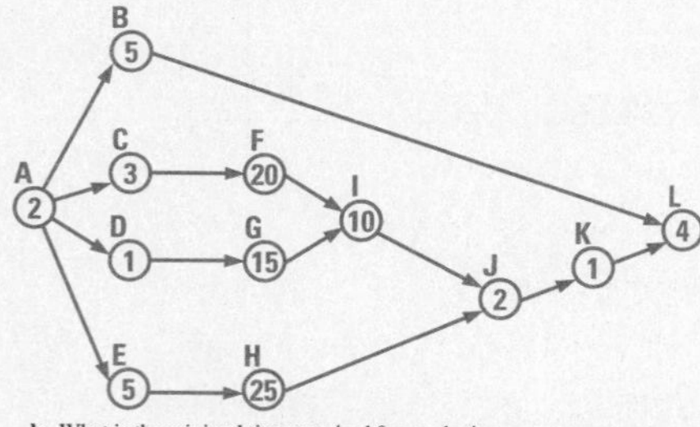

   b. What is the minimal time required for producing the musical through the last performance? 42 days

Name

2. In Brickton, 84% of the adult residents own their own homes and the rest rent. 58% of the homeowners favor a tax increase to pay for alley paving, while 18% of the renters favor this increase.
   a. Draw a probability tree to represent this situation.

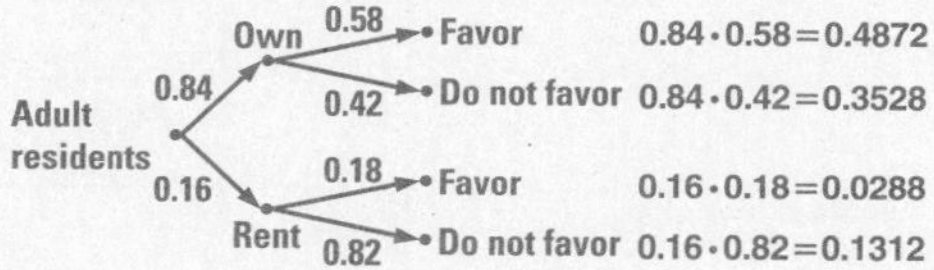

   b. What percent of adult residents who favor the tax increase to pay for alley paving? 51.6%
   c. If there are 17,400 adult residents, how many do not favor this tax increase? $\approx$8,422 residents
   d. If a randomly selected adult resident favors this tax increase, what is the probability that the resident is a renter? $= 5.6\%$

Uses Objective G

3. The segments of the grid at the right represent the streets of a section of a city, and the vertices represent the intersections.
   a. On the grid, draw a path that allows an ice cream truck to begin at *A* and end at *B* and visit each intersection exactly once. A sample is given.
   b. Is such a path possible that begins and ends at *A*? If so, draw it on the second grid. No

Name

LESSON MASTER 11-2

Questions on SPUR Objectives
See pages 713–717 for objectives.

Skills Objective A

In 1–4, draw a graph with the specified characteristics. Samples are given.

1. three vertices and four edges

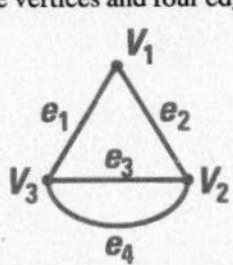
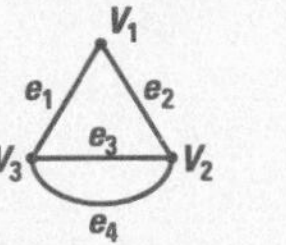

2. two vertices, a loop, and three parallel edges

3. three edges and four vertices, one of which is isolated

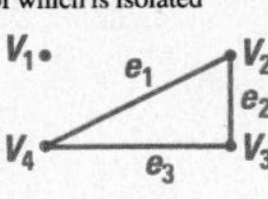

4. four vertices, four edges, and a crossing

5. Draw the graph G defined as follows:
(1) set of vertices: $\{v_1, v_2, v_3, v_4\}$
(2) set of edges: $\{e_1, e_2, e_3, e_4, e_5\}$
(3) edge-endpoint function:

edge	endpoints
e_1	$\{v_1, v_2\}$
e_2	$\{v_1, v_2\}$
e_3	$\{v_2, v_4\}$
e_4	$\{v_4\}$
e_5	$\{v_4\}$

Properties Objective B

6. a. What is a *simple graph*?
A graph with no loops and no parallel edges

b. Is the graph in Question 5 simple? Explain your answer.
No; it has both loops and parallel edges.

Name

▶ LESSON MASTER 11-2 *page 2*

7. Use the graph at the right.

a. Identify any loops.
e_5

b. Identify any isolated vertices.
v_6

c. Identify all vertices adjacent to v_5.
v_3, v_4

d. Identify all edges adjacent to e_3.
e_1, e_2, e_4, e_7

e. At the right, give the edge-endpoint function table for the graph.

edge	endpoints
e_1	$\{v_1, v_2\}$
e_2	$\{v_1, v_2\}$
e_3	$\{v_1, v_3\}$
e_4	$\{v_3, v_4\}$
e_5	$\{v_4\}$
e_6	$\{v_4, v_5\}$
e_7	$\{v_3, v_5\}$

Representations Objective I

8. Write the adjacency matrix for the directed graph below.

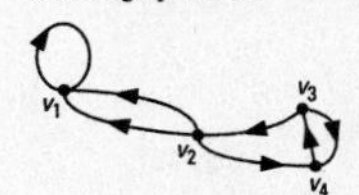

$$\begin{array}{c} \\ v_1 \\ v_2 \\ v_3 \\ v_4 \end{array} \begin{array}{c} v_1\ v_2\ v_3\ v_4 \\ \begin{bmatrix} 1 & 0 & 0 & 0 \\ 2 & 0 & 0 & 1 \\ 0 & 1 & 0 & 1 \\ 0 & 0 & 1 & 1 \end{bmatrix} \end{array}$$

9. Draw an undirected graph with the following adjacency matrix.

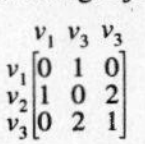

$$\begin{array}{c} \\ v_1 \\ v_2 \\ v_3 \end{array} \begin{array}{c} v_1\ v_3\ v_3 \\ \begin{bmatrix} 0 & 1 & 0 \\ 1 & 0 & 2 \\ 0 & 2 & 1 \end{bmatrix} \end{array}$$

Sample:

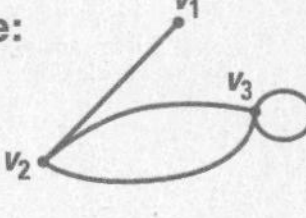

10. In the adjacency matrix for a simple graph, no element can be greater than what number? 1

Name

LESSON MASTER 11-3

Questions on SPUR Objectives
See pages 713–717 for objectives.

Skills Objective A

1. Draw a simple graph with five vertices of degrees 1, 2, 3, 3, and 3.
Sample:

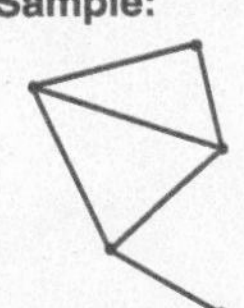

2. Draw a graph with three vertices of degrees 1, 6, and 1.
Sample:

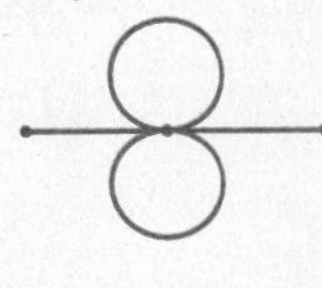

Properties Objective B

3. Refer to the graph at the right.

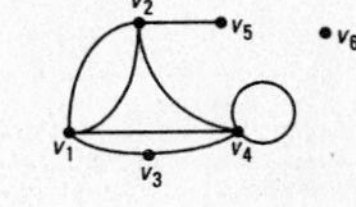

a. Give the degree of each vertex.
v_1: 4; v_2: 4; v_3: 2;
v_4: 5; v_5: 1; v_6: 0

b. Give the total degree of the graph.
16

4. A graph has five edges. What is its total degree? 10

5. *True or false.* The degree of any vertex is even. False

6. *True or false.* The total degree of any graph is even. True

7. *True or false.* Every graph has an odd number of vertices with even degree. False

8. *True or false.* Every graph has an even number of vertices with odd degree. True

Name

▶ LESSON MASTER 11-3 *page 2*

Properties Objective C

In 9 and 10, either draw a graph with the given properties, or explain why no such graph exists.

9. a simple graph with three vertices of degrees 1, 4, and 1
This graph does not exist, because vertices with the given degree could be drawn only if the vertex with degree 4 has a loop, which simple graphs do not allow.

10. a graph with six vertices of degrees 2, 2, 3, 3, 4, and 4
Sample:

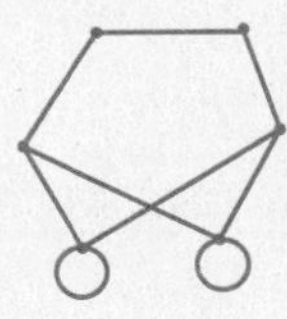

Uses Objective F

11. The Scholastic Bowl in each of five schools is scheduled to play every other team exactly once.

a. At the right, draw a graph to represent this situation.

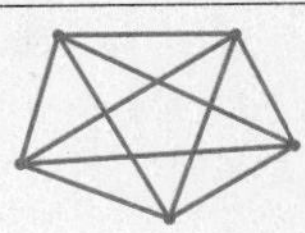

b. How many different pairings result?
10 pairings

12. At a bake-off, 19 contestants have baked their special cookie recipes. Is it possible for each contestant to sample the cookies of exactly five other contestants? Explain.
No; represent the situation as a graph. The 19 vertices each have degree 5, which contradicts the corollary stating that every graph has an even number of vertices of odd degree.

Name

LESSON MASTER 11-4

Questions on SPUR Objectives
See pages 713–717 for objectives.

Properties Objective B

1. Refer to the graph at the right. Describe, if possible. Samples given.
   a. a walk from v_2 to v_5 that is not a path.
   $v_2, e_1, v_1, e_2, v_2, e_1, v_1, e_7, v_5$
   b. a path from v_2 to v_6
   $v_2, e_4, v_3, e_{10}, v_7, e_9, v_6$
   c. a circuit starting at v_7 $v_1, e_{10}, v_3, e_5, v_4, e_6, v_5, e_8, v_6, e_9, v_7$
   d. an Euler circuit not possible

In 2–4, determine whether or not the graph is connected.

2. 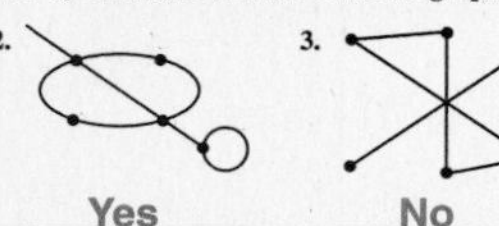 Yes
3. No
4. Yes

5. Consider the graph at the right.

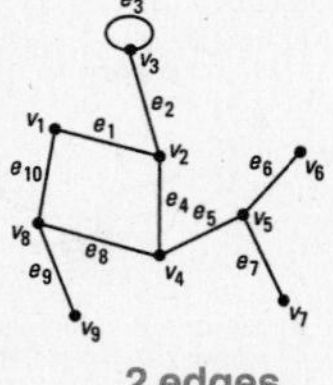

   a. If e_4 is removed, would the graph remain connected?
   Yes
   b. Give each edge whose removal (by itself) would keep the graph connected.
   $e_1, e_3, e_4, e_8, e_{10}$
   c. What is the maximum number of edges that can be removed simultaneously while keeping the graph connected? 2 edges

Name

▶ **LESSON MASTER 11-4** *page 2*

Properties Objective D

6. a. State the Euler Circuit Theorem.
   If a graph has an Euler circuit, then every vertex of the graph has even degree.
   b. Explain in your own words why the Euler Circuit Theorem is reasonable.
   Sample: For each edge leading to a vertex there must be another edge by which to exit, or vice versa for the first vertex. Because of this pairing of edges, each vertex must have even degree.

In 7–9, determine whether or not the graph has an Euler circuit. Justify your answer.

7. 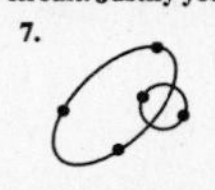
No; the graph is not connected.

8. Yes; the graph is connected, and each vertex has even degree.

9. the graph with adjacency matrix

$$\begin{array}{c} \\ v_1 \\ v_2 \\ v_3 \end{array}\begin{array}{c} \begin{array}{ccc} v_1 & v_2 & v_3 \end{array} \\ \begin{bmatrix} 0 & 0 & 4 \\ 0 & 0 & 2 \\ 4 & 2 & 1 \end{bmatrix} \end{array}$$

Yes; the graph is connected, and each vertex has even degree.

Properties Objective G

10. Suppose a camp counselor wants to check "lights out" at each cabin. Is it possible for her to start and end at her own cabin, C, and visit every cabin using each path given in the map exactly once? If so, draw the possible route on the map. If not, explain why.
No; "vertices" 2 and 4 have odd degree.

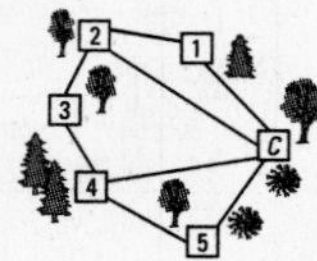

Name

LESSON MASTER 11-5

Questions on SPUR Objectives
See pages 713–717 for objectives.

Properties Objective B

1. Consider the graph at the right.

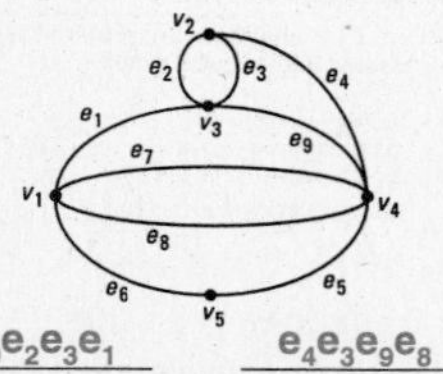

   a. List all the different walks of length 2 from v_1 to v_2.
   e_1e_2, e_1e_3, e_7e_4, e_8e_4
   b. List three different walks of length 4 from v_4 to v_1.
   Sample: $e_9e_3e_2e_1$ $e_9e_2e_3e_1$ $e_4e_3e_9e_8$

Representations Objective J

2. The adjacency matrix for a directed graph is
$$A = \begin{array}{c} \\ v_1 \\ v_2 \\ v_3 \\ v_4 \end{array}\begin{array}{c} \begin{array}{cccc} v_1 & v_2 & v_3 & v_4 \end{array} \\ \begin{bmatrix} 0 & 1 & 0 & 0 \\ 0 & 0 & 1 & 1 \\ 0 & 2 & 0 & 1 \\ 1 & 0 & 1 & 1 \end{bmatrix} \end{array}.$$

Use the fact that $A^4 = \begin{bmatrix} 2 & 3 & 4 & 5 \\ 5 & 10 & 8 & 12 \\ 6 & 9 & 13 & 16 \\ 6 & 12 & 9 & 14 \end{bmatrix}$ to answer the following.

   a. How many walks of length 1 are there from v_3 to v_2? 2 walks
   b. How many walks of length 4 are there from v_3 to v_2? 9 walks
   c. How many walks of length 4 are there from v_4 to v_4? 14 walks
   d. What does the 8 in A^4 indicate?
   There are 8 walks of length 4 from v_2 to v_3.

3. a. Give the adjacency matrix for the graph at the right.

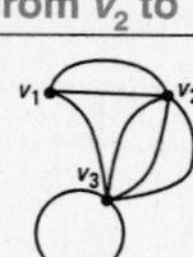

   b. How many walks of length 3 are there from v_1 to v_3? 21 walks
   c. How many walks of length 3 start at v_2? 99 walks

Name

LESSON MASTER 11-6

Questions on SPUR Objectives
See pages 713–717 for objectives.

Uses Objective H

1. In a laboratory, molecules of a liquid are changing phase in a flask. It is known that from one minute to the next, 15% of the liquid molecules become gaseous, while the rest remain liquid. At the same time, 30% of the gaseous molecules become liquid while the rest remain gaseous.

liquid to gas 15% gas to liquid 30%

   a. Give T, the transition matrix for this situation. $T = \begin{bmatrix} 0.85 & 0.15 \\ 0.3 & 0.7 \end{bmatrix}$
   b. After sufficient time, the substance will reach equilibrium so that the percent that is liquid and the percent that is gaseous become constant. Estimate these percents by calculating T^{10}.
   liquid, ≈ 67%; gas, ≈ 33%
   c. Find the exact percents by solving a system of equations.
   liquid, $66\frac{2}{3}$ %; gas, $33\frac{1}{3}$%

2. A large city has three major newspapers, the *Times*, the *Herald*, and the *Gazette*. A survey of readers who buy their newspapers at newsstands revealed they switched newspapers daily according to the directed graph below.
   a. Suppose that today 38% of the readers chose the *Times*, 45% chose the *Herald*, and 28% chose the *Gazette*. Based on the model, what percent of the readers would choose each newspaper tomorrow?
   Times 43.5%
   Herald 34.4%
   Gazette 22.1%

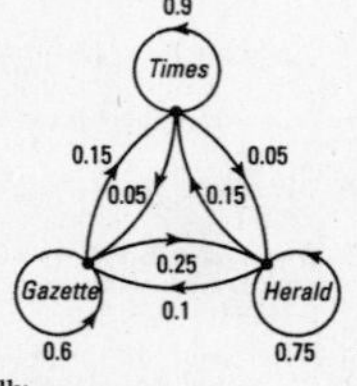

   b. What percent of the readers would eventually choose each newspaper after a long period of time?
   Times 60% *Herald* 26% *Gazette* 14%

Name

LESSON MASTER 12-1

Questions on SPUR Objectives
See pages 778–781 for objectives.

Skills Objective A

In 1–3, find the magnitude and direction of the given vector.

1. (-3, 7) $\sqrt{58}$, 113.2°
2. (-0.8, -0.6) 10, 216.9°
3. the arrow joining (2, -2) to (4, 9) $5\sqrt{5}$, 79.7°
4. Find all possible directions for a vector whose x-component is half its y-component. 63.4°, 243.4°
5. Find a polar representation of the vector (5, -1) [$\sqrt{26}$, 348.7°]

Uses Objective G

6. A plane's velocity is represented by [600, 120°], where the magnitude is measured in miles per hour and the direction is in degrees counterclockwise from due east.
   a. Sketch a vector for the velocity.

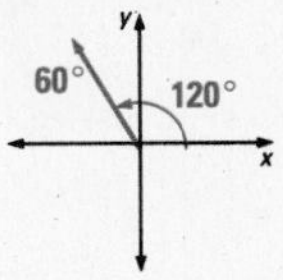

   b. Give the vector in component form.
   (-300, 519.6)
   c. Interpret the components.
   Each hour, the plane flies 300 miles to the west and 519.6 miles to the north.

7. A monkey is swinging from the end of a 24-foot rope. Its angle with the horizontal is 50°. Assume the rope is taut.

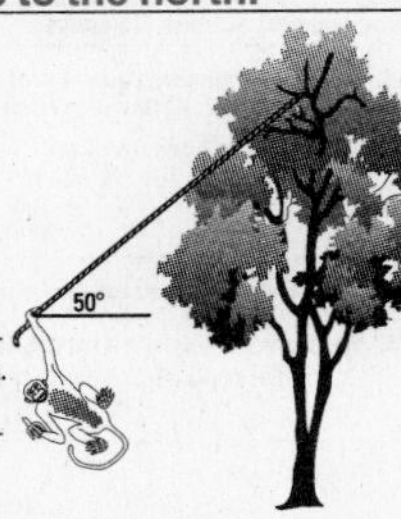

   a. Write a polar representation for the monkey's position, using the rope's knot on the tree branch as the origin.
   [24, 230°]
   b. Compute a component representation.
   (-15.4, -18.4)
   c. Interpret the components.
   The monkey is 15.4 feet to one side of the knot and 18.4 feet below it.

Name

▶ LESSON MASTER 12-1 *page 2*

Representations Objective I

8. Suppose $P = (4, -1)$ and $Q = (x, y)$ are points in a plan. If $\overrightarrow{PQ} = [8, \frac{\pi}{6}]$ find the coordinates of Q. (10.9, 3)

9. a. Find the component representation of [7, 330°].
   $\left(\frac{7\sqrt{3}}{2}, \frac{-7}{2}\right) \approx (6.1, -3.5)$
   b. Sketch the vector.

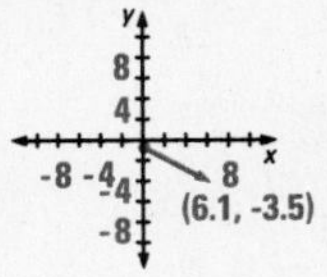

10. a. Give the endpoint of a vector with polar representation [2, -90°] and initial endpoint (3, 1).
   (3, -1)
   b. Sketch the vector.

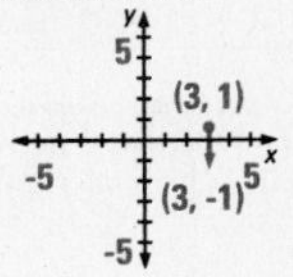

11. a. Find the component representation of the vector shown at the right.
   (-3, -3)
   b. Sketch the vector in standard position.

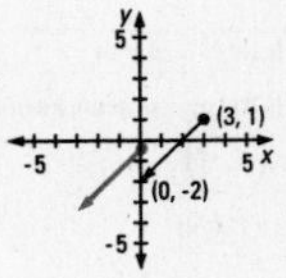

Name

LESSON MASTER 12-2

Questions on SPUR Objectives
See pages 778–781 for objectives.

Skills Objective B

In 1–4, let $\vec{u} = (-2, -5)$, $\vec{v} = (4, 1)$, and $\vec{w} = (-6, 0)$. Find the sum or difference.

1. $\vec{u} + \vec{w}$ (-8, -5)
2. $\vec{u} - \vec{v}$ (-6, -6)
3. $-\vec{u}$ (2, 5)
4. $\vec{w} - \vec{v} + \vec{u}$ (-12, -6)

In 5 and 6, let $\vec{s} = [4, 75°]$ and $\vec{t} = [1, 20°]$. Compute and express the answer in its polar representation.

5. $\vec{s} + \vec{t}$ [4.6, 64.8°]
6. $\vec{s} - \vec{t}$ [3.5, 88.45°]

Properties Objective E

7. Prove that if $\vec{v} + \vec{u} = \vec{v} + \vec{w}$, then $\vec{u} = \vec{w}$. Samples are given.
   Let $\vec{v} = (v_1, v_2)$, $\vec{u} = (u_1, u_2)$ and $\vec{w} = (w_1, w_2)$. Then $\vec{v} + \vec{u} = (v_1 + u_1, v_2 + u_2)$ and $\vec{v} + \vec{w} = (v_1 + w_1, v_2 + w_2)$. But, $\vec{v} + \vec{u} = \vec{v} + \vec{w}$, so $(v_1 + u_1, v_2 + u_2) = (v_1 w_1, v_2 w_2)$. Thus, $u_1 = w_1$ and $u_2 = w_2$. Therefore, $\vec{u} = (u_1, u_2) = (w_1, w_2) = \vec{w}$.

8. Show that $\vec{v} = (\cos 50°, 5 \sin 50°)$ is the opposite of $\vec{w} = (5 \cos 230°, 5 \sin 230°)$.
   $\vec{v} = (5 \cos 50°, 5 \sin 50°) \approx (3.2, 3.8)$.
   $\vec{w} = (5 \cos 230°, 5 \sin 230°) \approx (3.2, 3.8)$.
   Thus $\vec{v}$ and $\vec{w}$ are opposites.

Name

▶ LESSON MASTER 12-2 *page 2*

Uses Objective H

9. Two children push a friend on a sled with the forces shown at the right.

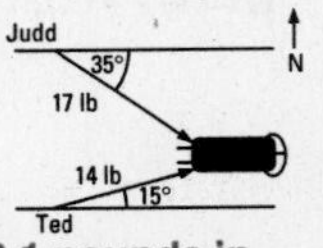

   a. Give the resultant force in polar form.
   [28.1, -12.6°]
   b. Interpret your answer to part a.
   The total force applied is 28.1 pounds in the direction 12.6° south of east.
   c. Which child is exerting more forward force? How much more? Judd; 0.4 lb

10. Relative to the water, a boat is moving with a speed of 25 mph in the direction 10° north of east. Due to the current which is moving 5° north of west, the boat is actually heading north relative to the land.
   a. Find the speed of the current. 24.7 mph
   b. Find the speed of the boat moving north. 6.5 mph

Representations Objective J

11. The vectors $\vec{u}$ and $\vec{v}$ are shown at the right. Sketch the following.

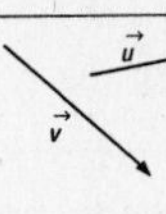

   a. $\vec{u} + \vec{v}$

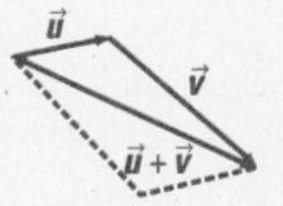

   b. $-\vec{u}$

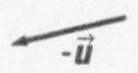

   c. $\vec{v} - \vec{u}$

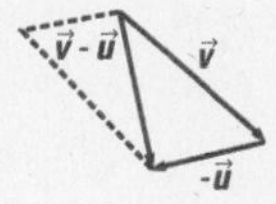

Name

LESSON MASTER 12-3

Questions on SPUR Objectives
See pages 778–781 for objectives.

Skills Objective B

In 1–4, let $\vec{u}$ = (-4, 12), and $\vec{v}$ = (-6, 1), and compute.

1. $\frac{2}{3}\vec{u}$ $\left(-\frac{8}{3}, 8\right)$
2. $5\vec{v}$ (-30, 5)
3. $\frac{2}{3}\vec{u} + 5\vec{v}$ $\left(-\frac{98}{3}, 13\right)$
4. $3\vec{u} - 4\vec{v}$ (12, 32)

Properties Objective E

5. Show that $\vec{v}$ = (-2, 5) and $\vec{w}$ = (12, -30) are parallel.
$\vec{w} = (12, -30) = -6(-2, 5) = -6\,\vec{v}$

6. Show that the line passing through (-2, -2) and (0, 8) is parallel to the vector $\vec{v}$ = (-1, -5).
$(0-(-2), 8-(-2)) = (2, 10) = -2(-1, -5) = -2\vec{v}$

Properties Objective F

In 7–9, is the given vector parallel to $\vec{u}$ = (12, 2)?

7. $\vec{v} = \left(-4, -\frac{2}{3}\right)$ Yes
8. $\vec{w}$ = (-24, 4) No
9. $\vec{n}$ = (12, 2) Yes
10. Are $\vec{u}$ = [2, 40°] and $\vec{v}$ = [3, 220°] parallel? Yes

Representations Objective I

11. Sketch $\vec{v}$ = (-2, -5) and $-2\vec{v}$ on the grid at the right.

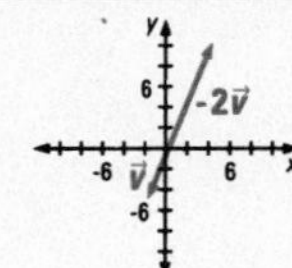

Name

12. a. Give the endpoint of a vector $\vec{u}$ which has polar representation [4, 120°] and starts at (3, -6). $(1, -6 + 2\sqrt{3})$
b. Give the endpoint of the vector $3\vec{u}$ if it starts at (2, -2). $(-3, -6 + 6\sqrt{3})$
c. Sketch both vectors on the grid at the right.

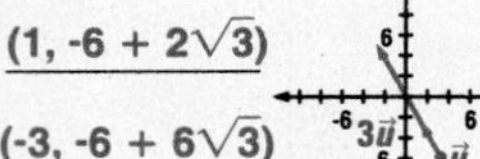

Representations Objective J

13. Given the vectors $\vec{u}$ and $\vec{v}$ shown at the right. Sketch the following.

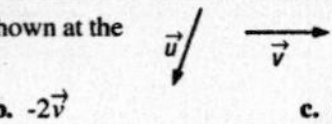

a. $3\vec{u}$

b. $-2\vec{v}$

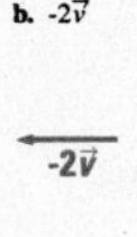

c. $3\vec{u} - 2\vec{v}$

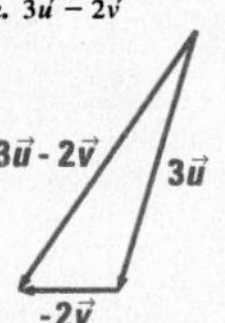

Representations Objective L

14. a. Find parametric equations of the line through (-1, 4) that is parallel to the vector $\vec{w}$ = (1, 6).
$\begin{cases} x = -1 + t \\ y = 4 + 6t \end{cases}$
b. Graph the line on the grid at the right.

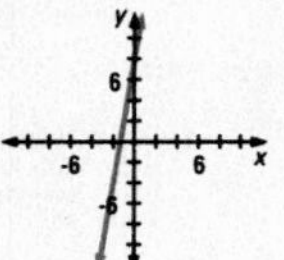

15. Write a vector equation for the line through (3, -2) that is parallel to the vector $\vec{u}$ = (5, -5).
$(x - 3, y + 2) = t(5, -5)$

Name

LESSON MASTER 12-4

Questions on SPUR Objectives
See pages 778–781 for objectives.

Skills Objective B

In 1–4, let $\vec{u}$ = (3, 8), $\vec{v}$ = (4, -2) and $\vec{w}$ = (-7, 6), and compute.

1. $\vec{v} \cdot \vec{w}$ -40
2. $\vec{u} \cdot \vec{u}$ 73
3. $\vec{u} \cdot (\vec{v} \cdot \vec{w})$ (-120, -320)
4. $(\vec{v} - \vec{w}) \cdot (\vec{u} + \vec{v})$ 29

Skills Objective D

In 5–8, find the measure of the angle between the two vectors.

5. (-3, -3) and (1, 2) 161.6°
6. (4, 6) and (2, 7) 17.7°
7. (-5, 0) and (0, -12) 90°
8. [4, 94°] and [19, 211°] 117°

Properties Objective E

9. Show that $\vec{v}$ = (-4, 7) and $\vec{w}$ = (-12, -9) are not orthogonal.
$\vec{v} \cdot \vec{w} = -4 \cdot -12 + 7 \cdot -9 = 48 - 63 = -15 \neq 0$

10. If $\vec{u}$ and $\vec{v}$ are perpendicular vectors, prove that for all nonzero real numbers j and k, $j\vec{u}$ and $k\vec{v}$ are perpendicular. Sample is given.
Let $\vec{u} = (u_1, u_2)$ and $\vec{v} = (v_1, v_2)$. Since $\vec{u}$ and $\vec{v}$ are perpendicular, $u_1v_1 + u_2v_2 = 0$. Also, $j\vec{u} = (ju_1, ju_2)$ and $k\vec{v} = (kv_1, kv_2)$. So $j\vec{u} \cdot k\vec{v} = ju_1 \cdot kv_1 + ju_2 \cdot kv_2 = jk(u_1, v_1) + jk(u_2, v_2) = jk(u_1, v_1 + u_2, v_2) = jk \cdot 0 = 0$. Therefore, $j\vec{u}$ and $k\vec{v}$ are perpendicular.

Name

Properties Objective F

In 11–13, determine whether $\vec{u}$ and $\vec{v}$ are perpendicular, parallel, or neither.

11. $\vec{u}$ = (7, 7), $\vec{v}$ = (-3, 8) neither
12. $\vec{u}$ = (4, -10), $\vec{v}$ = (-5, -2) perpendicular
13. $\vec{u}$ = (3, -5), $\vec{v}$ = (12, -20) parallel
14. Find x so that the vectors $\vec{u}$ = (10, -12) and $\vec{v}$ = (x, 5) are orthogonal. $x = 6$
15. Find all plane vectors with length $10\sqrt{2}$ that are orthogonal to $\vec{w}$ = (1, -7). (14, 2) or (-14, -2)

Representations Objective L

In 16 and 17, let $\vec{v}$ = (-2, 9). Write a vector equation for the line through P = (1, 4) that is

16. parallel to $\vec{v}$. $(x - 1, y - 4) = t(-2, 9)$
17. perpendicular to $\vec{v}$. $(x - 1, y - 4) = t(9, 2)$

Name

LESSON MASTER 12-5

Questions on SPUR Objectives
See pages 778–781 for objectives.

Representations Objective M

1. Which plane is described by the equation $z = 0$? *xy*-plane

2. Write an equation for the plane that is parallel to the *xz*-plane and is 8 units in the negative direction from the origin. $y = -8$

3. Let *M* be the plane parallel to the *yz*-plane that is 5 units in the positive direction from the *yz*-plane. Give a system of two linear equations that describes the intersection of *M* and the *xy*-plane. $\begin{cases} x = 5 \\ z = 0 \end{cases}$

4. Write an equation for the sphere with radius 12 and center (-2, 5, 0).
$(x + 2)^2 + (y - 5)^2 + z^2 = 144$

5. Find the center and radius of the sphere with equation $x^2 + y^2 + z^2 - 6x + 2z = 10$.
center: (3, 0, -1); radius: $2\sqrt{5}$

6. a. Sketch $P = (3, 0, -1)$ and $Q = (1, 2, 4)$ in the three-dimensional coordinate system at the right.
b. Write an equation for the sphere with center *P* and radius *PQ*.
$(x - 3)^2 + y^2 + (z + 1)^2 = 33$

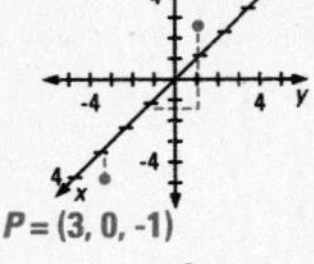

7. Write a system of two linear equations that describes the line parallel to the *z*-axis passing throught the point (5, 8, -4).

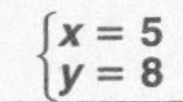

$\begin{cases} x = 5 \\ y = 8 \end{cases}$

Precalculus and Discrete Mathematics © Scott Foresman Addison Wesley

Name

LESSON MASTER 12-6

Questions on SPUR Objectives
See pages 778–781 for objectives.

Skills Objective C

In 1–6, let $\vec{u} = (3, -2, 1)$, and $\vec{v} = (-4, 4, 5)$, and compute.

1. $\vec{u} + \vec{v}$ (-1, 2, 6)
2. $-8\vec{v}$ (32, -32, -40)
3. $|\vec{u}|$ $\sqrt{14}$
4. $\vec{u} \cdot \vec{v}$ -15
5. $5\vec{u} - 3\vec{v}$ (27, -22, -10)
6. $\vec{u} \times \vec{v}$ (-14, -19, 4)

7. Find a vector orthogonal to both $\vec{r} = (1, 1, 3)$ and $\vec{s} = (-2, 0, 6)$. Sample: (6, -12, 2)

Skills Objective D

In 8–10, find the measure of the angle between the two vectors.

8. $\vec{u} = (2, 3, 4)$, $\vec{v} = (-6, 0, 3)$ 90°
9. $\vec{u} = (0, -1, 7)$, $\vec{v} = (8, -2, -2)$ 101.5°
10. $\vec{u} = (3, 6, -5)$, $\vec{v} = (-6, -12, 10)$ 180°

Properties Objective E

11. Prove that if $\vec{u}$, $\vec{v}$, and $\vec{w}$ are vectors in 3-space, then $\vec{u} \cdot (\vec{v} + \vec{w}) = \vec{u} \cdot \vec{v} + \vec{u} \cdot \vec{w}$. Sample is given.

Let $\vec{u} = (u_1, u_2, u_3)$, $\vec{v} = (v_1, v_2, v_3)$ and $\vec{w} = (w_1, w_2, w_3)$. Then, $\vec{u} \cdot (\vec{v} + \vec{w})$
$= (u_1, u_2, u_3) \cdot (v_1 + w_1, v_2 + w_2, v_3 + w_3)$
$= (u_1(v_1 + w_1), u_2(v_2 + w_2), u_3(v_3 + w_3))$
$= (u_1v_1 + u_1w_1, u_2v_2 + u_2w_2, u_3v_3 + u_3w_3)$
$= (u_1v_1, u_2v_2, u_3v_3) + (u_1w_1, u_2w_2, u_3w_3)$
$= \vec{u} \cdot \vec{v} + \vec{u} \cdot \vec{w}$

Precalculus and Discrete Mathematics © Scott Foresman Addison Wesley

Name

▶ LESSON MASTER 12-6 *page 2*

Properties Objective F

In 12–14, determine whether $\vec{u}$ and $\vec{v}$ are perpendicular, parallel, or neither.

12. $\vec{u} = (2, 8, 3)$, $\vec{v} = (-1, 6, 4)$ neither
13. $\vec{u} = (1, 4, -1)$, $\vec{v} = (1, -0.5, -1)$ perpendicular
14. $\vec{u} = (-8, -6, -2)$, $\vec{v} = (\frac{1}{3}, \frac{1}{4}, \frac{1}{12})$ parallel

15. Let $\vec{u} = (-2, y, 4)$ and $\vec{w} = (4, y - 5, -7)$. If are $\vec{u}$ and $\vec{w}$ orthogonal, find *y*. $y = 9$ or $y = -4$

Representations Objective K

In 16 and 17, let $\vec{u} = (1, 4, 0)$ and $\vec{v} = (3, -2, 6)$. Use the three-dimensional coordinate system at the right.

16. Sketch the vectors $\vec{u}$ and $\vec{v}$.

17. Find $\vec{u} - \vec{v}$.
(-2, -6, -6)

18. Sketch the vector $\vec{u} - \vec{v}$ in standard position.

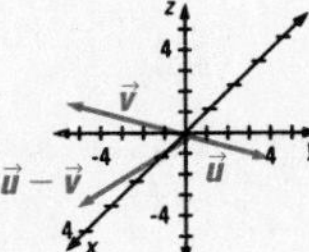

Precalculus and Discrete Mathematics © Scott Foresman Addison Wesley

Name

LESSON MASTER 12-7

Questions on SPUR Objectives
See pages 778–781 for objectives.

Representations Objective M

1. Let ℓ be a line passing through the two points (8, 3, -5) and (-7, -3, 1). Describe ℓ with
a. a vector equation.
Sample: $(x - 8, y - 3, z + 5) = t(15, 6, -6)$
b. parametric equations.
$\begin{cases} x = 8 + 15t \\ y = 3 + 6t \\ z = -5 - 6t \end{cases}$

2. Find a vector equation for the line through (-2, 5, -1) that is perpendicular to the plane given by $2x - 3y - 4z = 12$.
$(x + 2, y - 5, z + 1) = t(2, -3, -4)$

3. Find a vector perpendicular to the plane defined by the equation $x - 5y + 10z = 20$. (1, -5, 10)

4. Consider the line in 3-space through the point (4, -2, -2) that is parallel to the vector (7, 5, -2).
a. Find a vector equation for the line.
$(x - 4, y + 2, z + 2) = t(7, 5, -2)$
b. Find parametric equations for the line.
$\begin{cases} x = 4 + 7t \\ y = -2 + 5t \\ z = -2 - 2t \end{cases}$
c. Find a point other than (4, -2, -2) that lies on the line. Sample: (11, 3, -4)

5. Find an equation for the plane that is perpendicular to $\vec{u} = (2, 16, -10)$ and contains the point (3, -5, 0).
$2(x - 3) + 16(y + 5) - 10z = 0$ or $x + 8y - 5z = -37$

6. Show that the planes defined by the equations $2x + y - 4z = 5$ and $-x + 2y + 3z = 8$ are not parallel.
The vectors (2, 1, -4) and (-1, 2, 3), which are perpendicular to the planes, are not parallel.

Precalculus and Discrete Mathematics © Scott Foresman Addison Wesley

Name

▶ **LESSON MASTER 12-7** *page 2*

7. a. Find the intercepts of the plane defined by the equation $2x - 5y + z = 10$.
$x = 5, y = -2, z = 10$

b. Sketch the plane.

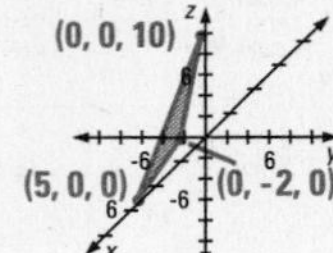

8. Let M be the plane defined by the equation $6x - 4y + 3z = 12$.
a. Sketch M.
b. Show that (3, 0, -2) is a point on the plane.
Sample: $6(3) - 4(0) + 3(-2) = 18 - 0 - 6 = 12$; since the point satisfies the equation, it is on the plane.

c. Show that the vector $\vec{u} = (-3, 2, -1.5)$ is perpendicular to M.
Sample: The vector $\vec{v} = (6, -4, 3)$ is perpendicular to M. Since $\vec{u} = (-3, 2, -1.5) = -\frac{1}{2}(6, -4, 3) = \frac{1}{2}\vec{v}$, $\vec{u}$ is parallel to $\vec{v}$ and thus perpendicular to M.

d. Find equation for the plane N that is parallel to M and passes through (3, -1, 4).
$6(x - 3) - 4(y + 1) + 3(z - 4) = 0$

Name

LESSON MASTER 13-1 **Questions on SPUR Objectives** See pages 836–839 for objectives.

Uses Objective D

1. What is the total distance traveled by a tour bus which travels at the rate of 55 mph for 2.5 hours, 40 mph for 30 minutes, and 25 mph for 15 minutes? **163.75 mi**

2. Use summation notation to express the total distance traveled by an object whose rate-time graph is given at the right.
$\sum_{i=1}^{6} r_i(t_i - t_{i-1})$

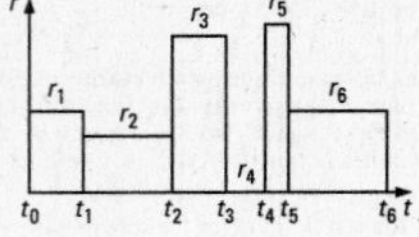

3. If a space probe travels in a straight line with an initial speed of 120 m/sec and a constant acceleration of 9.8 m/sec², then its velocity at time t seconds is given by $120 + 9.8t$. Find the distance it will have traveled in 8 seconds. **1273.6 m**

Uses Objective F

4. The rate-time graph below shows the speed of a truck during a trucker's 8-hour work day. Estimate the distance the trucker traveled.

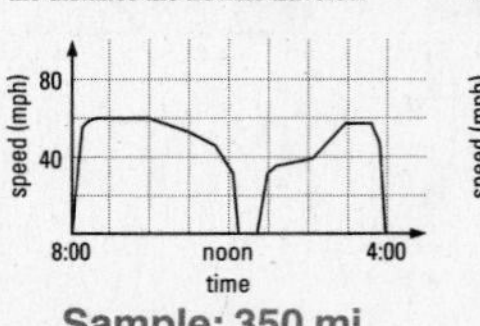

Sample: 350 mi

5. The rate-time graph below depicts a cyclist riding from home to work. From the graph, estimate the distance to work.

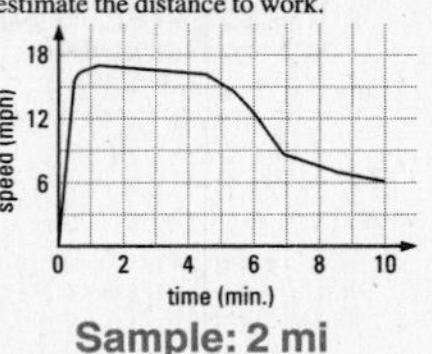

Sample: 2 mi

Name

LESSON MASTER 13-2 **Questions on SPUR Objectives** See pages 836–839 for objectives.

Skills Objective A

1. Consider the function f with $f(x) = x^3 + 2$ over the interval from 0 to 10. Let z_i be the rightmost endpoint of the ith subinterval. Evaluate $\sum_{i=1}^{5} f(z_i)\Delta x$. **3620**

2. For the function g with $g(x) = 2x^3 - 3$, calculate the Riemann sum over the interval $0 \le x \le 2$ for $\Delta x = 0.25$ when
a. z_i = the left endpoint of the ith subinterval. **0.125**
b. z_i = the right endpoint of the ith subinterval. **4.125**

3. a. Let $h(x) = \frac{1}{2}\sin x$. Evaluate the Riemann sum $\sum_{i=1}^{n} h(z_i)\Delta x$ over the interval from 0 to $\frac{\pi}{2}$ when z_i is the right endpoint of the ith subinterval, the subintervals are of equal width, and n has the given value.
i. $n = 4$ **≈0.592** ii. $n = 8$ **≈0.547** iii. $n = 16$ **≈0.524**

b. Which value of n provides an answer that is nearest the area under the graph of h? Why?
$n = 16$; The more subintervals, the better the estimate.

c. To what value might you expect the Riemann sum to converge as n increases? **0.5**

3. Use a computer or programmable calculator to evaluate the Riemann sum for the function f with $f(x) = x^2(\cos 2x - \sin x)$ over the interval from 0 to π when z_i is the right endpoint of the ith subinterval of equal width and n has the given value.

a. $n = 10$ **≈-2.615** b. $n = 50$ **≈-3.983**
c. $n = 100$ **≈-4.142** d. $n = 500$ **≈-4.268**

Name

▶ **LESSON MASTER 13-2** *page 2*

Uses Objective D

5. The graph below indicates the velocity of a Krazy Car along a track at an amusement park during a 2-minute ride.

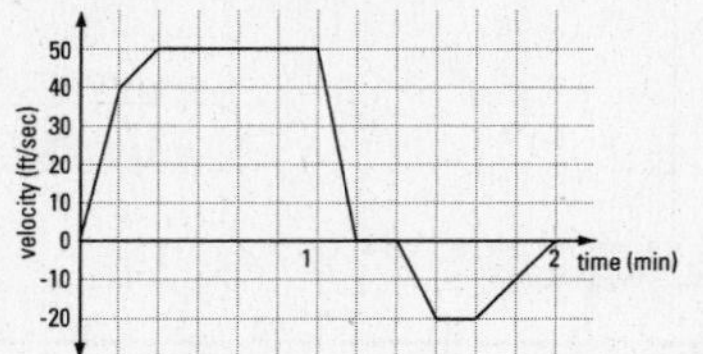

a. How far did the car travel in the first 2 minutes? **3400 ft**

b. At the end of the ride, what is the car's distance along the track from its position at the start of the ride? **2400 ft**

6. A runner accelerates from 14 ft/sec to 18 ft/sec during the last 5 seconds of a race. The runner's velocity t seconds after beginning to accelerate is given by $v(t) = 0.16t^2 + 14$. Estimate the distance the runner runs during these 5 seconds using a Riemann sum with 5 subintervals of equal width and
a. z_i = the left endpoint of the ith subinterval. **≈ 74.8 ft**
b. z_i = the right endpoint of the ith subinterval. **≈ 78.8 ft**

7. Which of the answers in Question 6 is closer to the exact distance? Why? (Hint: Sketch the velocity-time graph.)
a; Since the velocity function is concave up, the Riemann sum using the left endpoint provided a better estimate.

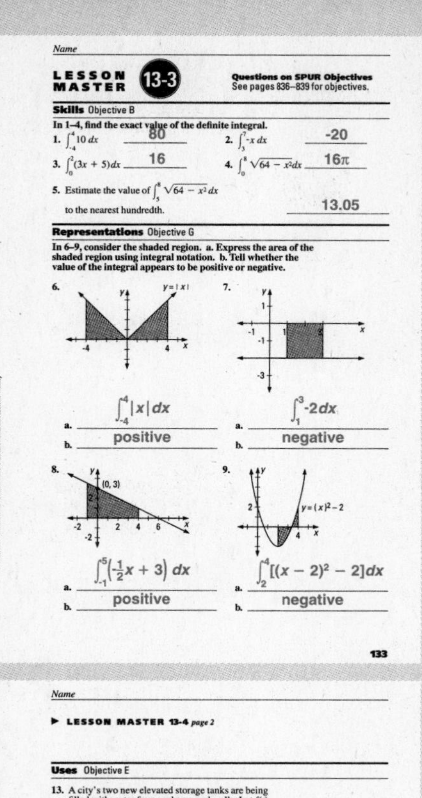

Name

LESSON MASTER 13-3

Questions on SPUR Objectives
See pages 836–839 for objectives.

Skills Objective B

In 1–4, find the exact value of the definite integral.

1. $\int_{-4}^{4} 10\,dx$ **80**
2. $\int_{3}^{5} -x\,dx$ **-20**
3. $\int_{0}^{2} (3x + 5)\,dx$ **16**
4. $\int_{0}^{8} \sqrt{64 - x^2}\,dx$ **16π**
5. Estimate the value of $\int_{5}^{8} \sqrt{64 - x^2}\,dx$ to the nearest hundredth. **13.05**

Representations Objective G

In 6–9, consider the shaded region. a. Express the area of the shaded region using integral notation. b. Tell whether the value of the integral appears to be positive or negative.

6. a. $\int_{-4}^{4} |x|\,dx$ b. positive
7. a. $\int_{1}^{3} -2\,dx$ b. negative
8. a. $\int_{-1}^{5} \left(-\frac{1}{2}x + 3\right) dx$ b. positive
9. a. $\int_{2}^{4} [(x - 2)^2 - 2]\,dx$ b. negative

Precalculus and Discrete Mathematics © Scott Foresman Addison Wesley

133

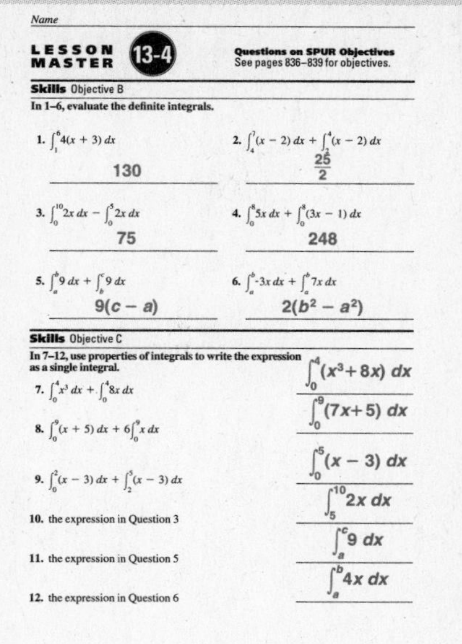

Name

LESSON MASTER 13-4

Questions on SPUR Objectives
See pages 836–839 for objectives.

Skills Objective B

In 1–6, evaluate the definite integrals.

1. $\int_{1}^{6} 4(x + 3)\,dx$ **130**
2. $\int_{2}^{7} (x - 2)\,dx + \int_{4}^{4} (x - 2)\,dx$ **$\frac{25}{2}$**
3. $\int_{0}^{10} 2x\,dx - \int_{0}^{5} 2x\,dx$ **75**
4. $\int_{0}^{8} 5x\,dx + \int_{0}^{8} (3x - 1)\,dx$ **248**
5. $\int_{a}^{b} 9\,dx + \int_{b}^{c} 9\,dx$ **$9(c - a)$**
6. $\int_{a}^{b} -3x\,dx + \int_{a}^{b} 7x\,dx$ **$2(b^2 - a^2)$**

Skills Objective C

In 7–12, use properties of integrals to write the expression as a single integral.

7. $\int_{0}^{4} x^3\,dx + \int_{0}^{4} 8x\,dx$ **$\int_{0}^{4} (x^3 + 8x)\,dx$**
8. $\int_{0}^{9} (x + 5)\,dx + 6\int_{0}^{9} x\,dx$ **$\int_{0}^{9} (7x + 5)\,dx$**
9. $\int_{0}^{2} (x - 3)\,dx + \int_{2}^{5} (x - 3)\,dx$ **$\int_{0}^{5} (x - 3)\,dx$**
10. the expression in Question 3 **$\int_{5}^{10} 2x\,dx$**
11. the expression in Question 5 **$\int_{a}^{c} 9\,dx$**
12. the expression in Question 6 **$\int_{a}^{b} 4x\,dx$**

Precalculus and Discrete Mathematics © Scott Foresman Addison Wesley

134

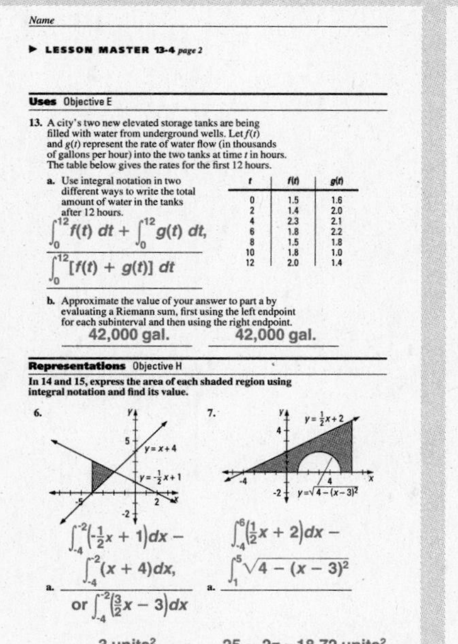

Name

► LESSON MASTER 13-4 *page 2*

Uses Objective E

13. A city's two new elevated storage tanks are being filled with water from underground wells. Let $f(t)$ and $g(t)$ represent the rate of water flow (in thousands of gallons per hour) into the two tanks at time t in hours. The table below gives the rates for the first 12 hours.

t	$f(t)$	$g(t)$
0	1.5	1.6
2	1.4	2.0
4	2.3	2.1
6	1.8	2.2
8	1.5	1.8
10	1.8	1.0
12	2.0	1.4

a. Use integral notation in two different ways to write the total amount of water in the tanks after 12 hours.
$\int_{0}^{12} f(t)\,dt + \int_{0}^{12} g(t)\,dt$, $\int_{0}^{12} [f(t) + g(t)]\,dt$

b. Approximate the value of your answer to part a by evaluating a Riemann sum, first using the left endpoint for each subinterval and then using the right endpoint.
42,000 gal. **42,000 gal.**

Representations Objective H

In 14 and 15, express the area of each shaded region using integral notation and find its value.

6. a. $\int_{-4}^{-2} \left(-\frac{1}{2}x + 1\right) dx - \int_{-4}^{-2} (x + 4)\,dx$, or $\int_{-4}^{-2} \left(\frac{3}{2}x - 3\right) dx$
b. 3 units²

7. a. $\int_{-4}^{6} \left(\frac{1}{2}x + 2\right) dx - \int_{1}^{5} \sqrt{4 - (x - 3)^2}$
b. $25 - 2\pi \approx 18.72$ units²

Precalculus and Discrete Mathematics © Scott Foresman Addison Wesley

135

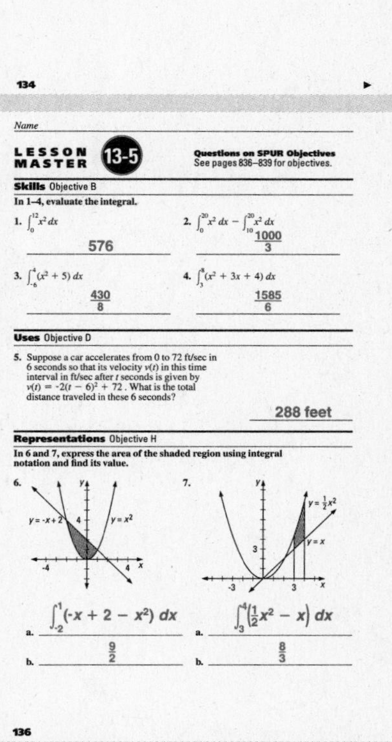

Name

LESSON MASTER 13-5

Questions on SPUR Objectives
See pages 836–839 for objectives.

Skills Objective B

In 1–4, evaluate the integral.

1. $\int_{0}^{12} x^2\,dx$ **576**
2. $\int_{0}^{20} x^2\,dx - \int_{10}^{20} x^2\,dx$ **$\frac{1000}{3}$**
3. $\int_{-6}^{4} (x^2 + 5)\,dx$ **$\frac{430}{8}$**
4. $\int_{3}^{8} (x^2 + 3x + 4)\,dx$ **$\frac{1585}{6}$**

Uses Objective D

5. Suppose a car accelerates from 0 to 72 ft/sec in 6 seconds so that its velocity $v(t)$ in this time interval in ft/sec after t seconds is given by $v(t) = -2(t - 6)^2 + 72$. What is the total distance traveled in these 6 seconds? **288 feet**

Representations Objective H

In 6 and 7, express the area of the shaded region using integral notation and find its value.

6. a. $\int_{-2}^{1} (-x + 2 - x^2)\,dx$ b. $\frac{9}{2}$
7. a. $\int_{3}^{4} \left(\frac{1}{2}x^2 - x\right) dx$ b. $\frac{8}{3}$

Precalculus and Discrete Mathematics © Scott Foresman Addison Wesley

136

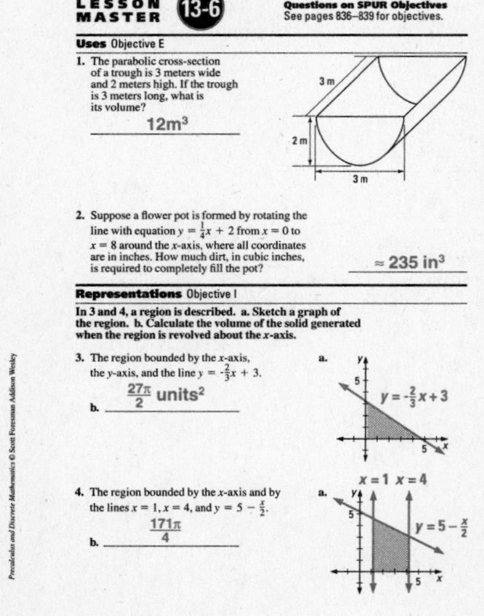

Name

LESSON MASTER 13-6

Questions on SPUR Objectives
See pages 836–839 for objectives.

Uses Objective E

1. The parabolic cross-section of a trough is 3 meters wide and 2 meters high. If the trough is 3 meters long, what is its volume? **12m³**

2. Suppose a flower pot is formed by rotating the line with equation $y = \frac{1}{4}x + 2$ from $x = 0$ to $x = 8$ around the x-axis, where all coordinates are in inches. How much dirt, in cubic inches, is required to completely fill the pot? **≈ 235 in³**

Representations Objective I

In 3 and 4, a region is described. a. Sketch a graph of the region. b. Calculate the volume of the solid generated when the region is revolved about the x-axis.

3. The region bounded by the x-axis, the y-axis, and the line $y = -\frac{2}{3}x + 3$.
b. $\frac{27\pi}{2}$ units²

4. The region bounded by the x-axis and by the lines $x = 1$, $x = 4$, and $y = 5 - \frac{x}{2}$.
b. $\frac{171\pi}{4}$

Precalculus and Discrete Mathematics © Scott Foresman Addison Wesley

137